Principles of ————

Trauma
Therapy

Principles of Trauma Therapy

A Guide to Symptoms, Evaluation, and Treatment

John Briere, Ph.D. & Catherine Scott, M.D.

University of Southern California

SAGE Publications
Thousand Oaks ■ London ■ New Delhi

For information:

Sage Publications, Inc.
2455 Teller Road
Thousand Oaks, California 91320
E-mail: order@sagepub.com

Sage Publications Ltd.
1 Oliver's Yard
55 City Road
London EC1Y 1SP
United Kingdom

Sage Publications India Pvt. Ltd.
B-42, Panchsheel Enclave
Post Box 4109
New Delhi 110 017 India

Printed in the United States of America on acid-free paper

Library of Congress Cataloging-in-Publication Data

Briere, John.
Principles of trauma therapy : a guide to symptoms, evaluation, and treatment / John Briere, Catherine Scott.
    p. cm.
Includes bibliographical references and index.
ISBN 0-7619-2920-7 (cloth) — ISBN 0-7619-2921-5 (pbk.)
   1. Post-traumatic stress disorder—Treatment. 2. Psychic trauma—Treatment. I. Scott, Catherine, MD. II. Title.
[DNLM: 1. Stress Disorders, Post-Traumatic—therapy. 2. Stress Disorders, Post-Traumatic—diagnosis. 3. Stress Disorders, Post-Traumatic—psychology. WM 170 B853p 2006] RC552.P67B7495 2006 616.85'2106—dc22dc22
                              2005027709

05 06 07 08 09 10 9 8 7 6 5 4 3 2 1

Acquiring Editor:	Arthur Pomponio
Editorial Assistant:	Veronica Novak
Production Editor:	Sanford Robinson
Copy Editor:	Pam Suwinsky
Typesetter:	C&M Digitals (P) Ltd.
Indexer:	Jean Casalegno
Cover Designer:	Michelle Kenny

Contents

Acknowledgments

The authors thank Janelle Jones, who read through many versions of this book and provided help with details large and small; Lucy Berliner, Megan Berthold, Chris Courtois, Constance Dalenberg, Marcia Goin, Rick Lasarow, George Simpson, and Jeff Uy for helpful advice and/or support; Jim High and Richard Loewenstein for helpful suggestions on the psychopharmacology chapter; and Sage project editor Sanford Robinson and freelance copy editor Pam Suwinsky, for their patience and direction.

JB thanks Cheryl Lanktree for all her love and support, and Bernard Brickman for his assistance and wisdom.

CS thanks her family, whose love makes everything possible: Ramona, Hans, David, Sarah, Rosannah, and Brian vonMoritz; Mimi and George Herschkowitz; Sheila Ryan and George Cavalletto and all of the Ryan-Cavallettos; Julie and Curtis Wallin; her sisters Shana Blake Hill, Elizabeth Frishkoff, Cheri Lowre, Cheryl Archbald, Allyson Rosen, Megan Berthold, and Janelle Jones, and her brother Hans Walser; Leanne, Rick, and Samantha Lasarow; Jeff and Brad Uy; Mark Ehrlich; and her parents Martha Ford Brady Petrou and Ron Petrou.

Introduction

T rauma seems to be an unavoidable part of the human condition. The history of humankind is not only the story of art and culture; it is also the story of war, subjugation of one group of people by another, domestic violence, and natural disaster. As a result, most people in Western society will experience at least one potentially traumatic event during their lives. Of these, a significant number of individuals will suffer lasting psychological distress, ranging from mild lingering anxiety to symptoms that interfere with all aspects of functioning.

The systematic study of the human response to trauma is relatively new. The modern field of traumatic stress was born in the aftermath of the Vietnam War, with the term "posttraumatic stress disorder" (PTSD) only introduced into the mental health lexicon in the mid-1980s. Since that time, we have learned that trauma is pervasive, and that the human response to trauma can be extremely complex. As our knowledge has grown, researchers and clinicians have developed a number of approaches to the treatment of posttraumatic stress and other trauma-related conditions. This information can be found in journal articles, books, and a handful of treatment manuals. Unfortunately, these sources are widely dispersed and are not always easily available to the practicing clinician. In addition, they tend to refer to a single theoretical orientation, generally focus on a single group of traumatized individuals (for example, sexual abuse survivors or motor vehicle accident victims), and often do not provide sufficient information on how to actually implement a given treatment approach.

In response, this book was written to be a hands-on, practical guide for clinicians working with adult and older adolescent trauma survivors. It outlines the essentials of treatment for people who have been traumatized by interpersonal violence, disasters, serious accidents, and other overwhelming events. Based in part on our experience directing the Psychological Trauma Program at Los Angeles County + University of Southern California Medical Center, it is intended as a resource for front-line mental health clinicians—as well as trainees in psychology, psychiatry, and social work—who require information on the actual practice of effective trauma-focused therapy. It is designed to be useful both for those clinicians working with clients who suffer from straightforward symptoms due to a one-time adult trauma and for those treating clients with more complex presentations, including clients who have experienced extensive childhood maltreatment.

The approach outlined in this book combines aspects of trauma-relevant cognitive-behavioral therapy with current thinking in the area of relational psychotherapy. Also included is information on trauma psychopharmacology, intended for medical practitioners and psychiatric trainees, as well as for nonmedical clinicians, who are often critical to their clients' pharmacological treatment.

Most of the techniques presented in this book are based on clinical research, and reflect the current science about working with traumatized individuals. However, clients seen in public mental health centers and general clinical practices are often more complex and potentially more challenging than those who are screened and selected to participate in randomized clinical trials (RCTs) (Spinazzola, Blaustein, & van der Kolk, 2005; Westen, Novotny, & Thompson-Brenner, 2004) and may be less responsive to RCT-developed treatment methodologies (Zayfert, et al., 2005). A recent meta-analysis concludes, in fact, that due to sample screening, participant drop-out, and other issues, the results of randomized clinical trials provide less guidance to clinicians in "real-world" settings than might be expected (Bradley, Greene, Russ, Dutra, & Westen, 2005). For this reason, we do not limit ourselves solely to interventions that have been fully validated in published treatment outcome research. For example, we include some ideas from modern psychodynamic or relational therapy, even though the complexity and, often, longer duration of such approaches do not lend themselves well to controlled scientific studies. In these cases, we attempt to provide research-based support for the underlying model. There are, however, newer, relatively experimental trauma treatment approaches that receive no attention in this book, primarily because they appear to lack meaningful (that is, empirically supportable) theoretical underpinnings.

Effective intervention requires accurate understanding and assessment of trauma and its effects, both in general and in the context of the individual, presenting client. For this reason, we begin this book with chapters on the nature of psychological trauma, the symptoms and disorders that can follow traumatic events, and an overview of the primary trauma-focused assessment strategies and instruments used in the field. We have tried to make this information as relevant to the treatment of traumatized individuals as possible.

In order to provide access to material beyond what can be reasonably addressed in a treatment guide, each chapter ends with suggested readings. We also include, throughout the text, references to the trauma literature, albeit typically citing only the most representative or integrative of articles and books. A complete list of references appears at the back of the book.

Working with trauma survivors can be stressful, and sometimes even vicariously traumatic. It often exposes us to the pain and suffering that comes from observing the worst that human beings can do to each other. However, this work also can be deeply satisfying and rewarding. Trauma survivors show us that human beings have a capacity to heal, to overcome enormous challenges, and to grow. We hope that this book will not only provide tools for those who work with traumatized clients, but will also—along the way—affirm the tremendous optimism and value inherent in this endeavor.

PART I

Trauma, Effects, and Assessment

T he first part of this book outlines the major types of traumatic events, their potential effects, and ways in which trauma and its outcomes can be assessed. Each of these areas is important to effective trauma therapy. Awareness of the major types of traumatic events and their known psychological effects can assist the clinician in understanding what the client has undergone and what his or her current symptomatic experience is likely to be. In addition, knowledge of the relevant diagnostic interviews and psychological tests allows the clinician to pinpoint, in an objective way, specific targets for clinical intervention.

1

What Is Trauma?

The term *psychological trauma* has been applied in so many contexts by so many people that it has lost some of its original meaning. Often, *trauma* is used to refer both to negative events that produce distress and to the distress itself. Technically, "trauma" refers only to the event, not the reaction, and should be reserved for major events that are psychologically overwhelming for an individual. The *Diagnostic and Statistical Manual of Mental Disorders,* 4th edition, Text Revision (*DSM-IV-TR;* American Psychiatric Association [APA], 2000) specifically defines a trauma as

> direct personal experience of an event that involves actual or threatened death or serious injury, or other threat to one's physical integrity; or witnessing an event that involves death, injury, or a threat to the physical integrity of another person; or learning about unexpected or violent death, serious harm, or threat of death or injury experienced by a family member or other close associate (Criterion A1). The person's response to the event must involve intense fear, helplessness, or horror (or in children, the response must involve disorganized or agitated behavior) (Criterion A2). (p. 463)

DSM-IV-TR provides a list of potentially traumatic events, including combat, sexual and physical assault, robbery, being kidnapped, being taken hostage, terrorist attacks, torture, disasters, severe automobile accidents, and life-threatening illnesses, as well as witnessing death or serious injury by violent assault, accidents, war, or disaster. Childhood sexual abuse is included even if it does not involve threatened or actual violence or injury.

Although the *DSM-IV-TR* definition is useful, some have criticized the requirement that trauma be limited to "threatened death or serious injury, or other threat to one's physical integrity," since many events may be traumatic even if life threat or injury is not an issue (Briere, 2004). The earlier *DSM-III-R* (APA, 1987) definition also included threats to *psychological* integrity as valid forms of trauma. Because *DSM-IV-TR* does not consider events to be traumatic if they are merely highly upsetting but not life threatening—for example, extreme emotional abuse, major losses or separations, degradation or humiliation, and coerced (but not physically threatened or forced) sexual experiences—it undoubtedly underestimates the extent of actual trauma in the general population. It also reduces the availability of a stress disorder diagnosis in some individuals who experience significant posttraumatic distress–since Criterion A is a prerequisite for the diagnosis of posttraumatic stress disorder (PTSD) or acute stress disorder (ASD).

The issue of whether an event has to satisfy current diagnostic definitions of trauma in order to be, in fact, "traumatic," is an ongoing source of discussion in the field. Our own conclusion is that an event is traumatic if it is extremely upsetting and at least temporarily overwhelms the individual's internal resources. This broader definition is used throughout this book, since people who experience major threats to psychological integrity can suffer as much as those traumatized by physical injury or life threat, and can respond equally well, we believe, to trauma-focused therapies. This is solely a treatment issue, however; the *DSM-IV-TR* version of trauma should be strictly adhered to when making a formal stress disorder diagnosis.

Major Types of Trauma

Surveys of the general population suggest that at least half of all adults in the United States have experienced at least one major traumatic stressor (Elliott, 1997; Kessler, Sonnega, Bromet, Hughes, & Nelson, 1995). Although such stressors are common, their ability to produce significant psychological disturbance varies as a function of a wide variety of other variables, as is discussed in Chapter 2. The following pages detail most of the major types of traumatic events potentially experienced by those seeking mental health services. There are myriad ways in which an individual can be traumatized, not all of which are easily expressed in an initial clinical interview. This is important to keep in mind—frequently, clients will not report events they have experienced unless they are specifically asked about those events in a nonjudgmental, supportive context (see Chapter 3). Each type of trauma is described only briefly; the reader is referred to the Suggested Reading section at the end of the chapter for references to more detailed information.

Natural Disasters

Natural disasters can be defined as large-scale, not directly human-caused, injury- or death-producing environmental events that adversely affect a significant number of people. Disasters are relatively common in the United States; surveys suggest that between 13 and 30 percent of individuals have been exposed to one or more natural disasters in their lifetimes (Briere & Elliott, 2000; Green & Solomon, 1995). Typical disasters include earthquakes, large fires, floods, avalanches, hurricanes, tornados, and volcanic eruptions. The extent of physical injury, fear of death, and property loss during disasters appear to be the most traumatizing aspects of these events (Briere & Elliott, 2000; Maida, Gordon, Steinberg, & Gordon, 1989; Ursano, Fullerton, & McCaughey, 1994). When mental health workers are involved in assisting disaster victims, it is usually within the context of governmental or quasi-governmental agencies (for example, the Red Cross) that have been mobilized relatively soon after the event. At such times, as described in Chapter 10, the clinician's initial job usually involves triage and providing support, comfort, and psychological "first aid," as opposed to trauma therapy, per se.

Mass Interpersonal Violence

Intentional violence that involves high numbers of injuries or casualties—but does not occur in the context of war—is a newer category in the trauma field. The Oklahoma City bombing on April 19, 1995 (North et al., 1999), the terrorist attacks on the World Trade Center and the Pentagon on September 11, 2001 (Galea et al., 2002), and the July 7, 2005, attacks on the London mass transit system are obvious cases of mass trauma. There is an unfortunately large number of other examples, however, including terrorist attacks throughout the world and mass human rights abuses by totalitarian regimes (Alexander & Brenner, 2001; Pfefferbaum et al., 2001). The September 11 attacks stimulated a dramatic increase in North American research on the effective short-term treatment of mass trauma, as described in Chapter 10. As noted later, this research suggests that it is as important to know what *not* to do as it is to know what *to* do when working acutely with victims of mass trauma. It is a goal of international groups like the International Society for Traumatic Stress Studies (ISTSS; http://www.istss.org) to disseminate this information worldwide, since there is little reason to believe that terrorist attacks or other mass traumas will decrease in the foreseeable future.

Large-Scale Transportation Accidents

Transportation accidents involve events such as airline crashes, train derailments, and maritime (for example, ship) accidents. These events often involve multiple victims and high fatality rates. Although the incidence of such events is not easily determined, large-scale transportation accidents can be especially traumatic to survivors, since such events frequently occur over a relatively extended period of time during which the victims are exposed to ongoing terror and fear of death. Immediate response to airliner accidents in the United States is controlled primarily by the Federal Aviation Administration (FAA) and the National Transportation Safety Board (NTSB), who work in concert with local emergency services, the relevant airline company, and others in providing assistance to traumatized survivors and their families.

House or Other Domestic Fires

Although fires are often listed as disasters in the trauma literature, a significant number of victims seen by trauma clinicians have experienced smaller-scale fires. These include house fires, often caused by smoking in bed or by electrical short circuits, and gas explosions due to leaking propane tanks, stoves, or heaters. Physical injuries from fire can be particularly traumatic. The lasting effects of serious burns—a long recovery period, reconstructive surgeries, the development of visible and/or painful scars, and sometimes chronic pain and reduced mobility—mean that the traumatic event, in some ways, continues and repeats over time (Gilboa, Friedman, Tsur, & Fauerbach, 1994). This sustained traumatization, in turn, can interfere with posttraumatic recovery.

Motor Vehicle Accidents

Approximately 20 percent of individuals in the United States have experienced a serious motor vehicle accident (MVA) (Blanchard & Hickling, 1997). A substantial number of these people go on to develop significant psychological disturbance, especially if the accident involved major injury or resulted in the death of others. In the latter case, grief and self-blame may increase subsequent psychological effects. In addition, survivors of major MVAs may sustain traumatic brain injury, which can further complicate assessment and treatment (Harvey & Bryant, 2002; Hickling, Gillen, Blanchard, Buckley, & Taylor, 1998). Despite the fact that serious MVAs are more likely than many other noninterpersonal traumas to produce PTSD and other forms of dysfunction, clinicians often inappropriately overlook such traumas when interviewing clients about negative life events.

Rape and Sexual Assault

Rape can be defined as nonconsensual oral, anal, or vaginal sexual penetration of an adolescent or adult (if the victim is a child, see "Child Abuse") through the use of threat or physical force, or when the victim is incapable of giving consent (for example, when under the influence of drugs or alcohol, or when he or she is otherwise cognitively impaired). The term *sexual assault* typically denotes any forced sexual contact short of rape, although some authorities consider sexual assault to involve any forced sexual contact, including rape. Using definitions similar to these, the prevalence of rape against women in the United States is reported to be 14–20 percent (Kilpatrick & Resnick, 1993; Koss, 1993; Tjaden & Thoennes, 2000). Rape and sexual assault rates for males are less clear, due in part to only recent social awareness that men can be sexually victimized, but are estimated to range between 2 and 4 percent (Elliott, Mok, & Briere, 2004; Tjaden & Thoennes, 2000). Peer sexual assault against adolescent women is, sadly, quite common as well; Singer, Anglin, Song, and Lunghofer (1995) found that, among students in six geographically and economically diverse high schools, 12–17 percent of adolescent women reported having been made to engage in at least one sexual act against their wishes. Because of the shame and secrecy associated with being a victim of rape or sexual assault in many cultures, it is likely that some victims do not identify themselves as such in research studies. As a result, the prevalence rates quoted are probably underestimates. Sexual assault and rape can be particularly devastating and traumatizing events, and are substantial risk factors for PTSD among women in the general population (Kessler et al., 1995).

Stranger Physical Assault

Stranger assault refers to muggings, beatings, stabbings, shootings, attempted strangulations, and other violent actions against a person not well known to the assailant. The motive for such aggression is often robbery or the (sometimes random) expression of anger, although in gang and "drive-by" situations the intent may also be to define or protect turf or to otherwise assert dominance. Although many acts of violence in relationships are directed more toward women than men, the reverse appears true for stranger physical assaults. In one study of inner-city psychiatric emergency room patients, for example, 64 percent of men reported having experienced at least one nonintimate physical assault, as opposed to 14 percent of women (Currier & Briere, 2000). Similarly, Singer et al. (1995) found that, depending on the research site, 3–33 percent of male adolescents described being shot at or shot, and 6–16 percent reported being attacked or stabbed with a knife.

Partner Battery

Partner battery (also known as *wife battering, spouse abuse,* or *domestic violence*) is usually defined as physically or sexually assaultive behavior by one adult against another in an intimate, sexual, and usually (but not inevitably) cohabiting relationship. In the majority of cases, there is emotional abuse as well (Straus & Gelles, 1990). There may also be threats toward or violence against children, pets, and/or property. In a large-sample survey of individuals in the United States who were married or living with a partner, 25 percent reported at least one incident of physical aggression in a domestic context, while 11.6 percent reported incidents of severe physical violence such as punching, kicking, or choking (Straus & Gelles, 1990). Rates of sexual assault of women by partners or spouses—irrespective of their history of physical battering—range from 9 to 15 percent (Elliott & Briere, 2003; Finkelhor & Yllo, 1985). Among women who are physically assaulted by a partner, concomitant rates of sexual assault as high as 45 percent have been reported (Campbell & Soeken, 1999).

Torture

Torture has been defined by the United Nations as "any act by which severe pain or suffering, whether physical or mental, is intentionally inflicted on a person for such purposes as obtaining from him [sic] or a third person information or confession, punishing him for an act he has committed or is suspected of having committed, or intimidating him or a third person . . ." (Vesti & Kastrup, 1995, p. 214). Regardless of function or context, methods of torture involve both physical and psychological techniques, including beatings, near strangulation, electrical shock, various forms of sexual abuse and assault, crushing or breaking of bones and joints, sensory deprivation, threats of death or mutilation, mock executions, being made to feel responsible for the death or injury of others, sleep deprivation, and being forced to engage in grotesque or humiliating acts. The incidence of torture is not known, although Amnesty International (2002) estimates that more than 111 nations currently sanction the use of—or at least tacitly allow—torture. Torture victims are dramatically overrepresented among refugees (Baker, 1992), although such individuals are rarely questioned about a potential torture history when they come in contact with North American mental health systems.

War

War is a common and relatively powerful source of enduring psychological disturbance. Posttraumatic difficulties have been described in veterans of the American Civil War and both world wars, as well as in those who fought in Afghanistan, Korea, Vietnam, the Persian Gulf (including Iraq), Israel, Armenia, the Falklands, Somalia, and Bosnia. War involves a very wide range of violent and traumatic experiences, including immediate threat of death and/or disfigurement, physical injury, witnessing injury and/or death of others, and involvement in injuring or killing others (both combatants and civilians) (Kulka et al., 1990; Weathers, Litz, & Keane, 1995). For some, war includes witnessing or participating in atrocities, as well as undergoing rape, capture, and prisoner-of-war experiences such as confinement, torture, and extreme physical deprivation. These traumas, in turn, can produce a variety of symptoms and disorders. Most U.S. war veterans who seek psychological services today were combatants or support personnel in Iraq, Vietnam, or Korea. Although the Veterans' Administration provides care for many war veterans with service-connected injuries or disabilities in the United States, it is not uncommon for veterans to present to non–VA mental health centers and clinicians.

Child Abuse

Childhood sexual and physical abuse, ranging from fondling to rape and from severe spankings to life-threatening beatings, is quite prevalent in North American society. Studies of retrospective child abuse reports in the United States suggest that approximately 25–35 percent of women and 10–20 percent of men, if asked, describe being sexually abused as children, and approximately 10–20 percent of men and women report experiences congruent with definitions of physical abuse (Briere & Elliott, 2003; Finkelhor, Hotaling, Lewis, & Smith, 1990). Several studies suggest that 35–70 percent of female mental health patients self-report, if asked, a childhood history of sexual abuse (Briere, 1992). Many children are psychologically abused and/or neglected, as well, although these forms of maltreatment are harder to quantify in terms of incidence or prevalence (Erickson & Egeland, 2002; Hart, Brassard, Binggeli, & Davidson, 2002). As is described in later chapters, child abuse and neglect not only produces significant, sometimes enduring, psychological dysfunction, it is also associated with a greater likelihood of being sexually or physically assaulted later in life (Classen, Palesh, & Aggarwal, 2005).

Emergency Worker Exposure to Trauma

Because emergency workers often encounter potentially traumatic phenomena, including fatal injury, traumatic amputation, disembowelment, severe burns, and extreme victim distress, it is not surprising that those who help the traumatized may become traumatized themselves. Among those known to be at risk for such work-related stress are firefighters, rescue workers, paramedics and other emergency medical personnel, individuals involved in the identification and handling of deceased trauma victims, emergency mental health and crisis intervention workers, and law enforcement personnel (Berah, Jones, & Valent, 1984; Fullerton, Ursano, & Wang, 2004; Rivard, Dietz, Martell, & Widawski, 2002). Psychotherapists who treat trauma survivors may also develop a form of vicarious traumatization (Dalenberg, 2000; Goin, 2002; Pearlman & Saakvitne, 1995).

The Problem of Combined and Cumulative Traumas

The listing of separately described traumas presented may give the erroneous impression that such traumas are independent of one another—in other words, that undergoing one trauma does not necessarily increase the likelihood of experiencing another. This is generally true of noninterpersonal traumas such as disasters or house fires. However, a number of studies demonstrate that victims of interpersonal traumas are at statistically greater risk of additional interpersonal traumas. This is especially true in what is known as *revictimization:* those who have experienced childhood abuse are considerably more like to be victimized again as adults (Classen et al., 2002; Tjaden & Thoennes, 2000). In addition, many clinicians have noticed that some clients seem to have more than their normal share of adult traumas: lifestyle, environmental, behavioral, personality, and/or social issues appear to increase the likelihood of the individual being repeatedly victimized.

The relationship among different traumas, and the symptoms and difficulties they cause in a given individual's life history, can be complex. Childhood abuse, for example, may produce various symptoms and maladaptive behaviors in adolescence and adulthood (for example, substance abuse, indiscriminate sexual behavior, and reduced danger awareness via dissociation or denial) that, in turn, increase the likelihood of later interpersonal victimization. These later traumas may then lead to further behaviors and responses that are additional risk factors for further trauma, and subsequent, potentially even more complex mental health outcomes (Briere & Jordan, 2004). Because both childhood and adult traumas can produce psychological difficulties, current symptomatology in adult survivors may represent (1) the effects of childhood trauma that have lasted into adulthood, (2) the effects of more recent sexual or physical assaults, (3) the additive effects of childhood trauma *and* adult assaults (for example, flashbacks to both childhood and adult victimization experiences), and/or (4) the exacerbating interaction of childhood trauma and adult assault, such as especially severe, regressed, dissociated, or self-destructive responses to the adult trauma.

This complicated mixture of multiple traumas and multiple symptomatic responses is well known to trauma-focused clinicians, who sometimes find it difficult to connect certain symptoms to certain traumas, and other symptoms to other traumas, or, in fact, to discriminate trauma-related symptoms from less trauma-specific symptoms. Although this task is often daunting, the remaining chapters of this book describe assessment and treatment approaches that clarify these various trauma-symptom connections or, in some cases, provide alternative ways of approaching multitrauma-multisymptom presentations.

Suggested Reading

Breslau, N., Davis, G. C., Andreski, P., & Peterson, E. L. (1991). Traumatic events and post-traumatic stress disorder in an urban population of young adults. *Archives of General Psychiatry, 48,* 216–222.

Koss, M. P. (1993). Detecting the scope of rape: A review of prevalence research methods. *Journal of Interpersonal Violence, 8,* 198–222.

March, J. S. (1993). What constitutes a stressor? The "criterion A" issue. In J. R. T. Davidson & E. B. Foa (eds.), *Posttraumatic stress disorder: DSM-IV and beyond.* Washington, DC: American Psychiatric Association Press.

Norris, F. (1992). Epidemiology of trauma: Frequency and impact of different potentially traumatic events on different demographic groups. *Journal of Consulting and Clinical Psychology, 60,* 409–418.

Read, J., & Fraser, A. (1998). Abuse histories of psychiatric inpatients: To ask or not to ask? *Psychiatric Services, 49,* 355–359.

2

The Effects of Trauma

This chapter is divided into two sections. The first discusses those individual, social, and trauma-specific variables that are most associated with the development of posttraumatic symptoms in older adolescents and adults. These various contributors to (and moderators of) posttraumatic outcomes are relevant to clinical practice because, as it turns out, two people exposed to a similar trauma may respond in remarkably different ways—one may present with only mild, transient symptoms, whereas the other may develop a full-blown stress disorder that endures for months or years. Current research indicates that only a minority of those exposed to a Criterion A trauma, as defined by the *Diagnostic and Statistical Manual of Mental Disorders (DSM-IV-TR;* American Psychiatric Association [APA], 2000) go on to develop posttraumatic stress disorder (Breslau, Davis, Andreski, & Peterson, 1991)—the rest are either less affected or respond with other symptoms, such as depression or generalized anxiety. The specific extent and type of symptom expression is associated with a number of variables, often referred to as *risk factors* for traumatic stress. In some cases, intervention aimed at these risk factors may lead to decreased posttraumatic response and less risk for future disorders.

The second section of this chapter describes the major forms that posttraumatic symptomatology can take. Clinical outcomes include not only the three major trauma-specific disorders (acute stress disorder [ASD], posttraumatic stress disorder [PTSD], and brief psychotic disorder with marked stressor [BPDMS]), but also a number of other, more generic responses or disorders that can arise from exposure to trauma.

What Makes Trauma Responses More Likely, More Intense, or More Complicated?

The amount and type of posttraumatic symptomatology an individual experiences are a function of at least three domains: (1) variables specific to the victim, (2) characteristics of the stressor, and (3) how those around the victim respond to the victim.

Victim Variables

Victim variables refer to those aspects of the victim that were in place before the trauma but that nevertheless are associated with a likelihood of sustained posttraumatic stress.

Major victim-specific risk factors include:

- Female gender (Breslau, Chilcoat, Kessler, & Davis, 1999; Leskin & Sheikh, 2002)
- Age, with younger or older individuals being at greater risk than those in mid-adulthood (Atkeson, Calhoun, Resick, & Ellis, 1982; Koenen et al., 2002)
- Race, with African Americans and Hispanics—as compared to Caucasians—at higher risk (Kulka et al., 1990; Ruch & Chandler, 1983)
- Lower socioeconomic status (Kulka et al., 1990; Rosenman, 2002)
- Previous psychological dysfunction or disorder (Brady, Killeen, Brewerton, & Lucerini, 2000; Kulka et al., 1990)
- Less functional coping styles (Fauerbach, Richter, & Lawrence, 2002; Silver, Holman, McIntosh, Poulin, & Gil-Rivas, 2002)
- Family dysfunction and/or a history of psychopathology (Bassuk, Dawson, Perloff, & Weinreb, 2001; Breslau et al., 1991)
- Previous history of trauma exposure (Breslau et al., 1999; Ozer, Best, Lipsey, & Weiss, 2003)
- A hyperreactive or dysfunctional nervous system (Southwick, Morgan, Vythilingam, & Charney, 2003; Yehuda, Halligan, Golier, Grossman, & Bierer, 2004)
- Genetic predisposition (Segman et al., 2002; Stein, Jang, Taylor, Vernon, & Livesley, 2002)
- Greater distress at the time of the trauma or immediately thereafter (Brewin, Andrews, & Rose, 2000; Roemer, Orsillo, Borkovec, & Litz, 1998)

This last characteristic, distress during or after the trauma (often referred to as *peritraumatic distress*), is a major predictor of risk for PTSD. In fact, as described by *DSM-IV-TR* Criterion A2, a stressful event is not considered to be a trauma unless the individual reports feelings of horror, fear, or helplessness at the time it happened or soon thereafter. Other peritraumatic responses, such as anger, shame, and guilt, are also likely to increase the risk of posttraumatic reactions (for example, Andrews, Brewin, Rose, & Kirk, 2000; Leskela, Dieperink, & Thuras, 2002). Although sometimes considered a trauma characteristic (as implied by *DSM-IV-TR*), peritraumatic distress is probably as much a victim variable as it is an index of trauma severity. Those who experience especially high levels of distress at the time of a trauma would seemingly be more at risk for posttraumatic difficulties for a number of reasons, including preexisting (that is, pretrauma) problems in stress tolerance and affect regulation, prior trauma exposure, and a cognitive predisposition to view life events as outside of their control or as potential threats.

The Role of Gender and Race

It makes sense that many of the victim characteristics listed would be associated with greater posttraumatic difficulties. For example, individuals with lower socioeconomic status, less functional coping styles, family histories of mental disorder, histories of previous trauma exposure, genetic predisposition to PTSD, and reduced stress tolerance, as well as those who are especially young or older, all might have greater vulnerability to traumatic events. On the other hand, the demographic variables of gender and race are less intuitively obvious risk factors. There is no reason to expect that women or people of color are inherently less hardy, or in some other way especially prone to trauma effects. Nevertheless, these groups are more likely than others to meet diagnostic criteria for PTSD in both clinical and nonclinical samples.

As it turns out, being a woman or a non-Caucasian in American society is a risk factor for traumatic stress in large part because women and racial/ethnic minorities are more frequently exposed to events that produce posttraumatic disturbance (Briere, 2004). In other words, the higher rate of PTSD in these demographic groups is not due to a decreased ability to handle stress, but rather to the fact that—as a result of broad social factors such as racial and sexual inequality—these individuals are more likely to experience trauma than other groups of people. For example, in the National Vietnam Veterans Readjustment Study (Kulka et al., 1988), the rate of PTSD in veterans was considerably lower for Caucasians (14 percent) than for Hispanics (28 percent) or African Americans (19 percent). However, it was determined that Hispanics and African Americans were also more likely to be exposed to high combat stress than Caucasians (and, although not highlighted in that study, probably more likely to be victimized prior to joining the military). When race differences in level of combat exposure were controlled statistically, the difference in PTSD between Caucasians and African Americans disappeared, and the Caucasian-Hispanic difference decreased significantly. Similarly, although Kessler, Sonnega, Bromet, Hughes, and Nelson (1995) estimate the lifetime prevalence of PTSD to be 10.4 percent for women and 5.0 percent for men, they suggest that these sex differences are largely due to women's greater likelihood of exposure to PTSD-producing traumas—especially sexual abuse and rape—than men's. When the likelihood of trauma exposure is equivalent for both sexes (for example, natural disasters), PTSD rates are approximately equal between men and women (Yehuda, 2004).

Characteristics of the Stressor

In addition to victim variables, a number of trauma characteristics appear to affect posttraumatic outcome. These include:

- Intentional acts of violence (as opposed to noninterpersonal events) (Briere & Elliott, 2000; Green, Grace, Lindy, & Gleser, 1990)
- The presence of life threat (Holbrook, Hoyt, Stein, & Sieber, 2001; Ullman & Filipas, 2001)
- Physical injury (Briere & Elliott, 2000; Foy, Resnick, Sipprelle, & Caroll, 1987)
- The extent of combat exposure during war (Goldberg, True, Eisen, & Henderson, 1990; Kulka et al., 1990)
- Witnessing death (Selley et al., 1997), especially when the scene is grotesque (Epstein, Fullerton, & Ursano, 1998)
- The loss of a friend or loved one due to a trauma (Green et al., 1990)
- Unpredictability and uncontrollability (Carlson & Dalenberg, 2000; Foa, Zinbard, & Rothbaum, 1992)
- Sexual (as opposed to nonsexual) victimization (Breslau et al., 1991)

The impact of these trauma characteristics on the development of posttraumatic stress is significant. Irrespective of victim variables, certain traumatic events (for example, rape) are known to produce a much greater likelihood of PTSD than others (for example, natural disasters). Thus, just as it is erroneous to consider only trauma variables when attempting to predict posttraumatic stress in an individual, it is also erroneous to assume that posttraumatic reactions are solely due to individual or demographic variables.

Social Response, Support, and Resources

Psychological support by family members, friends, and others is known to reduce the intensity of posttraumatic stress. Such support includes accepting (that is, nonblaming, nonstigmatizing) responses after the trauma disclosure, caring and nurturing from loved ones, and the availability of helpers and support or aid agencies after a traumatic event (for example, Berthold, 2000; Coker et al., 2002; Lee, Isaac, & Janca, 2002). Social response to the victim is not independent of trauma characteristics or victim variables, however. Some traumatic events are more socially acceptable than others (for example, the victim of a hurricane or earthquake may be seen by some people as more innocent and worthy of compassion than a rape victim), and certain trauma survivors (for example, racial minorities, homosexuals, undocumented immigrants, prostitutes, the homeless), are more likely to receive prejudicial treatment than others. Above and beyond these complexities, however, most studies suggest that social support is one of the most powerful determinants of the ultimate effects of trauma. This fact highlights the social/relational aspect of trauma recovery, including, as we will see, the importance of the therapeutic relationship in trauma treatment.

Types of Posttraumatic Responses

As noted previously, potentially traumatic events vary in type and frequency, and their psychological effects are moderated by a host of victim-specific and social/cultural variables. It is not surprising, therefore, that a number of different symptoms and disorders have been associated with exposure to traumatic events. The most significant of these are described in the following pages. It is important to note, however, that not all psychological injury can be encompassed by a list of symptoms or disorders. Trauma can alter the very meaning we give to our lives, and can produce feelings and experiences that are not easily categorized in diagnostic manuals. These more existential impacts include profound emptiness, loss of connection with one's spirituality, or disruption in one's ability to hope, trust, or care about oneself or others (Herman, 1992a). For this reason, rarely will a diagnosis or set of psychological test results encompass the full breadth of trauma impact. On the other hand, diagnosis and symptom description allow clinicians to refer to a common language and knowledge base and can assist in the development of a useful treatment plan.

Depression

Events that are overwhelming enough to produce posttraumatic stress can also produce clinical levels of depression (Kessler et al., 1995). When posttraumatic and depressive symptoms arise from the same traumatic events, victims often report themes of grief and loss, abandonment and isolation. The significant overlap among posttraumatic stress, grief, and depression, as well as the connection between posttraumatic depression and heightened suicide potential, means that depression should always be considered in work with those who have been traumatized.

Complicated or Traumatic Grief

Grief is a normal response to loss and often resolves naturally over time. When the loss involves a sudden, traumatic (perhaps violent or gruesome) death or disruption of an individual's life, however, this response may become more complicated, and may be associated with lasting mental health problems (Prigerson et al., 1999). For example, traumatic loss may be accompanied by clinical depression, PTSD, substance abuse, or, in some cases, serious physical illness (for example, Shear & Smith-Caroff, 2002; Zisook, Chentsova-Dutton, & Shuchter, 1998). In this regard, a "complicated" or "traumatic" grief disorder following traumatic loss has been proposed (Horowitz et al., 1997; Prigerson et al., 1999), involving posttraumatic symptoms such as "intense intrusive thoughts, distressing yearnings, feeling excessively alone and empty, excessively avoiding tasks reminiscent of the deceased, unusual sleep disturbances, and maladaptive levels of loss of interest in personal activities" (Horowitz et al., 1997, p. 904). Although not codified in *DSM-IV*, such symptoms are commonly found among those exposed to natural disasters, terrorist attacks, and other events that produce death or other major loss.

Major Depression

As mentioned earlier, a number of studies indicate that those who have been exposed to a major trauma are at risk of developing a major depressive disorder, and depression is one of the most common comorbid disorders for PTSD (Breslau et al., 1991; Kessler et al., 1995). Some symptoms of major depression (particularly insomnia, psychomotor agitation, and decreased inability to concentrate) overlap with symptoms of PTSD, which may complicate assessment. In addition, many trauma survivors present with a chief complaint of depressed mood, and do not initially report their history of trauma exposure. As a result, clinicians evaluating trauma victims should be alert to depressive symptoms, including:

- Extreme sadness or dysphoria related to irrevocable loss
- Hopelessness regarding the likelihood of future traumatic events
- Worthlessness, excessive guilt, or thoughts about having deserved a traumatic event
- Suicidality
- Loss of interest in former pleasurable activities
- Decreased ability to concentrate
- Psychomotor agitation or retardation
- Anorexia and/or weight loss

- Fatigue and loss of energy
- Sleep disturbance, either insomnia or hypersomnia

When depression is a significant component of an individual's posttraumatic picture, pharmacotherapy may be indicated in addition to psychotherapy (see Chapter 11).

Psychotic Depression

Trauma is known to be associated with psychosis as well as with depression (Davidson, 1994). It is not unexpected, therefore, that major depression with psychotic features has been linked to posttraumatic stress. What is more surprising is that PTSD is as much as four times more common among depressed individuals with psychotic symptoms than among depressed individuals without psychosis (for example, Zimmerman & Mattia, 1999).

This elevated risk of PTSD in those with psychotic depression may be explained in several ways. First, extreme trauma can produce both psychosis and depression, such that some individuals present with both sets of symptoms simultaneously. Second, those with a predisposition to psychotic depression may be at risk for PTSD by virtue of decreased affect regulation abilities or a tendency to become cognitively disorganized when stressed. Third, it is likely that some of the "psychotic" symptoms in those PTSD sufferers with comorbid depression actually represent severe intrusive symptomatology associated with posttraumatic stress. For example, victims of rape and domestic violence frequently report hearing the perpetrator calling their name or making derogatory comments, and victims of gun violence often report hearing gunshots. Regardless of the reason for the association among posttraumatic stress, depression, and psychosis, the assessing clinician should be alert to the possibility of significant trauma exposure in those who complain both of psychotic and depressive symptoms.

Anxiety

Because trauma involves the experience of danger and vulnerability, posttraumatic outcomes often involve symptoms of anxiety. Such responses can be divided into three clusters: generalized anxiety, panic attacks, and posttraumatic phobias.

Generalized Anxiety

Generalized anxiety disorder is known to be both a risk factor for developing posttraumatic stress in response to a trauma (for example, Koenen et al., 2002) and a syndrome that may follow trauma exposure (for example, Freedman et al., 2002). In addition, many individuals report an increase in nonspecific anxiety symptoms after a traumatic event (for example, Mayou, Bryant, & Ehlers, 2001). Because anxiety is probably a final common pathway for a variety of etiological factors, some of which are not trauma related, the presence of generalized anxiety in any given individual does not necessarily mean that he or she has a trauma history. In traumatized individuals, however, such nonspecific anxiety often reflects the impact of threatening events and should be addressed in any comprehensive trauma therapy.

Panic

Historically, panic attacks (usually lasting from 10 minutes to an hour and characterized by symptoms such as palpitations, sweating, and feelings of impending doom) and panic disorder have not been considered trauma-related phenomena. Yet, *DSM-IV-TR* notes that panic attacks can arise from especially stressful events and major losses, and many trauma survivors report episodes of panic following interpersonal victimization (for example, Falsetti & Resnick, 1997). According to *DSM-IV-TR*, such episodes are not considered evidence of panic disorder, since diagnostic criteria require that panic attacks not be linked to a specific event. Regardless of whether the diagnostic criteria for panic disorder are met, panic attacks can be overwhelming and terrifying experiences that require intervention from clinicians, including possible pharmacotherapy, as is discussed in later chapters.

Despite the decoupling of posttraumatic panic and formal panic disorder in *DSM-IV*, recent research suggests a significant comorbidity between panic disorder and posttraumatic stress in the general population (for example, Leskin & Sheikh, 2002). In other words, PTSD is often associated with panic attacks, even when such attacks are not obviously attributable to trauma-related triggers. As a result, the clinician should inquire about episodes of panic when evaluating those suffering from trauma exposure, and should consider the possibility that panic attacks in a given trauma survivor may represent a form of posttraumatic stress.

Phobic Anxiety

Most models of the etiology of "irrational" fears (that is, phobias) tend to stress conditioned fear responses to stimuli associated with prior upsetting events, although some do emphasize more genetic aspects of phobia development (Kendler, Myers, & Prescott, 2002). In line with conditioning theory, many of the avoidant symptoms of PTSD and ASD are implicitly phobic: they involve efforts to avoid people, places, and situations that are reminiscent of a given trauma, primarily because of the fear that has become associated with those stimuli. In addition, both social phobias and specific phobias have been found to be comorbid with posttraumatic stress (Kessler et al., 1995; Zayfert, Becker, Unger, & Shearer, 2002) and to be more prevalent among those exposed to trauma (Mayou et al., 2001).

Stress Disorders

The hallmark of extreme traumatization is often considered to be PTSD or ASD, each of which is categorized as an anxiety disorder in *DSM-IV-TR*. Although these responses represent only a subset of the symptoms that can arise from trauma, they are obviously quite prevalent among the trauma-exposed. A related disorder, brief psychotic disorder with marked stressors, is sometimes included among the stress disorders, but is considered separately later in this chapter.

PTSD

Posttraumatic stress disorder is the best known trauma-specific diagnosis in *DSM-IV-TR*. As presented in Table 2.1, the symptoms of PTSD are divided into three clusters: reexperiencing of the traumatic event, avoidance of trauma-relevant stimuli and numbing of general responsiveness, and persistent hyperarousal. Typically, reexperiencing presents as flashbacks and intrusive thoughts and/or memories of the trauma, as well as distress and physiologic reactivity upon exposure to stimuli reminiscent of the event. Avoidance symptoms may be cognitive (for example, avoiding or suppressing upsetting thoughts, feelings, or memories), behavioral (for example, avoiding activities, people, places, or conversations that might trigger memories of the stressor), dissociative (for example, amnesia for all or parts of the stressor, depersonalization) and at least partially physiologic (for example, emotional numbing). The third PTSD symptom cluster, hyperarousal, may present as "jumpiness" (a lowered startle threshold), irritability, sleep disturbance, or attention/concentration difficulties. The reexperiencing symptoms of PTSD are often the first to fade over time, whereas avoidant and hyperarousal symptoms typically are more enduring (for example, McFarlane, 1988).

In contrast to acute stress disorder (described next), PTSD can only be diagnosed once a month has elapsed since the stressor. The symptoms do not have to appear within a certain time period after the trauma; in some instances "there may be a delay of months, or even years, before symptoms appear" (APA, 2000, p. 466). Such delayed PTSD appears to be relatively rare, however (for example, Bryant & Harvey, 2002).

Table 2.1   *DSM-IV-TR* Diagnostic Criteria for Posttraumatic Stress Disorder

A. The person has been exposed to a traumatic event in which both of the following were present:
    (1) the person experienced, witnessed, or was confronted with an event or events that involved actual or threatened death or serious injury, or a threat to the physical integrity of self or others
    (2) the person's response involved intense fear, helplessness, or horror. **Note:** In children, this may be expressed instead by disorganized or agitated behavior.

B. The traumatic event is persistently reexperienced in at least one of the following ways:
    (1) recurrent and intrusive distressing recollections of the event, including images, thoughts, or perceptions. **Note:** In young children, repetitive play may occur in which themes or aspects of the trauma are expressed.
    (2) recurrent distressing dreams of the event. **Note:** In children, there may be frightening dreams without recognizable content.
    (3) acting or feeling as if the traumatic event were recurring (includes a sense of reliving the experience, illusions, hallucinations, and dissociative flashback episodes, including those which occur on awakening or when intoxicated). **Note:** In young children, trauma-specific reenactment may occur.
    (4) intense psychological distress at exposure to internal or external cues that symbolize or resemble the traumatic event
    (5) physiological reactivity on exposure to internal or external cues that symbolize or resemble the traumatic event

C. Persistent avoidance of stimuli associated with the trauma and numbing of general responsiveness (not present before the trauma), as indicated by three (or more) of the following:
    (1) efforts to avoid thoughts, feelings, or conversations associated with the trauma
    (2) efforts to avoid activities, places, or people that arouse recollections of the trauma
    (3) inability to recall an important aspect of the trauma
    (4) markedly diminished interest or participation in significant activities
    (5) feelings of detachment or estrangement from others
    (6) restricted range of affect (e.g., unable to have loving feelings)
    (7) sense of foreshortened future (e.g., does not expect to have a career, marriage, children, or a normal life span)

D. Persistent symptoms of increased arousal (not present before the trauma), as indicated by two (or more) of the following:
    (1) difficulty falling or staying asleep
    (2) irritability or outbursts of anger
    (3) difficulty concentrating
    (4) hypervigilance
    (5) exaggerated startle response

Table 2.1 (Continued)

E. Duration of the disturbance (symptoms in Criteria B, C, or D) is more than 1 month.

F. The disturbance causes clinically significant distress or impairment in social, occupational, or other important areas of functioning.

Specify if: **Acute:** if duration is less than 3 months
                 Chronic: if duration is 3 months or more,

Specify if: **With Delayed Onset:** if onset of symptoms is at least 6 months after the stressor

Source: APA (2000), p. 467. Reprinted with permission from the *Diagnostic and Statistical Manual of Mental Disorders, Fourth Edition, Text Revision* (copyright © 2000), American Psychiatric Association.

As is noted more extensively later in the chapter under "Complex PTSD," *DSM-IV* acknowledges several "associated features" of PTSD that are especially prevalent following interpersonal victimization. These include dissociation, cognitive distortions, and more personality disorder-like difficulties in areas such as identity and affect regulation. In addition, up to 80 percent of those with PTSD have at least one other psychological disorder (Kessler et al., 1995; Spinazzola, Blaustein, & van der Kolk, 2005). Common comorbidities include major depression, substance abuse, and the various anxiety disorders (Breslau et al., 1991; Kessler et al., 1995). For this reason, a detailed assessment for PTSD should consider these sequelae as well.

ASD

The diagnosis of acute stress disorder is new to *DSM-IV*. The primary function of this category is to recognize and codify those intrusive, avoidant (especially dissociative), and hyperarousal-related psychological reactions to an acute stressor that occur relatively immediately after the traumatic event has transpired, and that may help in identifying those who will progress to later PTSD. The relevant symptoms must last for at least 2 days but not exceed 4 weeks in duration. The specific symptoms of ASD are presented in Table 2.2.

ASD is noteworthy for its similarity to PTSD, except that it is diagnosed more acutely, has fewer effortful avoidance and hyperarousal requirements, and includes more dissociative symptomatology. Especially prominent dissociative features listed in *DSM-IV* are psychic numbing and detachment, as well as depersonalization and/or derealization. As these differences suggest, there is not a one-to-one relationship between ASD and later PTSD. Some individuals with severe acute responses, especially those with significant dissociation, will initially meet criteria for ASD, but will fail to meet criteria for PTSD when

Table 2.2   *DSM-IV-TR* Diagnostic Criteria for Acute Stress Disorder

A. The person has been exposed to a traumatic event in which both of the following were present:
   (1) the person experienced, witnessed, or was confronted with event(s) that involved actual or threatened death or serious injury, or a threat to the physical integrity of self or others
   (2) the person's response involved intense fear, helplessness, or horror

B. Either while experiencing or after experiencing the distressing event, the individual has three (or more) of the following dissociative symptoms:
   (1) a subjective sense of numbing, detachment, or absence of emotional responsiveness
   (2) a reduction in awareness of his or her surroundings (e.g., "being in a daze")
   (3) derealization
   (4) depersonalization
   (5) dissociative amnesia (i.e., inability to recall an important aspect of the trauma)

C. The traumatic event is persistently reexperienced in at least one of the following ways: recurring images, thoughts, dreams, illusions, flashback episodes, or a sense of reliving the experience; or distress upon exposure to reminders of the traumatic event.

D. Marked avoidance of stimuli that arouse recollections of the trauma (e.g., thoughts, feelings, conversations, activities, places, people).

E. Marked symptoms of anxiety or increased arousal (e.g., difficulty sleeping, irritability, poor concentration, hypervigilance, exaggerated startle response, motor restlessness).

F. The disturbance causes clinically significant distress or impairment in social, occupational, or other important areas of functioning or impairs the individual's ability to pursue some necessary task, such as obtaining necessary assistance or mobilizing personal resources by telling family members about the traumatic experience.

G. The disturbance lasts for a minimum of 2 days and a maximum of 4 weeks and occurs within 4 weeks of the traumatic event.

H. The disturbance is not due to the direct physiological effects of a substance (e.g., a drug of abuse, a medication) or a general medical condition, is not better accounted for by Brief Psychotic Disorder, and is not merely an exacerbation of a preexisting Axis I or Axis II disorder.

Source: APA (2000), p. 471. Reprinted with permission from the *Diagnostic and Statistical Manual of Mental Disorders, Fourth Edition, Text Revision* (copyright © 2000), American Psychiatric Association.

30 days have elapsed. Conversely, some individuals who do not meet criteria for ASD initially, because they do not have dissociative symptoms, will meet criteria for PTSD at 1 month posttrauma (Harvey & Bryant, 2002).

Individuals with acute stress reactions sometimes present with labile affect and psychomotor agitation or retardation, although these symptoms are not included in the *DSM-IV* criteria. Psychotic or near-psychotic symptoms also may be present, especially when the stressor is severe or the victim is particularly vulnerable psychologically. These may include transient cognitive loosening, briefly overvalued ideas or delusions involving persecution or outside control, and auditory hallucinations with trauma-related content. When psychotic features are prominent, however, the appropriate diagnosis is usually brief psychotic disorder, as noted later in this chapter, or major depression with psychotic features.

Some argue that there is insufficient evidence for the existence of ASD as a disorder separate from early PTSD (for example, Marshall, Spitzer, & Liebowitz, 1999), and that the dissociative symptoms emphasized by the ASD diagnostic criterion set are not necessarily a regular part of early onset posttraumatic stress (Harvey & Bryant, 2002). Regardless of whether ASD is discriminable from PTSD on any dimension other than its time of onset, it is a useful diagnosis for those suffering from severe symptoms immediately after accidents, major disasters, mass trauma, or interpersonal victimization.

A Note Regarding Differential Diagnosis of Stress Disorders

Clinicians are sometimes unclear about how to describe someone who suffers from significant posttraumatic symptoms, but either (1) has not experienced a formal Criterion A event, or (2) has experienced such an event, but his or her symptoms do not quite reach the threshold for PTSD. Generally, if an individual has not met Criterion A, but describes anxiety or depressive symptoms that meet criteria for another Axis I anxiety or depressive disorder, that disorder may best describe the person's clinical state. If symptoms do not meet anxiety or depressive disorder criteria, the diagnosis of *adjustment disorder* (a rather loosely defined diagnosis that captures anxiety, depressive, and behavioral disturbances in response to stressful life events) may be relevant. If the individual has experienced a Criterion A stressor, but does not fully meet all of the criteria for PTSD (perhaps reporting two avoidance symptoms instead of three, or describing significant avoidance and hyperarousal, but no reexperiencing)—in the absence of another codable Axis I diagnosis—the diagnosis of *anxiety disorder not otherwise specified* may be applied.

Dissociation

The *DSM-IV* describes *dissociation* as "a disruption in the usually integrated functions of consciousness, memory, identity, or perception of the environment" (p. 519). Central to most definitions is the notion of a variation in normal consciousness that arises from reduced or altered access to one's thoughts, feelings, perceptions, and/or memories, typically in response to a traumatic event, that is not attributable to an underlying medical disorder (Briere & Armstrong, in press).

The *DSM-IV* lists five dissociative disorders:

1. *Depersonalization disorder,* involving perceptual alienation and separation from one's body

2. *Dissociative amnesia,* consisting of psychogenic, clinically significant inability to access memory

3. *Dissociative fugue,* characterized by extended travel with associated identity disturbance

4. *Dissociative identity disorder* (formerly multiple personality disorder), involving the experience of having two or more personalities within oneself

5. *Dissociative disorder not otherwise specified* (DDNOS), used when significant dissociative symptoms are present but cannot be classified into one of the preceding diagnostic categories

Despite the range of dissociative disorders, dissociative phenomena traditionally have been considered manifestations of a single underlying state or trait, for example, "dissociation" or "dissociativity." Some clinicians view dissociative symptoms on a continuum, such that phenomena such as dissociative identity disorder or fugue states are thought to represent more severe dissociation than, say, depersonalization (for example, Bernstein, Ellason, Ross, & Vanderlinden, 2001). Other researchers note, however, that dissociative symptoms tend to form a number of only moderately correlated clusters (for example, Briere, Weathers, & Runtz, 2005; Ross, Joshie, & Currie, 1991). These latter analyses suggest that "dissociation" is to some extent a misnomer—the construct appears to refer to a cluster of diverse, phenomenologically distinct experiences that differ in form but ultimately produce a similar outcome, that is, mental avoidance of emotional distress.

Although the phenomenology of dissociative responses has yet to be resolved, it is clear that dissociation is often related to trauma. Each of the dissociative disorders (other than dissociative disorder not otherwise specified) is linked to traumatic events in *DSM-IV*, albeit not always exclusively. Among the stressors related to dissociative symptoms in the trauma literature are child abuse (for example, Chu, Frey, Ganzel, & Matthews, 1999), combat (for example, Bremner et al., 1992), sexual and physical assaults (for example, Cooper, Kennedy, & Yuille, 2001), and natural disasters (for example, Koopman, Classen, & Speigel, 1996). This trauma-dissociation relationship probably explains the prominence of dissociative symptoms in the diagnostic criteria for ASD, as well as the significant comorbidity between persistent dissociation and PTSD (Briere, Scott, & Weathers, 2005). However, one study suggests that, although most dissociative responses occur in those with a trauma history, the majority of those exposed to a trauma—in the absence of other risk factors—will not describe major dissociative symptomatology (Briere, in press). As well, some dissociative responses are associated with childhood neglect experiences and/or early, insecure parent-child attachment (Main & Morgan, 1996; Ogawa, Sroufe, Weinfield, Carlson, & Egeland, 1997)—phenomena that also can be viewed as a form of trauma (Cassidy & Mohr, 2001), albeit not defined as such in *DSM-IV*.

Somatoform Responses

Somatoform responses are physical or bodily symptoms that are strongly influenced by psychological factors. Especially relevant to trauma survivors are somatization disorder and conversion reaction.

Somatization Disorder

Individuals with *somatization disorder* endorse a wide variety of symptoms (pain, gastrointestinal, sexual, and neurological) whose only commonality is their somatic focus and the fact that they cannot be explained based on medical phenomena alone. A related disorder, *undifferentiated somatoform disorder,* requires only one physical complaint for which no medical explanation can be found or for which the symptom(s) exceeds its expected intensity. Somatization has been linked repeatedly to a history of childhood maltreatment, especially sexual abuse (for example, Walker et al., 1993), as well as other traumatic events (Beckham et al., 1998; Ursano, Fullerton, Kao, & Bhartiya, 1995). The reason for the connection between trauma and somatization is unclear. Possibilities include the effects of sustained autonomic arousal on organ systems especially responsive to sympathetic activation, and preoccupation with somatic vulnerability when the trauma involved the survivor's body, such as chronic pelvic pain in sexual abuse survivors (Briere, 1992b). In addition, somatization may serve as an idiom of distress for some cultures and subcultures that do not accept the validity of psychological symptoms (Kirmayer, 1996).

Although somatization is often related to trauma, many trauma survivors have more obviously "real" medical problems (Schnurr & Green, 2004). In such cases, somatic complaints may reflect identifiable underlying illness, as well as, in some cases, sensitivity to bodily distress—perhaps especially in sexual abuse survivors with gastrointestinal and pelvic complaints.

Conversion

According to *DSM-IV, conversion* refers to "symptoms or deficits affecting voluntary motor or sensory function that suggest a neurological or other general medical condition" when "(p) psychological factors are judged to be associated with the symptom or deficit because the initiation or exacerbation of symptoms or deficit is preceded by conflicts or stressors" and the symptom(s) cannot be fully explained medically (APA, 2000, p. 498). Typical conversion symptoms include paralysis, loss of ability to speak, abnormal movements, deafness, blindness, and seizures.

Conversion disorder may occur after a major stressor (for example, combat or the recent death of a significant other), although it may also arise from extreme psychological conflict (usually with associated guilt) and the availability of secondary gain. When trauma is contributory, the stressors most frequently implicated in the clinical literature are child abuse (for example, Roelofs, Keijsers, Hoogduin, Naring, & Moene, 2002; Sar, Akyüz, Kundakci, Kiziltan, & Dogan, 2004), combat (for example, Neill, 1993), and torture (for example, Van Ommeren et al., 2002).

Both somatization and conversion appear to vary by culture and sometimes reflect ethnocultural models or explanations for psychological distress (Kirmayer, 1996). Whatever their cultural functions, conversion responses are considerably more frequent in some other societies than in North America (Leff, 1988).

Brief Psychotic Disorder With Marked Stressor

Brief psychotic disorder with marked stressor (BPDMS) appeared in *DSM-III-R* (APA, 1987) as "Brief Reactive Psychosis." BPDMS is noteworthy for the fact that it often begins quite abruptly and may be quite florid in nature. The diagnosis requires at least one of four psychotic symptoms: delusions, hallucinations, disorganized speech, or grossly disorganized or catatonic behavior. Like other acute psychotic conditions, BPDMS is sometimes accompanied by extreme agitation, emotional distress, and confusion. *DSM-IV* lists suicide attempts as an associated feature, and notes that those with this disorder may require close supervision. The duration of BPDMS ranges from 1 day to less than 1 month, although this time frame is somewhat questionable. See Table 2.3 for the *DSM-IV-TR* criteria for this disorder.

Table 2.3   *DSM-IV-TR* Criteria for Brief Psychotic Disorder

A. Presence of one (or more) of the following symptoms:
    (1) delusions
    (2) hallucinations
    (3) disorganized speech (e.g., frequent derailment or incoherence)
    (4) grossly disorganized or catatonic behavior

Note: Do not include a symptom if it is a culturally sanctioned response pattern.

B. Duration of an episode of the disturbance is at least 1 day but less than 1 month, with eventual full return to premorbid level of functioning.

C. The disturbance is not better accounted for by a Mood Disorder With Psychotic Features, Schizoaffective Disorder, or Schizophrenia and is not due to the direct physiological effects of a substance (e.g., a drug of abuse, a medication) or a general medical condition.

Specify: **With Marked Stressor(s)** (brief reactive psychosis): if symptoms occur shortly after and apparently in response to events that, singly or together, would be markedly stressful to almost anyone in similar circumstances in the person's culture
Without Marked Stressor(s): if psychotic symptoms do not occur shortly after, or are not apparently in response to events that, singly or together, would be markedly stressful to almost anyone in similar circumstances in the person's culture
With Postpartum Onset: if onset within 4 weeks postpartum.

Source: APA (2000), p. 332. Reprinted with permission from the *Diagnostic and Statistical Manual of Mental Disorders, Fourth Edition, Text Revision* (copyright © 2000), American Psychiatric Association.

It is not always clear whether a psychotic episode that follows a traumatic stressor is, in fact, BPDMS. In some cases, for example, the psychosis may be trauma related, but may persist for several months or longer (APA, 2000, p. 331). Because these symptoms exceed the (somewhat arbitrary) one month limit, they cannot be diagnosed as BPDMS—regardless of how trauma related they appear. In other instances, apparent psychotic responses to a marked stressor may represent the trauma-related activation of a latent predisposition toward psychosis, or the acute exacerbation of an already existing—but previously undetected—psychotic illness. It also is not uncommon for a severe trauma to produce or trigger depression with psychotic features, as noted earlier in this chapter—a diagnosis that takes precedence over BPDMS (APA, 2000, p. 332). As well, it appears that some chronic psychotic states are associated, at least in part, with childhood traumatic events (Read, 1997), suggesting that not all trauma-related psychosis is necessarily "brief." Finally, some cases of severe posttraumatic stress may include psychotic symptoms (for example, paranoid ideation, looseness of thought, or hallucinations) in the context of a more prominent ASD or PTSD presentation (Davidson, 1994; Pinto & Gregory, 1995). It has been estimated, for example, that 30–40 percent of treatment-seeking Vietnam combat veterans with PTSD experience at least some hallucinations and/or delusions (David, Kutcher, Jackson, & Mellman, 1999). In all of the latter cases, of course, BPDMS is not a diagnostic option, since the 1-month period has obviously passed.

Drug and Alcohol Abuse

Substance abuse and substance dependence (the latter occurring when there is also tolerance, withdrawal symptoms, and inability to sustain abstinence) are relatively common among those exposed to traumatic events, perhaps especially those who have experienced interpersonal violence (Ouimette & Brown, 2003). Further, as would be expected, those with substance abuse problems are more likely than most other groups to report a history of trauma exposure and to present with symptoms of PTSD (Najavits, 2002; Ouimette, Moos, & Brown, 2003). The comorbidity of trauma, PTSD, and substance abuse is widely discussed in both the substance abuse and trauma fields, primarily because such comorbidity can complicate assessment and interfere with treatment (Brown, Read, & Kahler, 2003; Najavits, 2002).

There are at least three major reasons why trauma, PTSD, and substance abuse may overlap (Brown & Wolfe, 1994): (1) because trauma survivors seek out psychoactive substances as a way to "self-medicate" posttraumatic distress; (2) because those who abuse substances are more easily victimized or otherwise prone to trauma exposure; and/or (3) because substance abuse leads to more symptomatology (for example, PTSD) in those exposed to trauma. In general, of these three possibilities, it appears that self-medication is the most common explanation: Chilcoat and Breslau (1998), for example, found that individuals with PTSD were four times more likely to abuse alcohol or drugs than those without PTSD (irrespective of trauma history), whereas substance abuse was not a predictor of subsequent trauma exposure or PTSD. Nevertheless, some studies do suggest that substance abuse increases the likelihood of victimization (for example, Cottler, Compton, Mager, Spitznagel, & Janca, 1992; Resnick, Yehuda, & Acierno, 1997) and other trauma exposure, such as automobile accidents (Ursano et al., 1999). In fact, clinical experience with substance-abusing survivors suggests a "vicious circle":

- Early trauma exposure (for example, childhood sexual abuse) increases the likelihood of additional traumas later in life (see Chapter 1).
- The accumulation of these traumas leads to significant posttraumatic stress and dysphoria.

- Increased distress motivates the use of drugs and alcohol as "self-medication."
- Drug and alcohol abuse leads to decreased environmental awareness and involvement in "risky" behaviors.
- These effects increase the likelihood of additional trauma and posttraumatic distress.
- Increased distress potentially leads to more substance abuse (Allen, 2001; Becker, Rankin, & Rickel, 1998; Briere, 2004; McFarlane, 1998).

Complex Posttraumatic Presentations

"Complex PTSD"

Although not listed in *DSM-IV*, "complex PTSD" (Herman, 1992b), also known as "disorder of extreme stress, not otherwise specified" (DESNOS; Pelcovitz et al., 1997) or "self-trauma" disturbance (Briere, 2002a), is frequently described in the clinical literature. Such complex post-traumatic outcomes are thought to arise from severe, prolonged, and repeated trauma, almost always of an interpersonal nature (van der Kolk et al., 1996). Examples of such stressors are extended child abuse, torture, captivity as a prisoner of war or concentration camp internee, and chronic spouse abuse.

Reflecting its chronic and often developmental etiology, this more complex presentation includes the somatic and dissociative problems described previously, as well as chronic difficulties in identity, boundary awareness, interpersonal relatedness, and affect regulation (van der Kolk, Roth, Pelcovitz, Sunday, & Spinazzola, 2005; Herman, 1992a,b). In the absence of sufficient affect regulation skills, for example, traumatized individuals may have to rely on external ways of reducing activated abuse-related distress, often referred to as *tension reduction behaviors* (Briere, 1996, 2002a). Such behaviors include compulsive or indiscriminant sexual behavior (Brennan & Shaver, 1995), binging and purging (Kendler et al., 2000), self-mutilation (Briere & Gil, 1988), suicidality (Zlotnick, Donaldson, Spirito, & Pearlstein, 1997), and other "impulse control" problems (Herpertz et al., 1997). Inadequate affect regulation may also lead to drug and alcohol abuse (Grilo et al., 1997), which, as described previously, may then increase the likelihood of further trauma and additional negative outcomes (Acierno, Resnick, Kilpatrick, Saunders, & Best, 1999).

The relational and identity disturbance subsumed under complex PTSD or DESNOS includes the tendency to be involved in chaotic and frequently maladaptive relationships, to have difficulty negotiating interpersonal boundaries, and reduced awareness of one's entitlements and needs in the presence of compelling others (Allen, 2001; Briere & Spinazzola, 2005). This set of problems is often attributed to a history of inadequate parent-child attachment (Brennan & Shaver, 1998; Sroufe, Carlson, Levy, & Egeland, 1999), typically as a result of childhood abuse or neglect (Cole & Putnam, 1992; Elliott, 1994).

Interestingly, despite the inclusion of "PTSD" in "complex PTSD"—as well as the frequent presence of comorbid PTSD in such cases—the reliving, avoidant, and hyperarousal symptoms of posttraumatic stress disorder are not included in this symptom cluster (Herman, 1992a; Pelcovitz et al., 1997). It has yet to be determined, in fact, whether complex PTSD is (1) a discrete syndrome, (2) the associated features of PTSD, or (3) as we generally believe, a wide range of outcomes that vary from person to person as a function of the variables described at the outset of this chapter (Briere & Spinazzola, 2005).

Borderline Personality Disorder

DSM-IV describes *borderline personality disorder* as a chronic disturbance in which there is "a pervasive pattern of instability of interpersonal relationship, self-image, and affects, and marked impulsivity beginning by early adulthood and present in a variety of contexts" (APA, 2000, p. 706). The *DSM-IV* criteria for this disorder are presented in Table 2.4.

Most traditional theories of borderline personality development (for example, Kernberg, 1976) trace the genesis of this disorder to dysfunctional parental (primarily maternal) behavior in the first several years of the child's life. They assert that the soon-to-be-borderline child is rewarded for enmeshed dependency and punished (often through abandonment) for independence. There is, however, limited empirical support for this specific model. Instead, a number of studies indicate that borderline personality disorder is generally associated with severe and extended childhood trauma, neglect, and loss (Herman, Perry, & van der Kolk, 1989; Ogata et al., 1990). The symptoms of borderline personality disorder are relatively similar to those of complex PTSD, involving problems in identity, affect regulation, and interpersonal relatedness. Unfortunately, the term *borderline personality* has acquired a negative valence for many mental health practitioners, indicating someone who is difficult to work with, emotionally overreactive, and often manipulative, rather than someone who suffers deeply as a result of adaptations to negative life events. For this reason, we rarely refer to borderline personality disorder, per se, in this book, but rather consider such symptoms a form of chronic relational disturbance arising from adverse developmental events and processes.

Table 2.4   *DSM-IV-TR* Criteria for Borderline Personality Disorder

A pervasive pattern of instability of interpersonal relationships, self-image, and affects and marked impulsivity beginning by early adulthood and present in a variety of contexts, as indicated by five (or more) of the following:

(1) frantic efforts to avoid real or imagined abandonment. **Note:** Do not include suicidal or self-mutilating behavior covered in Criterion 5.

(2) a pattern of unstable and intense interpersonal relationships characterized by alternating between extremes of idealization and devaluation

(3) identity disturbance: markedly and persistently unstable self-image or sense of self

(4) impulsivity in at least two areas that are potentially self-damaging (e.g., spending, sex, substance abuse , reckless driving, binge eating). **Note:** Do not include suicidal or self-mutilating behavior covered in Criterion 5.

(5) recurrent suicidal behavior, gestures, or threats, or self-mutilating behavior

(6) affective instability due to a marked reactivity of mood (e.g., intense episodic dysphoria, irritability , or anxiety usually lasting a few hours and only rarely more than a few days)

(7) chronic feelings of emptiness

(8) inappropriate, intense anger or difficulty controlling anger (e.g., frequent displays of temper, constant anger, recurrent physical fights)

(9) transient, stress-related paranoid ideation or severe dissociative symptoms

Source: APA (2000), p. 710. Reprinted with permission from the *Diagnostic and Statistical Manual of Mental Disorders, Fourth Edition, Text Revision* (copyright © 2000), American Psychiatric Association.

Medical Sequelae of Trauma

Individuals with psychological disorders also have been shown to have increased risk for physical health complications, especially in the case of PTSD (Schnurr & Green, 2004; Zayfert, Dums, Ferguson, & Hegel, 2003). Although the nature of the relationship between trauma and physical illness has not been well elucidated, PTSD sufferers have been shown to have increased rates of back pain, hypertension, arthritis, lung disease, nervous system diseases, circulatory disease, cancer, stroke, digestive disorders, and endocrine disorders, among others (Dobie et al., 2004; Frayne et al., 2004). PTSD also has been associated with lower overall physical health status, higher use of medical services, and higher health care costs (Frayne et al., 2004; Walker et al., 2003). This association appears especially high in victims of chronic interpersonal violence. Surveys of women seeking medical care have repeatedly shown that intimate partner violence, sexual abuse, and sexual assault are correlated with physical health outcomes such as musculoskeletal disorders, chronic pelvic pain, sexual dysfunction, and gastrointestinal complaints (Briere, 1992b; Campbell, 2002). For this reason, as noted in Chapter 3, assessment of traumatized individuals should include evaluation of physical—as well as mental—health status.

Trauma Syndromes in Non-Western Cultures

As indicated at the beginning of this chapter, posttraumatic presentations are influenced by a variety of individual and environmental variables. People from different cultures or subcultures often experience trauma and express posttraumatic symptoms in ways that diverge from the mainstream North American society (Friedman & Jaranson, 1994). For example, it appears that individuals from non-Anglo-Saxon cultures "often fail to meet PTSD diagnostic criteria because they lack avoidant/numbing symptoms despite the presence of reexperiencing and arousal symptoms" (Marsella, Friedman, Gerrity, & Scurfield, 1996, p. 533). Further, in some cultures, classic PTSD symptoms are often accompanied by more somatic and dissociative symptoms than are found in North American groups (Marsella et al., 1996).

Growing clinical awareness that not all posttraumatic stress responses are captured by the PTSD diagnosis, especially in non-Anglo-American cultures, has led to the concept of *culture-bound* stress responses. It should be noted, however, that PTSD itself should be considered partially culture bound, since it best describes the posttraumatic symptomatology of those born or raised in Anglo/European countries. Appendix I of the *DSM-IV* lists several culture-bound syndromes that appear to involve dissociation, somatization, and anxiety-related stress responses (for example, *attaques de nervios*, *dhat*, *latah*, *pibloktoq*, *shin-byung*, and *susto*), although none are inevitably posttraumatic in etiology.

Suggested Reading

Brewin, C. R., Andrews, B., & Valentine, J. D. (2000). Meta-analysis of risk factors for posttraumatic stress disorder in trauma-exposed adults. *Journal of Consulting and Clinical Psychology, 68,* 748–766.

Briere, J., & Jordan, C. E. (2004). Violence against women: Outcome complexity and implications for treatment. *Journal of Interpersonal Violence, 19,* 1252–1276.

Davidson, J. R. T., & Foa, E. B. (Eds.). (1993). *Posttraumatic stress disorder: DSM-IV and beyond.* Washington, DC: American Psychiatric Press.

Harvey, A. G., & Bryant, R. A. (2002). Acute stress disorder: a synthesis and critique. *Psychological Bulletin, 128,* 886–902.

Herman, J. L. (1992). *Trauma and recovery: The aftermath of violence—from domestic abuse to political terror.* New York: Basic Books.

Marsella, A. J., Friedman, M. J., Gerrity, E. T., & Scurfield, R. M. (Eds.). (1996). *Ethnocultural aspects of posttraumatic stress disorder: Issues, research, and clinical applications.* Washington, DC: American Psychological Association.

van der Kolk, B. A., McFarlane, A. C., & Weisaeth, L. (1996). *Traumatic stress: The effects of overwhelming experience on mind, body, and society.* New York: Guilford.

3

Assessing Trauma and Posttraumatic Outcomes

C hapter 2 outlined the various symptoms and psychological disorders that can arise from trauma exposure. The current chapter describes the various ways in which these posttraumatic outcomes—and the events that produced them—can be assessed. Although we strongly support the use of empirically validated assessment instruments and structured diagnostic interviews, it is also true that most "real-world" clinical assessments occur in the context of less formal, relatively unstructured interchanges between the client and clinician during an intake session. Although more subjective, and thus more prone to interpretative error, observation of client responses can yield important information that has direct implications for subsequent treatment. For this reason, we begin with the clinical interview, and then move on to the application of more standardized methodologies.

Assessment in the Clinical Interview

Immediate Concerns

Most of this chapter addresses assessment approaches that allow the clinician to evaluate specific trauma-related symptoms or dysfunction. Such assessment is necessary to ensure that whatever interventions occur are best suited to the client's specific needs. However, the evaluation of the client's immediate level of safety, psychological stability, and readiness for further assessment and treatment is even more critical.

Life Threat

Most obviously, the first focus of assessment in any trauma-related situation is whether the client is in imminent danger of loss of life or bodily integrity, or is at risk for hurting others. This includes—in the case of immediate accident, disaster, or physical attack—assessment of whether the client is medically stable. In cases of ongoing interpersonal violence, it is also very important to determine whether the client is in danger of victimization from others in the near future. Most generally, the hierarchy of assessment is as follows:

1. Is there danger of imminent death (for example, by bleeding, internal injuries, toxic or infectious agents), or immediate danger of loss of limb or other major physical functioning?

2. Is the client incapacitated (for example, through intoxication, brain injury or delirium, severe psychosis) to the extent that he or she cannot attend to his or her own safety (for example, wandering into streets, or unable to access available food or shelter)?

3. Is the client acutely suicidal?

4. Is the client a danger to others (for example, homicidal, or making credible threats to harm someone), especially when means are available (for example, a gun)?

[*Note:* #3 and #4 are of equal importance.]

5. Is the client's immediate psychosocial environment unsafe (for example, is he or she immediately vulnerable to maltreatment or exploitation by others)?

The first goal of trauma intervention, when any of these issues are present, is to ensure the physical safety of the client or others, often through referral or triage to emergency medical or psychiatric services, law enforcement, or social service resources. It is also important, whenever possible, to involve supportive and less-affected family members, friends, or others who can assist the client in this process.

Psychological Stability and Stress Tolerance

Psychological stability is also very important. A common clinical error is to immediately assess for psychological symptoms or disorders in a trauma survivor without first determining his or her overall level of psychological homeostasis. Individuals who have recently experienced a traumatic event, such as a rape or mass disaster, may still be in a state of crisis at the time of assessment—in some cases psychologically disorganized to the extent that they are unable to fully comprehend their current situation, let alone respond to a clinician's inquiries or interventions. In such instances, as is true with some cases of debilitating longer-term trauma impacts, psychological assessment may not only further challenge the survivor's fragile equilibrium, but may also lead to compromised assessment results. For this reason, the first step in the mental health evaluation of trauma victims should be to determine the individual's relative level of psychological stability. When it appears that the client is overwhelmed or cognitively disorganized, stabilizing interventions (for example, reassurance, psychological support, or reduction in the level of environmental stimuli) should be provided before more detailed evaluation is pursued.

In some cases, however, although the trauma survivor may appear superficially stable following a traumatic event, he or she may suddenly display extreme distress, high anxiety, intrusive posttraumatic symptoms, or sudden outbursts of anger when faced with even superficial inquiry about the event. As described later in this chapter, these reactions are referred to as *activation responses*—intense, often intrusive, trauma-specific psychological states that are triggered by reminders of the traumatic event. Although some level of activation is normal—even desirable—during treatment, and most survivors in research studies do not report negative effects of trauma evaluation, per se (Carlson, Newman, Daniels, Armstrong, Roth, & Lowenstein, 2003; Walker et al., 1997), assessment-related activation may be psychologically destabilizing if the individual does not have sufficient capacities to internally regulate his or her distress. As a result, it is important to determine the extent to which trauma issues can be discussed with a given survivor without unduly "retraumatizing" him or her. When excessive activation is likely, it is usually preferable to at least temporarily defer significant questions about or discussion of traumatic material (Najavits, 2002). The decision to avoid significant discussion of trauma with a trauma survivor should be made carefully, however, given the often helpful effects of talking about traumatic memories (see Chapter 4) and the sometimes immediate need for assessment.

At the risk of repetition, the usual components of assessment should be initiated only after the traumatized person's immediate safety, psychological stability, and capacity to discuss traumatic material have been verified. Failure to adequately evaluate these preconditions may result in unwanted outcomes, ranging from unnecessary client distress to, in extreme cases, emotional harm.

Assessing Trauma Exposure

Once the clinician has determined that the client is safe and reasonably stable, the specifics of trauma exposure and response can be investigated. In many cases, the clinician begins by asking about the traumatic event or events, including the nature of the trauma and its characteristics (for example, severity, duration, frequency, level of life threat). Because it is logical to start with events and then move on to outcomes, assessment of trauma exposure is presented here before the assessment of trauma effects. In some cases, however, the client's emergent psychological state is obviously of greater initial concern than how he or she got that way. For example, except in some forensic situations, the evaluation of an acute rape victim often will focus more immediately on her or his emotional functioning and psychological symptoms than on the specifics of the rape itself. In other cases, however, especially when the trauma is farther in the past and the client is not currently acutely distressed, it is reasonable to begin with a trauma history.

Although one might assume that traumatized individuals easily disclose the events that bring them to therapy, this is not always the case. In fact, several studies indicate that many trauma survivors are reluctant to volunteer detailed (or any) information in this area unless directly asked, due to embarrassment, a desire to avoid reactivating traumatic memories, or the clinician's own avoidance of such information (Read & Fraser, 1998). For example, Briere and Zaidi (1989) surveyed the admission charts of a randomly selected group of women presenting to a psychiatric emergency room (PER), and found that only 6 percent documented a history of childhood sexual abuse. In a second phase of the study, PER clinicians were requested to routinely ask female patients about any history of childhood sexual victimization. When charts from this phase were examined, documentation of a sexual abuse history increased more than tenfold. Further, sexual abuse history assessed in Phase 2 was associated with a wide variety of presenting problems, including suicidality, substance abuse, multiple Axis I diagnoses, and an increased rate of borderline personality disorder.

We recommend that each client, whatever the presenting complaint, be assessed for trauma history as part of a complete mental health evaluation. When this occurs will vary according to the clinical situation. Often, as described previously, traumatized clients present with a chief complaint, such as depression, suicidality, generalized anxiety, or unexplained panic attacks, that does not obviously include the trauma. In such cases, it is advisable to explore with the individual the symptoms that bring him or her in for treatment before delving into the possibility of trauma exposure. This allows the client to develop an initial sense of trust and rapport with the evaluator, before answering what may be perceived as intrusive (if not irrelevant) questions about traumatic experiences.

Many individuals, especially those who have never before been evaluated by a mental health professional, respond to questions about trauma history, particularly child abuse and other forms of interpersonal victimization, with embarrassment and/or guardedness. It is not uncommon for clients to ask, "Why do you need to know that?" upon being queried about specifics of their trauma history. Victims of interpersonal violence who have been repeatedly hurt and betrayed by others may be especially reluctant to share intimate details with an evaluator whom they have just met.

Even those clients whose chief complaints are related to a particular acute or past traumatic event may balk at being asked questions about their past. The victim of an earthquake who complains of acute anxiety, for example, may not want to answer questions about child abuse, feeling that such details are not relevant to his or her current situation. Likewise, the recent rape victim may interpret questions about other sexual assaults and childhood sexual abuse as implicit criticism from the evaluator, or as a subtle message that he or she in some way "asks" to be victimized.

In light of such concerns, general guidelines for assessment of trauma exposure include the following:

- Establish an initial level of trust and rapport before assessing trauma.
- Spend some time at the beginning of the assessment interview exploring the client's overt reason for presenting for clinical services, whatever it may be.
- Ask questions in an empathic and nonjudgmental manner.
- Become comfortable talking about details of sexual abuse and violence experiences with clients; victims of interpersonal traumas may be especially sensitive to nuances in the clinician's voice and body language. For example, certain clients may avoid reporting disturbing experiences if they believe that the clinician will be too upset by such material or will make negative judgments.
- Use behavioral definitions. For example, a woman who was sexually assaulted and forced to perform oral sex on a man but was not vaginally penetrated may not believe that she was in fact raped. It is rarely sufficient to ask, "Were you ever raped?" Instead, a better question might be, "Did anyone ever do something sexual to you that you didn't want, or make you do something sexual to them?"
- Remember that trauma is deeply personal and that the client may fear being stigmatized. In the course of a trauma-focused interview, clients may disclose information that they have never told anyone before. The clinician should keep this possibility in mind, and respond to such disclosures with visible support.
- Be aware that disclosure of trauma history may bring up intense feelings, including shame, embarrassment, and anger. Clients may respond in a variety of

ways—some may cry, others may become agitated and anxious, and some may withdraw. Still others may become irritable and even hostile toward the interviewer. In such contexts, gentle support and validation of the client's feelings and reactions may be especially important.

- Repeat assessments as necessary—some clients may not disclose certain trauma-related information at the initial evaluation, but may do so later, when they feel more comfortable with the clinician and the treatment process.

Some evaluators find it helpful to preface questions about trauma exposure with an opening that frames assessment in a supportive and nonjudgmental context. Examples of such opening statements might include:

- "If it is okay with you, I'd like to ask you some questions about your past. These are questions that I ask every client I see, so I can get a better sense of what [he or she] has been through."
- "I'd like to ask you some questions about experiences you may have had in the past. If you feel uncomfortable at any time, please let me know. Okay?"
- "Sometimes people have experienced things in their pasts that affect how they are feeling now. If it is okay, I'd like to ask you some questions about things that may have happened to you."

Other clinicians prefer to integrate assessment of trauma history into the flow of the initial interview. What follows are two examples of how this might be accomplished with different clients. These examples are not intended to provide an exhaustive list of potential trauma exposures; rather, they illustrate ways of approaching traumatic material in a nonthreatening and organic way in the context of a mental health evaluation.

- For those clients who appear reluctant to discuss interpersonal information, a trauma history can be gathered at the same time as medical history is assessed. This formalizes the questioning and places it in the context of other, more routine, questions that are generally experienced as both necessary and nonthreatening. The flow of questions in such a scenario might follow a pattern such as:

  - "Do you have any medical problems?"
  - "Are you in any physical discomfort right now?"
  - "What medications are you currently taking?"
  - "Do you have any allergies to medications?"
  - "Have you ever had any surgeries?"
  - "Have you ever been in a car accident? Were you injured? Did you receive medical attention?"
  - "Have you ever been in a disaster such as a fire, earthquake, or flood? Were you injured? Did you receive medical attention?"
  - "Have you ever had a head injury? Did you lose consciousness? Did you receive medical attention?"

- "Have you ever witnessed a violent event, such as a shooting?"
- "Have you ever been assaulted by anyone? How old were you? Were you injured? Did you receive any medical attention afterward?"
- "Has anyone every forced you to do something sexual against your will? Has anyone ever touched you sexually in a way that made you feel uncomfortable? Did you receive medical attention for this?"

[Follow with childhood trauma exposure questions.]

- For those patients who are willing to discuss their family and relationships, an alternative scenario for questioning might follow a different pattern:

  - "Where did you grow up?"
  - "What was your childhood like?"
  - "Who did you grow up with?"
  - "When you were a child what was home like?"
  - "Were both parents at home?"
  - "Did you witness any violence at home when you were a child?"
  - "How were you punished when you were a child?"
  - "When you were a child was anyone abusive to you in any way?" (In some cases, this question alone will prompt the client to report all of their childhood abuse experiences.)
  - "Did anyone ever do anything sexual to you when you were a child, or make you do something sexual to them?"

[Follow with more detailed childhood trauma questions.]

  - "Have you ever been in a car accident? Were you injured? Did you receive any medical attention afterward?"
  - "As an adult, were you ever attacked by anyone? How old were you? Were you injured? Did you receive any medical attention afterward?"

[Follow with other adult trauma questions.]

Given potential client reluctance in this area, and the likelihood that some traumas will be overlooked in an informal assessment interview, trauma assessment is probably best accomplished when the clinician refers to a predefined list of potential traumas during the evaluation interview. This structured approach ensures not only that trauma exposure will be formally assessed, but also that all relevant types of trauma will be explored. Included in Appendix 1 of this book is an instrument that can be used to evaluate the client's life history of traumatic events, the Initial Trauma Review-3 (ITR-3). This is a behaviorally anchored, semi-structured interview that allows the clinician to assess most major forms of trauma exposure. It also inquires about subjective distress in response to these traumas, as required by the

DSM-IV A2 criterion for PTSD and ASD. The clinician should feel free to paraphrase the items of the ITR-3 in such a way that the process is supportive and nonstigmatizing, and to add any additional traumas that he or she thinks are relevant to the client's situation. There are also a number of other instruments available in the psychological literature (for example, the Stressful Life Events Screening Questionnaire, developed by Goodman, Corcoran, Turner, Yuan, and Green, 1998; and the Traumatic Events Scale, developed by Elliott, 1992) that the clinician may use to review a client's trauma history. In addition, some psychological tests of traumatic stress include traumatic event reviews, as described later in this chapter.

In the Psychological Trauma Program at Los Angeles County + University of Southern California Medical Center, trainees often initially assess trauma history in a relatively unstructured manner, asking questions as appropriate in the context of the dynamics of the interview and the client's presenting complaints. In the second session, they more formally assess trauma exposure using the ITR-3. Asking about trauma on both occasions often yields a more thorough and complete history.

Evaluating the Effects of Trauma

For the purposes of this book, the effects of trauma can be divided into two categories: *process* responses, involving impacts of traumatization that are readily determined during the interview, and *symptom* responses, involving the more classic markers or forms of psychological disturbance.

Process Responses

Considerable information may be gained by observing the traumatized client's behavior during the clinical interview or therapy session. Because this form of assessment is based on the clinician's perceptions, and thus is influenced both by clinical experience and personal subjectivity, data gathered in this manner are not always as valid as the results of standardized testing. On the other hand, the alert and perceptive evaluator often can discern things that are rarely, if ever, tapped by psychometric tests. Such information can be divided into four areas: activation responses, avoidance responses, affect dysregulation, and relational difficulties.

Activation Responses. As described in greater detail in Chapter 8, activation responses are the sudden emergence of posttraumatic emotions, memories, and/or cognitions in response to some sort of triggering stimulus. Some of these responses may be sensory reexperiencing of the traumatic event; in other cases the response is less extreme, involving sudden emotional distress or anxiety. Although extreme activation is generally to be avoided, in most cases lower levels of such responses can provide information regarding both severity of the client's current posttraumatic stress and the degree to which his or her trauma memories can be readily activated by the external environment.

Typically, the clinician's intent is not to trigger activation, but rather to be alert to its emergence during the interview or during therapy. For example, the clinician interviewing a burn patient in his hospital room a week after a fire may watch carefully for changes in facial expression, tone of voice, verbal content, or even respirations when the patient is gently asked about his or her trauma experience. Or, a child sexual abuse survivor may be observed for changes in emotion, body position, eye movement, or verbal syntax while he or she discusses a childhood molestation experience.

When the trauma is relatively recent, a moderate level of activation is often a good sign, indicating that the client is not in a highly avoidant or numbed state and that his or her traumatic material is available for internal processing. Especially easily triggered and intensely experienced activation, however, may suggest more severe posttraumatic stress and may indicate that unwanted intrusive symptoms can be triggered by a wide variety of stimuli in the environment. In a similar vein, easily triggered activation in chronic traumatic states (for example, tearfulness and distress in a combat veteran when discussing war experiences that occurred 30 years prior to the interview) may indicate inadequate processing, since, in the uncomplicated case, posttraumatic stress would be expected to resolve—or at least decrease—naturally over that time period.

The attuned examiner or therapist may find that consistent attention to an individual's emotional, verbal, and motor reactivity to trauma cues provides continuous information regarding (1) the level of posttraumatic stress the person is experiencing, and (2) the extent to which traumatic reexperiencing is being blocked through dissociation or other avoidance responses. Information regarding the client's level of posttraumatic activation can assist not only in diagnosis and assessment, but may also indicate his or her level and type of response to the exposure component of trauma therapy (see Chapter 8).

Avoidance Responses. Observational assessment of avoidance in trauma survivors generally involves attention to both inferred underactivation—the relative absence of expected activation—and the visible presence of avoidance activities. In the former case, avoidance can be hypothesized when activation would be expected (for example, in a recent sexual assault victim) but where little or no significant emotional reactivity is observed (for example, describing the event in an especially detached or overly matter-of-fact manner). In the latter, the clinician is able to detect direct evidence of dissociation or substance use, or the client informs the clinician of effortful avoidance (for example, no longer driving a car after a motor vehicle accident).

Underactivation can occur as a result of a number of different defensive mechanisms that are not, by themselves, visible, although their effects may be inferred. They include:

- *Emotional numbing.* The client displays reduced emotional reactivity to trauma triggers as a result of severe posttraumatic stress (see Chapter 2).
- *Dissociative disengagement.* The client engages in subtle cognitive-emotional separation or disengagement from potentially upsetting stimuli, but does so without exhibiting overt signs of dissociation, per se.
- *Thought suppression.* The client cognitively blocks or suppresses emotionally upsetting thoughts or memories.
- *Denial.* The client acknowledges the traumatic event, but develops a theory or perspective that reduces the perceived threat or seriousness associated with the trauma.
- *Anxiolysis without obvious intoxication.* The client uses a psychoactive substance (for example, alcohol or a benzodiazepine) prior to the session that is not evident during treatment or evaluation but that blocks anxious responses to trauma triggers.

Underactivation is often both difficult to identify and hard to pin down in terms of the specific mechanism involved. For example, when a trauma survivor presents as less upset than the circumstances might warrant (for example, a calm and nontraumatized demeanor one day after involvement in a major automobile accident with multiple fatalities), potential mechanisms include those listed as well as the possibility that the client is not engaging in avoidance at all, but, instead, is especially resilient to stress. Despite this uncertainty, the experienced trauma clinician often learns to discriminate various types of defensive avoidance strategies from psychological health, whether through increased sensitivity to subtle avoidance mechanisms or through a growing sense of when a posttraumatic response would logically occur.

Explicit signs of avoidance, on the other hand, usually involve the use of mechanisms that are visible to the clinician or are expressed directly. Most typically, these include:

- *Visible dissociative symptoms.* The client "spaces out," demonstrates obvious fixity of gaze (for example, the "thousand-mile stare"), moves in a disconnected manner, or seems to enter a different identity state.

- *Self-reported dissociation.* The client describes symptoms such as depersonalization (for example, out-of-body experiences) or derealization (for example, feeling like he or she is in a dream).
- *Intoxication.* The client comes to the session visibly intoxicated on drugs or alcohol.
- *Effortful avoidance.* The client describes behaviors consistent with the effortful avoidance cluster of PTSD symptoms, such as avoiding people, places, or situations that might trigger posttraumatic intrusions or distress. Effortful avoidance is also evidenced in the session by visible attempts to avoid discussing traumatic material. Missed sessions also may reflect effortful avoidance.

The excessive presence of emotional avoidance in the evaluation or treatment session typically signals a greater likelihood of posttraumatic stress (Plumb, Orsillo, Luterek, 2004), an increased chance of chronicity (Lawrence, Fauerbach, & Munster, 1996), and potentially greater difficulties dealing with the exposure component of therapy (Jaycox, Foa, & Morral, 1998). In addition, client reports of effortful avoidance may indicate specific areas in which the client is having especially intrusive experiences (for example, avoidance of sexual activity because it triggers flashbacks to a rape). Such information may allow the clinician to explore Cluster B (reliving) PTSD symptoms that otherwise might not be identified or disclosed. It is important to note, however, that avoidance is typically a coping response that the survivor uses to maintain psychological stability in the face of potentially destabilizing trauma memories. As a result, although such responses typically indicate traumatic stress, they are not necessarily maladaptive at the moment they occur—especially early in the recovery process.

Affect Dysregulation. Some trauma survivors are prone to visible difficulties with affect regulation. Affect regulation refers to the individual's relative capacity to tolerate painful internal states (*affect tolerance*) and to internally reduce such distress without resorting to dissociation or other avoidance techniques (*affect modulation*). Affect regulation problems appear to arise from, among other phenomena, extreme and/or early trauma exposure (Pynoos, Steinberg, & Piacentini, 1999; Schore, 2003), and, as noted earlier, are associated with subsequent distress-avoidance symptoms such as substance abuse, impulsivity, self-injurious behavior, and other seemingly "personality disorder"-level responses (van der Kolk, Roth, Pelcovitz, Sunday, & Spinazzola, 2005). Individuals with reduced affect regulation capacities may be less able to process traumatic memories in therapy without becoming overwhelmed by the associated painful emotions. The risk of overwhelming trauma survivors with too much therapeutic exposure is of sufficient concern that some clinicians (for example, Briere, 2002a; Cloitre, Koenen, Cohen, & Han, 2002; Linehan, 1993a) consider affect dysregulation to be a central issue for those with more complex traumas. In other cases, typically when the trauma is less severe and occurs later in life, affect regulation difficulties may be less relevant. In any case, however, a complete assessment of the trauma victim should include such issues so that the treating clinician can either address them in therapy (see Chapter 6) or be satisfied that otherwise effective therapy is unlikely to retraumatize the client.

Problems with affect regulation may be identified in the assessment or therapy session by any of the following signs:

- Mood swings that are not attributable to a bipolar or cyclothymic disorder
- Very short (for example, measured in hours), yet symptomatically intense depressive episodes that seem to resolve spontaneously
- Sudden, extreme, emotional distress during the session, with apparent difficulty calming down or shifting to a more positive emotional state thereafter
- A tendency to act out, self-mutilate, become aggressive, make suicide attempts or gestures, or otherwise engage in sudden tension reduction behaviors when upset or distressed
- Sudden dissociative responses in the context of strong emotionality

When such signs suggest affect regulation difficulties, the clinician should evaluate the possibility that (1) the client has a history of severe or early child abuse and neglect, and/or (2) he or she has a personality disorder characterized by affective instability (although see Chapter 2 for cautions about overgeneralizing from the borderline personality disorder diagnosis). In such cases, as noted in Chapter 8, therapeutic intervention (especially exposure activities) often must be carefully titrated to the client's existing capacity to regulate painful feelings.

Relational Disturbance. Relational information is obtained in the interview by observing the client's responses to the clinician and to the therapy environment. Such information can also be extracted from the content of client disclosures regarding important others in his or her life. In general, these responses signal underlying cognitive schemas, assumptions, and beliefs (as well as their associated affects) that the individual carries regarding important interpersonal figures and relationships.

Central relational issues (and their associated intra-interview signs) are discussed following.

ALERTNESS TO INTERPERSONAL DANGER. Because many trauma survivors have been hurt, betrayed, or otherwise maltreated in interpersonal relationships, they may respond to evaluation or treatment with hypervigilance to physical or emotional danger (Courtois, 1988; Herman, 1992a). In extreme cases, this response may take on nearly paranoid proportions: the recent victim of torture or rape may covertly examine the clinical setting for possible weapons, hidden spyholes, or hiding places for other people; the refugee from a totalitarian state may scrutinize the clinical process for evidence of governmental collusion; the stalking or battering victim may voice fears that he or she was followed to the session or that the clinician is in communication with his or her perpetrator; and the Vietnam veteran may position himself for ready access to the nearest doorway.

Although such responses are not always part of the clinical presentation of trauma survivors, even those less severely affected may display signs of hyperalertness to potential aggression, boundary violation, unfair criticism, or other potential dangers. The client may question the evaluator or therapist regarding his or her intentions, the appropriateness or relevance of various assessment questions, and the intended use of the information gathered from the session. Sexual trauma victims may evidence special distrust of male interviewers, and those with highly punitive parents may be hypersensitive to the possibility of negative evaluation by the clinician.

The presence of such preoccupations may indicate a specific sensitivity to evaluation and interactions with authority figures. More typically, however, the fact that danger schemas are easily triggered in the survivor signals a generalized expectation of potential injury in interpersonal situations, and is, most basically, a reflection of posttraumatic stress.

ABANDONMENT ISSUES. Individuals with histories of childhood neglect or rejection may signal abandonment concerns during assessment and treatment— both by their description of significant others in their lives and by their responses to the clinician. There may be a preoccupation with themes of needing people or relationships (sometimes regardless of the valence or health of those connections), fears or expectations of abandonment or loss in relationships, or historical renditions that seem excessively characterized by being left or rejected. In the session, clients with abandonment concerns may become especially attached to the clinician, even over a very short period of time; they may be reluctant to allow termination of the interview, and may seem especially "clingy" or dependent. On occasion, they may express anger or despair regarding the examiner's perceived insufficient caring or support and the brevity of the evaluation or therapy session, or concern that the clinician is not sufficiently attuned to their emotional experience. Also common is the tendency for clinician unavailability (for example, while on vacation or during personal emergencies) to trigger abandonment schemas and produce anger or despondency.

As might be expected, it is not always easy to detect abandonment fears in the evaluation interview or the first sessions of treatment—it may only be later in psychotherapy that the client's underlying preoccupation with relationships and avoiding abandonment becomes clear. As noted in Chapter 9, however, such issues are highly relevant in work with those who were neglected or maltreated early in life. Not only do they represent potential sources of distress and conflict as the client encounters the constraints of the treatment process, but the underlying dysfunctional schemas they reflect are important targets for psychological intervention.

NEED FOR SELF-PROTECTION THROUGH INTERPERSONAL CONTROL. The experience of helplessness that arises from interpersonal victimization may lead to a later need for personal control in relation to others. Often, this manifests as an insistence on autonomy, a tendency to micromanage one's interactions with others so that one's own safety and self-determination are intact, and negative responses to control, perceived manipulation, or influence by other people. This interpersonal style may also manifest as difficulty with authority figures who, by definition, have some degree of implicit control over the trauma survivor.

Those individuals with a high need for control may engage in behaviors that seek to maximize their own autonomy during interpersonal interactions—including those that take place in the evaluation or treatment session. For example, the trauma survivor may attempt to control the session by speaking in a continuous manner, thereby keeping the clinician from exerting verbal influence over the assessment or treatment process. In such instances, interruptions by the clinician may be ignored or may prompt irritation or anger. Similarly, the client may resist interview questions that lead away from whatever topic he or she is discussing, viewing the clinician's desire to gain historical or psychological information as an attempt to overtake the client's agenda or autonomy. Such behaviors arise from a fear of being revictimized by others, and often reflect underlying relational anxiety—a posttraumatic state that leads to interpersonal rigidity and sometimes an almost compulsive self-protectiveness.

Signs of a need for interpersonal control should be viewed as potential evidence of a history of (1) highly controlling, intrusive, or abusive caretakers earlier in life, (2) early emotional neglect associated with a chaotic childhood environment, and/or (3) later trauma experiences that were especially characterized by extended helplessness, such as torture or forced confinement.

The immediate implications of this interpersonal style are for the assessment process itself: it may be quite difficult to steer the control-focused survivor into domains that the clinician (but not the client) feels are important to evaluate and treat, including current symptomatology, prior history, and level of interpersonal functioning. Clinical experience suggests that the clinician will be most effective in this regard to the extent that he or she does not overly challenge the client's need for interpersonal control, but rather works to reassure him or her—both verbally and nonverbally—of the benign intent of the clinical process. In some cases, this will require considerable patience on the part of the clinician.

CAPACITY TO ENTER INTO AND SUSTAIN A CLINICAL RELATIONSHIP. Psychological assessment and treatment typically requires that the client enter into a working relationship with the clinician. Unfortunately, victims of interpersonal traumas such as child abuse, rape, torture, or partner violence may experience any sort of intimate connection to an authority figure as potentially dangerous—no matter how "safe" that figure is deemed by others (McCann & Pearlman, 1990). For example, in the normal process of therapy, the clinician may inadvertently activate victimization-related flashbacks, threat-related cognitions, or conditioned fears in the client that disrupt what otherwise might be a good working alliance. For this reason, one of the goals of assessment is to determine both the client's most obvious relational triggers and his or her overall capacity to form an ongoing relationship with the clinician. In cases where the relational capacities of the client are impaired, the therapist should be especially alert to potential difficulties with trust, boundaries, and safety—phenomena that may need to be addressed (or at least taken into account) before much overt trauma-related material can be processed.

To varying degrees, trauma survivors (especially those who were repeatedly victimized in childhood) may show evidence of some or all of the relational issues described here. On a practical level, such disturbances may result in responses and behaviors that are often labeled as "difficult," "manipulative," "demanding," or "disordered." Reframing such responses as the probable effects of trauma rather than as necessarily evidence of an underlying personality disorder may allow the clinician to approach the client in a more accepting, nonjudgmental, and therapeutically constructive manner.

The relational dynamics listed may also intrude upon the assessment process itself. The same trauma-related activations that discourage an effective therapeutic relationship may cause the client to produce test or interview responses that are compromised by extensive avoidance, fear, anger, or restimulated trauma memories. Although victimization-related hypervigilance, distrust, and traumatic reexperiencing are not easily addressed in the immediate context of psychological assessment, the clinician should do whatever he or she can to promote and communicate respect, safety, and freedom from judgment. Typically, this will involve:

- A positive, nonintrusive demeanor
- Acknowledgement of the client's distress and immediate situation

- A clear explanation of the assessment process (including the goals of the evaluation and its intended use)
- Explicit boundaries regarding confidentiality and the limits of the assessment inquiry

In addition, it may be helpful to avoid excessively direct or intrusive questions that might feel demeaning or interrogating, and, instead, work to facilitate the client's self-disclosure at his or her own pace and level of specificity. When assessment communicates respect and appreciation for the victim's situation, he or she is more likely to be forthcoming about potentially upsetting, humiliating, or anxiety-producing traumas and symptoms.

Symptom Responses

Above and beyond the process signs of trauma response presented thus far, an obvious goal of trauma assessment is to determine the victim's current mental status and level of psychological functioning, and to inquire about the major symptoms known to be associated with trauma exposure. During a full work-up, whether trauma-focused or otherwise, the client should ideally be evaluated for the following forms of disturbance:

- Altered consciousness or mental functioning (for example, dementia, confusion, delirium, cognitive impairment, or other organic disturbance)
- Psychotic symptoms (for example, hallucinations, delusions, thought disorder, disorganized behavior, "negative" signs)
- Evidence of self-injurious or suicidal thoughts and behaviors
- Potential danger to others
- Mood disturbance (for example, depression, anxiety, anger)
- Substance abuse or addiction
- Personality dysfunction
- Reduced ability to care for self

In combination with other information (for example, from the client, significant others, and outside agencies or caregivers), these interview data provide the basis for diagnosis and an intervention plan in most clinical environments. However, when the presenting issue potentially includes posttraumatic disturbance, the classic mental status and symptom review is likely to miss important information. Individuals with significant trauma exposure—perhaps especially victims of violence—do not always disclose the full extent of their trauma history or their posttraumatic symptomatology unless directly asked, and thus require specific, concrete investigation in these areas.

When there is a possibility of trauma-related disturbance, the assessment interview should address as many (if not all) of the following additional components as is possible, many of which were outlined in the previous chapter:

- Symptoms of posttraumatic stress
  - Intrusive/reliving experiences such as flashbacks, nightmares, intrusive thoughts and memories
  - Avoidance symptoms such as behavioral or cognitive attempts to avoid trauma-reminiscent stimuli, as well as emotional numbing
  - Hyperarousal symptoms such as decreased or restless sleep, muscle tension, irritability, jumpiness, or attention/concentration difficulties
- Dissociative responses
  - Depersonalization or derealization experiences
  - Fugue states
  - "Spacing out" or cognitive-emotional disengagement
  - Amnesia or missing time
  - Identity alteration or confusion
- Substance abuse
- Somatic disturbance
  - Conversion reactions (for example, paralysis, anesthesia, blindness, deafness)
  - Somatization (excessive preoccupation with bodily dysfunction)
  - Psychogenic pain (for example, pelvic pain or chronic pain that cannot be explained medically)
- Sexual disturbance (especially in survivors of sexual abuse or assault)
  - Sexual distress (including sexual dysfunction and/or pain)
  - Sexual fears and conflicts
- Trauma-related cognitive disturbance
  - Low self-esteem
  - Helplessness
  - Hopelessness
  - Excessive or inappropriate guilt
  - Shame
  - Overvalued ideas regarding the level of danger in the environment
  - Idealization of the perpetrator or inaccurate rationalization or justification of the perpetrator's behavior
- Tension reduction activities
  - Self-mutilation
  - Bingeing/purging
  - Excessive or inappropriate sexual behavior
  - Compulsive stealing
  - Impulsive aggression
- Transient posttraumatic psychotic reactions
  - Trauma-induced cognitive slippage or loosened associations

- Trauma-induced hallucinations (often trauma congruent)
- Trauma-induced delusions (often trauma congruent, especially paranoia)
• Culture-specific trauma responses (for example, *attaques de nervios*), if relevant, when assessing individuals from other countries or cultures

This list may be more comprehensive than is relevant for certain posttraumatic presentations (for example, the survivor of a motor vehicle accident), although most of the components may be appropriate for chronic traumas (for example, extended child abuse or political torture). Some review of these symptoms is usually indicated in a comprehensive evaluation, even if it is followed by a more structured diagnostic interview.

The assessment of the reexperiencing and dissociative symptoms associated with posttraumatic stress can be challenging, especially if the client has not described his or her symptoms to anyone before, and views them as bizarre, or even, perhaps, psychotic. Both reexperiencing and dissociation involve a change in level of consciousness and awareness of one's surroundings, which can be difficult to put into words. Suggested interview approaches and questions in this area are presented next.

• *Posttraumatic nightmares.* Some clients may not report nightmares that they only indirectly associate with the trauma in question—as a result, asking simply if they have nightmares about the event may not be sufficient. For example, a rape victim may not dream about the rape, but may have nightmares about being chased down a dark alley, or about being attacked by animals or evil spirits. Clarifying questions may include:
  - "Do you have bad or frightening dreams?"
  - "What are your dreams about?"
  - "Do you ever dream about bad things that have happened to you?"
• *Flashbacks.* Many clients will not know the meaning of the word *flashback*, and may need a more descriptive explanation. More detailed questions include:
  - "Do you ever have visions of [the trauma] that flash into your mind?"
  - "Do you ever feel like the [trauma] is still happening to you?"
  - "Do you ever feel like you are reliving the [trauma]?"
  - "Do you ever hear the voice of the person who hurt you?"
  - "Do you ever hear the sound of the [gunshot/accident/other trauma-relevant sound]?"
• *Intrusive thoughts.* Some clients report intrusive or ego-dystonic thoughts that intrude "out of nowhere" and/or that are a major source of ongoing preoccupation. Questions that may assist in the exploration of such cognitive symptoms include:
  - "Do you think about the [trauma] a lot? All the time?"
  - "Do you find that you can't get the thought of the [trauma] out of your mind?"

    – "Does thinking about the [trauma] make it hard for you to concentrate on other things?"

    – [*For those with associated insomnia*] "When you can't sleep at night, are there thoughts that keep you awake?"

- *Dissociation.* Because dissociation is an internal process that may be difficult for the client to express to others, the clinician often can assist the client by asking questions specific to the dissociative experience. Broken down by symptom type, these include:

Depersonalization

– "Do you ever feel like you are outside of your body?"
– "Do you ever feel that you can't recognize parts of your body, or that they change size or shape?"
– "Do you ever feel like you are watching things that happen to you from outside of yourself?"

Derealization

– "Do you ever feel like you are living in a dream?"
– "Do you ever feel like people and things around you are not real?"

Fugue states

– "Have you ever found yourself somewhere far away and wondered how you got there?"
– "Have you ever traveled a significant distance from home without realizing it?"

Cognitive-emotional disengagement

– "Do you find out that you 'space out' while at work or at home and lose track of what you are doing?"
– "Do other people tell you that you sometimes seem 'a million miles away' or 'out of it'?"

Amnesia or missing time

– "Are there important things in your life that you can't remember very well or at all?"
– "Do you ever have experiences where you 'zone out' for a few minutes and then find out that a much longer amount of time has passed?"

Identity alteration

– "Do you ever forget your own name or think you have a different name?"
– "Do you ever feel like there are different people inside you?"

Psychosis in the Context of Posttraumatic Response

Because dissociation and posttraumatic stress can sometimes involve reduced contact with—and altered perceptions of—the external environment, discriminating such responses from the symptoms of psychosis is not always easy. At times, the boundaries between posttraumatic reexperiencing and hallucinations; between reasonable posttraumatic fears, overvalued ideas and paranoid delusions; and between anxiety-related cognitive fragmentation and frank thought disorganization may become blurred. In addition, severe trauma-related dissociation may appear indistinguishable from withdrawn, internally preoccupied psychotic states. As mentioned earlier, there is a relationship between trauma and psychosis: psychotic depression and PTSD are frequently comorbid, and severe trauma can lead to brief psychotic reactions. As well, those with underlying psychotic processes may be at increased risk for victimization due to decreased levels of vigilance or self-care. However, it is important to exercise caution before jumping to the conclusion that a trauma survivor is psychotic—not the least because treatments for psychotic disorders are not typically effective for posttraumatic stress. In some instances, the clinical presentation may be so ambiguous as to make a definitive determination impossible; in such cases, clients should be carefully followed in treatment with frequent reassessments.

In differentiating psychosis from posttraumatic stress, the following, if present, may suggest a posttraumatic rather than psychotic process:

- *Reexperiencing, as opposed to hallucinations*
  - The content of the perceptions is trauma-related (for example, hearing the voice of the perpetrator or another sound associated with the trauma). Note, however, that a prior trauma history can affect the content of psychotic hallucinations and delusions, as well (Ross, Anderson, & Clark, 1994).
  - The perceptions occur in the context of a triggering experience or trauma-related anxiety.
  - The perceptions are not interactive: they do not, for example, "talk back" to the survivor.
  - The perceptions are not bizarre.
- *Posttraumatic expectations as opposed to delusions*
  - The content of the ideas or fears is related to the traumatic event.
  - The client is able to express an understanding that such ideas or fears are not reasonable (for example, a woman who was raped may fear all men and may not want to be alone with men due to fears of being further victimized, although she may be able to cognitively express that not every man is a rapist).
- *Trauma-induced fragmentation as opposed to loosened associations*
  - The fragmentation or disorganization occurs only when the client is talking about upsetting or trauma-related subjects, and not throughout the client's discourse.
  - The level of disorganization decreases as the client becomes less anxious.

Conversely, the following, if present, may suggest a psychotic rather than posttraumatic process:

- *Hallucinations as opposed to reexperiencing*
  - At least some of the content of the perceptions is not trauma-related (for example, hearing the voices of others not involved in the trauma).
  - The perception is interactive, and/or the client is observed by others to be talking or laughing to himself or herself.
- *Delusions as opposed to posttraumatic expectations*
  - The content of the ideas/fears is not simply related to the traumatic event, but extends to other areas (for example, a woman who was raped states that not only will all men potentially hurt her, but believes that the CIA is wiretapping her home).
- *Loosened associations as opposed to trauma-induced fragmentation*
  - The cognitive slippage occurs throughout the client's discourse, whether the client is anxious or not, and irrespective of the topic of conversation.

The Structured Interview

Although an informal mental status examination and symptom review can reveal many forms of posttraumatic disturbance, the unstructured nature of such approaches often means that certain symptoms or syndromes may be overlooked or inadequately assessed. In fact, it is estimated that up to half of actual cases of PTSD are missed during unstructured clinical interviews (Zimmerman & Mattia, 1999). For this reason, some clinicians and most researchers use structured clinical measures when evaluating posttraumatic stress, especially PTSD. The most commonly used of these structured interviews are discussed next.

The Clinician-Administered PTSD Scale (CAPS)

The CAPS (Blake et al., 1995) is considered the "gold standard" of structured interviews for posttraumatic stress disorder. The CAPS has several helpful features, including standard prompt questions and explicit, behaviorally anchored rating scales, and assesses both frequency and intensity of symptoms. It generates both dichotomous and continuous scores for current (1 month) and lifetime ("worst ever") PTSD. In addition to the standard 17 PTSD items, the CAPS also contains items tapping posttraumatic impacts on social and occupational functioning, improvement in PTSD symptoms since a previous CAPS assessment, overall response validity, and overall PTSD severity, as well as items addressing guilt and dissociation.

Unfortunately, the CAPS may require an hour or longer for complete administration, may sometimes provide more information than actually is needed clinically, and focuses only on PTSD.

The Acute Stress Disorder Interview (ASDI)

When the diagnostic issue is ASD, as opposed to PTSD, the clinician may find the ASDI (Bryant, Harvey, Dang, & Sackville, 1998) useful. This interview consists of 19 items that evaluate dissociative, reexperiencing, effortful avoidance, and arousal symptoms. Although relatively new, the ASDI has good reliability and validity and can be administered in a relatively short period of time (Bryant et al., 1998).

The Structured Interview for Disorders of Extreme Stress (SIDES)

The SIDES (Pelcovitz et al., 1997) was developed as a companion to existing interview-based rating scales for PTSD. The 45 items of the SIDES measure the current and lifetime presence of DESNOS and each of six symptom clusters: Affect Dysregulation, Somatization, Alterations in Attention or Consciousness, Self-Perception, Relationships with Others, and Systems of Meaning. Item descriptors contain concrete behavioral anchors in order to facilitate clinician ratings. The SIDES interview has good interrater reliability and internal consistency (Pelcovitz et al., 1997).

The Structured Clinical Interview for DSM-IV Dissociative Disorders-Revised (SCID-D)

The SCID-D (Steinberg, 1994) evaluates the existence and severity of five dissociative symptoms: amnesia, depersonalization, derealization, identity confusion, and identity alteration. This interview provides diagnoses for the five major *DSM-IV* dissociative disorders (presented in Chapter 2), along with acute stress disorder (although we recommend the ASDI for the latter). Also evaluated by the SCID-D are "intra-interview dissociative cues," such as alterations in demeanor, spontaneous age regression, and trancelike appearance, which are coded in a postinterview section.

The Brief Interview for Posttraumatic Disorders (BIPD)

Although the preceding (and other) diagnostic interviews are clearly helpful tools, we have included the BIPD (Briere, 1998) in Appendix 2 for those who desire a broader band, somewhat less structured interview. This measure, which can be photocopied or otherwise reproduce for general clinical use, is relatively easily and quickly administered. It reviews all those symptoms associated with PTSD, acute stress disorder, and brief psychotic disorder with marked stressors. On the other hand, the semi-structured format of the BIPD means that it is somewhat less objective than the CAPS or ASDI, and it does not provide as many detailed definitions regarding specific symptom criteria.

Psychological Tests

In contrast to clinical interviews, structured or otherwise, most psychological tests are self-administered, in the sense that the client completes a paper inventory using a pencil or pen. Standardized psychological tests have been normed on demographically representative samples of the general population, so that a specific score on such measures can be compared to what would be a "normal" value for that scale or test. We strongly recommend the use of such tests, since they provide objective, comparative data on psychological functioning (both trauma-specific and general) in trauma survivors. A number of testing instruments are briefly described below. Not discussed are projective tests, although one (the Rorschach Ink Blot Test; Rorschach, 1981/1921) also can be helpful in the assessment of posttraumatic states (Luxenberg & Levin, 2004; Armstrong & Kaser-Boyd, 2003). The interested reader should consult the Suggested Reading list at the end of this chapter for books and articles that address in greater detail the psychometric evaluation of traumatized individuals.

Generic Tests

A variety of psychological measures can be used to assess generic (that is, non-trauma-specific) psychological symptoms in adolescent and adult trauma survivors. Several of these assess anxiety, depression, somatization, psychosis, and other symptoms relevant to Axis I of *DSM-IV*. Because posttraumatic distress often includes such symptoms, a good psychological test battery should include at least one generic measure in addition to more trauma-specific tests.

Examples of generic tests include:

- Minnesota Multiphasic Personality Inventory, 2nd edition (MMPI-2: Butcher, Dahlstrom, Graham, Tellegen, & Kaemmer, 1989)
- Minnesota Multiphasic Personality Inventory for Adolescents (MMPI-A: Butcher, Williams, Graham, Archer, Tellegen, Ben-Porath, & Kaemmer, 1992)

- Psychological Assessment Inventory (PAI: Morey, 1991)
- Millon Clinical Multiaxial Inventory, 3rd edition (MCMI-III: Millon, Davis, & Millon, 1997), and
- Symptom Checklist-90-Revised (SCL-90-R: Derogatis, 1983)

Each of these tests (especially the PAI and MCMI-III) also provides some information on the personality-level (that is, Axis II) difficulties associated with the complex posttraumatic outcomes described in Chapter 2. In addition, three (the MMPI-2, PAI, and MCMI-III) include PTSD scales—although these scales are typically only moderately effective in identifying actual cases (and non-cases) of posttraumatic stress disorder (Briere, 2004; Carlson, 1997). Most major generic instruments also include validity scales, used to detect client under- or overreporting of symptoms. Such scales can be helpful in identifying denial, exaggeration, and some cases of malingering. However, traumatized individuals—by virtue of the unusual quality of some posttraumatic symptoms—tend to score higher than others on negative impression (overreporting) scales, even when not attempting to malinger or otherwise distort their responses (for example, Jordan, Nunley, & Cook, 1992).

Trauma-Specific Tests

Although generic tests can detect many of the more nonspecific symptoms associated with trauma, as well as other comorbid disorders that might be present, psychologists often use more specific tests when assessing posttraumatic stress, dissociation, and trauma-related self-capacity disturbance (Carlson, 1997). The most common of these instruments are presented below.

For Posttraumatic Stress and Associated Symptoms

- *Posttraumatic Stress Diagnostic Scale (PDS).* The PDS (Foa, 1995) evaluates exposure to potentially traumatic events, characteristics of the most traumatic event, 17 symptoms corresponding to *DSM-IV* PTSD criteria, and the extent of symptom interference in the individual's daily life. The PDS has high internal consistency ($\propto$ = .92 for the 17 symptom items) and good sensitivity and specificity with respect to a PTSD diagnosis (.82 and .77, respectively). This measure has not been normed on the general population and thus does not yield standardized T-scores. Instead, PTSD symptom severity estimates are based on extrapolation from a clinical sample of 248 women with trauma histories.
- *Davidson Trauma Scale (DTS).* The DTS (Davidson et al., 1997) is a 17-item scale measuring each *DSM-IV* symptom of PTSD on five-point frequency and severity scales. This measure yields a total score, as well as Intrusion, Avoidance/Numbing, and Hyperarousal scale scores, although there are no

norms available for interpreting symptom severity on these scales. The DTS has good test-retest reliability and internal consistency, as well as concurrent validity. Criterion validity has been assessed vis-à-vis the SCID, where the DTS was found to have a sensitivity of .69 and a specificity of .95 in detecting PTSD.

- *Detailed Assessment of Posttraumatic Stress (DAPS).* The DAPS (Briere, 2001) yields *DSM-IV* diagnoses for PTSD and ASD, as well as measuring a number of associated features of posttraumatic stress. Normed on general population individuals with a history of trauma exposure, the DAPS has validity scales (Positive Bias and Negative Bias) and clinical scales that evaluate lifetime exposure to traumatic events (Trauma Specification and Relative Trauma Exposure), immediate responses to a specified trauma (Peritraumatic Distress and Peritraumatic Dissociation), PTSD symptom clusters (Reexperiencing, Avoidance, and Hyperarousal), and three associated features of posttraumatic stress: Trauma-specific Dissociation, Suicidality, and Substance Abuse. This measure has good sensitivity (.88) and specificity (.86) with respect to a CAPS diagnosis of PTSD.
- *Trauma Symptom Inventory (TSI).* The TSI (Briere, 1995) is a 100-item instrument that evaluates the overall-level posttraumatic symptomatology experienced by an individual over the prior six months. It has been normed on the general population and has been shown to have good reliability and validity. The TSI has three validity scales (Response Level, Atypical Response, and Inconsistent Response) and 10 clinical scales (Anxious Arousal, Depression, Anger/Irritability, Intrusive Experiences, Defensive Avoidance, Dissociation, Sexual Concerns, Dysfunctional Sexual Behavior, Impaired Self-Reference, and Tension Reduction Behavior). It is often used to index more complex or wide-ranging posttraumatic outcomes.
- *Trauma Symptom Checklist for Children* (TSCC). Although often used to evaluate the trauma-related symptomatology in children, the TSCC (Briere, 1996) is also used to assess adolescents up to age 17. This measure is normed on more than 3,000 individuals under age 18, and consists of two validity scales (Underresponse and Hyperresponse) and six clinical scales (Anxiety, Depression, Anger, Posttraumatic Stress, Dissociation, and Sexual Concerns).

For Affect Regulation, Interpersonal Relatedness, and Identity Problems

- *Trauma and Attachment Belief Scale (TABS).* The TABS (Pearlman, 2003; formerly the Traumatic Stress Institute Belief Scale) is a normed instrument that measures disrupted cognitive schemas and need states associated with complex trauma exposure. It evaluates disturbance in five areas: Safety, Trust, Esteem, Intimacy, and Control. There are reliable subscales for each of these domains, rated both for "self" and "other." In contrast to more symptom-based tests, the TABS evaluates the self-reported needs and expectations of trauma survivors as they describe self in relation to others. For this reason, the TABS is helpful in understanding important assumptions that the client carries regarding his or her relationships to others, including the therapist.

- *Inventory of Altered Self Capacities (IASC).* The IASC (Briere, 2000a) is a standardized test of difficulties in the areas of relatedness, identity, and affect regulation. The scales of the IASC assess the following domains: Interpersonal Conflicts, Idealization-Disillusionment, Abandonment Concerns, Identity Impairment, Susceptibility to Influence, Affect Dysregulation, and Tension Reduction Activities. Scores on the IASC have been shown to predict childhood trauma history, adult attachment style, interpersonal problems, suicidality, and substance abuse history in various samples. The Idealization-Disillusionment, Susceptibility to Influence, and Abandonment Concerns scales are useful in warning of potentially therapy-disrupting issues or dynamics that emerge in work with some survivors of more complex and severe trauma.

For Dissociation

- *Dissociative Experiences Scale (DES).* The DES (Bernstein & Putnam, 1986) is the most often used of the dissociation measures, although it is not normed on the general population. The DES taps "disturbance in identity, memory, awareness, and cognitions and feelings of derealization or depersonalization or associated phenomena such as deja vu and absorption" (Bernstein & Putnam, 1986, p. 729). A score of 30 or higher on the DES correctly identified 74 percent of those with DID and 80 percent of those without DID in a large sample of psychiatric outpatients (Carlson et al., 1993).
- *Multiscale Dissociation Inventory (MDI).* Based on data suggesting that dissociation is a multidimensional phenomenon, the MDI (Briere, 2002b) is a normed clinical test that consists of six scales (Disengagement, Depersonalization, Derealization, Memory Disturbance, Emotional Constriction, and Identity Dissociation). Together, these scores form an overall dissociation profile. The MDI is reliable and correlates as expected with child abuse history, adult trauma exposure, PTSD, and other measures of dissociation, including the DES. The Identity Dissociation scale had a specificity of .92 and a sensitivity of .93 with respect to a diagnosis of dissociative identity disorder (Briere, 2002b).

Assessment of Physical Health

A trauma evaluation is not complete without an assessment regarding the client's self-reported physical health status. At some point in the interview, the clinician (whether a medical or nonmedical practitioner) should ask if the client has any active medical conditions, whether he or she is in any current physical distress, and whether he or she takes any medications (including over-the-counter medications, vitamins, and herbal supplements). This part of the interview is especially relevant for traumatized individuals, because, as described in Chapter 2, those with PTSD are at increased risk for physical health problems. In addition, some medical conditions (such as endocrine problems, neurological disorders, and traumatic brain injury) can mimic the symptoms of PTSD (Kudler & Davidson, 1995).

Given this complexity, and the fact that somatization is more common in traumatized individuals, the determination of which symptoms are due to actual medical illness (and require medical intervention) often can be quite challenging. In health care settings that provide services to indigent, uninsured, or undocumented clients, or where, for various other reasons, clients have difficulty obtaining medical care, concerns about medical complications may be especially relevant. In such instances, the mental health clinician may be the client's primary point of contact with the health care system. We therefore recommend that therapists refer traumatized clients for full medical examinations and regular medical follow-ups.

Suggested Reading

Briere, J. (2004). *Psychological assessment of adult posttraumatic states: Phenomenology, diagnosis, and measurement* (2nd ed.). Washington, DC: American Psychological Association.

Carlson, E. B. (1997). *Trauma assessments: A clinician's guide.* New York: Guilford.

Pelcovitz, D., van der Kolk, B. A., Roth, S., Mandel, F., Kaplan, S., & Resick, P. (1997). Development of a criteria set and a structured interview for disorders of extreme stress (SIDES). *Journal of Traumatic Stress, 10,* 3–16.

Schnurr, P. P., & Green, B. L. (2004). *Trauma and health: physical health consequences of exposure to extreme stress.* Washington, DC: American Psychological Association.

Simon, R. I. (Ed.). (1995). *Posttraumatic stress disorder in litigation: Guidelines for forensic assessment.* Washington, DC: American Psychiatric Press.

Stamm, B. H. (Ed.). (1996). *Measurement of stress, trauma and adaptation.* Lutherville, MD: Sidran.

Wilson, J., & Keane, T. (Eds.). (2004). *Assessing psychological trauma and PTSD: A practitioner's handbook* (2nd ed.). New York: Guilford.

PART II

Clinical Interventions

O nce the client's trauma history and posttraumatic symptoms have been determined, trauma therapy can be initiated. We begin the treatment part of this book by outlining general issues relevant to trauma therapy; the more technical aspects of treatment follow.

We refer throughout these chapters to the integration of cognitive-behavioral, psychodynamic, and eclectic approaches in the treatment of trauma effects. It is our position that the various components of these methods can be combined into a single, broad therapeutic approach—one that can be adapted to the potentially wide range of symptoms and needs of each client. Nevertheless, these models are quite different from one another, and some of their originators may disagree with the idea of combining their techniques with those of other clinicians. In our experience, however, effective therapy almost always consists of a variety of interventions and theoretical models—whether acknowledged by the clinician or not. For example, many good cognitive-behavioral therapists use psychodynamic techniques in their work with clients, and many psychodynamic interventions are, at their base, translatable into cognitive-behavioral principles.

A review of the existing literature on the treatment of posttraumatic states, in combination with clinical experience, suggests that effective therapy—irrespective of underlying theory—can usually be broken down into a number of broad components, the exact combination of which varies according to the client's specific clinical needs. These minimally consist of:

- An overall approach that is respectful and positive, and that provides support and validation in the context of a therapeutic relationship
- Psychoeducation on trauma and trauma symptoms
- Some form of stress reduction or affect regulation training
- Cognitive interventions that address harmful or debilitating trauma-related beliefs, assumptions, and perceptions
- Opportunities to develop a coherent narrative about the traumatic event
- Memory processing, usually involving guided self-exposure to trauma memories
- Processing of relational issues in the context of a positive therapeutic relationship
- Exploration activities that increase self-awareness and self-acceptance

Many of these interventions may occur within the same therapy session, and may be hard to distinguish from one another during the treatment process. Nevertheless, they represent, to some extent, separate processes and goals. For this reason, each receives detailed attention in the following chapters. We also include in Part II chapters on the treatment of acute trauma (that is, traumas that have very recently occurred) and the psycho-pharmacology of posttraumatic states.

4

Central Issues
in Trauma Treatment

A Basic Philosophy of Trauma, Recovery, and Growth

Although much of this book is devoted to the technical aspects of treatment, we start this chapter with philosophical issues associated with trauma therapy. This is because the way in which the clinician views trauma and trauma-related outcomes, and what he or she believes to be the overbridging goals and functions of treatment, have significant effects on the process and outcome of therapy.

Perspectives on trauma and its treatment vary among clinicians, and a variety of clinical models can inform effective psychotherapy. The approach that we advocate in this book emphasizes the probably innate tendency for humans to process trauma-related memories and to move toward more adaptive psychological functioning. As discussed in more detail later in this book (Chapter 8), many of the "reliving" symptoms of posttraumatic stress disorder (PTSD) can be conceptualized as recovery algorithms that humans have evolved over time in response to trauma exposure (Briere, 1996, 2002a; Horowitz, 1978). The intrinsic function of these reliving experiences appears to be to process and integrate upsetting material. This implies that individuals who present with trauma-related symptoms are, in a sense, attempting to "metabolize" or internally resolve distressing thoughts, feelings, and memories. This perspective reframes many posttraumatic symptoms as adaptive and recovery focused rather than as inherently pathological. It also suggests that therapeutic exposure (see Chapter 8) and other approaches to processing traumatic memories may work by optimizing those activities in which the client is already engaged, as opposed to imposing entirely new or alien techniques. Seen in this light, traumatized individuals are not collections of symptoms, but rather people who, at some level, are attempting to recover—albeit not always successfully.

A second philosophical notion offered in this book is that trauma can result in growth. Like many other therapists who work in this area, we have found that adversity and distress—beyond their capacity to disrupt and injure—often push people to develop in positive ways. As documented by various studies, this may involve new levels of psychological resilience, additional survival skills, greater self-knowledge and self-appreciation, increased empathy, and a more broad and complex view of life in general (for example, O'Leary, 1998; Siegel & Schrimshaw, 2000; Updegraff & Taylor, 2000). The recently widowed person may learn new independence, the survivor of a heart attack may develop a more healthy perspective on life's priorities, and the person exposed to a catastrophic event may learn important things about his or her resilience in the face of tragedy. The implication is not that someone is "lucky" when bad things happen, but, rather, that not all outcomes associated with adversity are inevitably negative. The message is not that one should "look on the bright side," which can easily be seen as dismissive and unempathic. Instead, we suggest that the survivor's life, although perhaps irrevocably changed, is not over, and that future good things are possible.

Of course, some traumatic events are so overwhelming that they make growth extremely difficult; they may involve so much loss that it seems impossible (if not disrespectful) to suggest any eventual positive outcomes to the client. Survivors of chronic traumas such as severe childhood abuse or torture may feel that they have been permanently injured. In other cases, life experiences may have pushed some survivors so far into avoidance and defense that they cannot easily see beyond the immediate goals of pain avoidance and psychological survival. Even in these instances, however, treatment should not necessarily be limited to symptom reduction; it may also include the possibility of new insights and skills. In less tragic circumstances, it may even be possible to suggest that adversity can make the survivor more, as opposed to less.

This philosophy may appear to be a distraction from the technical job of trauma treatment. Clearly, an injured person first needs attention to immediate safety and life support, and help with painful symptoms; it is often only later that the more complicated and subtle aspects of recovery and growth become salient. Yet, ultimately, some of the best interventions in posttraumatic psychological injury are implicitly existential and hopeful. This perspective can also be beneficial for the therapist—the possibility that the client can not only recover, but also may gain in some way from traumatic experience, brings tremendous richness and optimism to the job of helping hurt people.

Respect and Positive Regard

One of the implications of this philosophy is that the traumatized client should be seen as someone who, despite being confronted with potentially overwhelming psychic pain and disability, is struggling to come to terms with his or her history—and, perhaps, to grow beyond it. It is often hard to be in therapy, especially when (as is outlined in the next chapters) such treatment requires one to feel things that one would rather not feel and think about things that one would rather not consider. The easy choice, in many cases, is to block awareness of the pain and avoid the thought—to "let sleeping dogs lie." It is a braver choice, when the option is available, to confront one's memories and their attendant psychological distress and attempt to integrate them into the fabric of one's life. It may be that—in order to survive pain—the client engages in some level of resistance in order to avoid being exposed to the full experience of relived trauma during treatment. Such a response is logical and should be understood as such by the clinician. It does not take away from the fact that the client deserves considerable respect for being willing to revisit painful events and to choose awareness over the apparent (although typically false) benefits of denial and avoidance.

Continuous appreciation of the client's bravery is a central task for the trauma-specialized clinician—acknowledging the courage associated with the client's mere physical presence during the therapy hour, and taking note of the strength that is required to confront painful memories when avoidance is so obviously the less challenging option. When the therapist can accomplish a respectful and positive attitude, the therapy process almost always benefits. Although the client may not completely believe the therapist's positive appraisal of him or her, visible therapist respect assists greatly in establishing a therapeutic rapport, increasing the likelihood that the client will make him- or herself psychologically available to the therapeutic process.

Hope

Hope is also intrinsic to effective trauma treatment. Repeated experience of painful things (including painful symptoms) may cause the client to expect continuing despair as an inevitable part of the future. In this light, part of the task of therapy is to reframe trauma as challenge, pain as (at least in part) awareness and growth, and the future as opportunity. This in no way means that the clinician should be Pollyannaish about the client's experiences and current distress; it is very important that the client's perceptions be acknowledged and understood. However, it is rarely a good idea for the therapist to accept and therefore inadvertently reinforce the helplessness, hopelessness, and demoralization that the client may infer from life experiences; to do so is, to some extent, to share in the client's injury. Instead, the challenge is to acknowledge the sometimes incredible hurt that the client has experienced, while, at the same time, gently suggesting that his or her presence in treatment signals implicit strength, adaptive capacity, and hopefulness for the future.

Instilling hope does not mean that the therapist promises anything. For a variety of reasons (for example, genetic or biological influences, the possibility of premature termination, treatment interference through substance abuse, especially complex and severe symptomatology, new traumas, and so on), not every client experiences complete symptom remission. Because we cannot predict the future, we cannot guarantee that things will go well for any given person. Yet, an overall positive view of the client and his or her future is often justified and helpful. Even when not treated, many of those individuals exposed to major trauma will experience significant symptom reduction over time (Freedman & Shalev, 2000), probably as a function of the innate self-healing processes described in Chapter 3. Even more important, having completed trauma-focused treatment is associated with greater symptom reduction than not having done so (Foa, Keane, & Friedman, 2000). For such reasons, it is generally appropriate to communicate guarded optimism regarding the client's future clinical course and to note signs of improvement whenever they occur.

Ultimately, hope is a powerful antidote to the helplessness and despair associated with many major traumas and losses. Although not typically described as a therapeutic goal, the instillation of hope is a powerful therapeutic action (Meichenbaum, 1994; Najavits, 2002). It takes advantage of the ascribed power and knowledge of the clinician to communicate, with some credibility, that things are likely to get better. The impact of this message for many trauma survivors should not be underestimated.

Central Treatment Principles

Beyond a general philosophy of trauma and recovery, there are a number of basic principles of effective trauma-focused treatment. Although these principles apply most directly to psychotherapy, they also are relevant to other treatment methodologies, including psychopharmacology.

Provide and Ensure Safety

Because trauma is about vulnerability to danger, safety is a critical issue for trauma survivors (Herman, 1992a; Najavits, 2002; Cook et al., 2005). It is often only in perceived safe environments that those who have been exposed to danger can let down their guard and experience the relative luxury of introspection and connection. In therapy, safety involves, at minimum, the absence of physical danger, psychological maltreatment, exploitation, or rejection. Physical safety means that the survivor perceives, and comes to expect, that there is no likelihood of physical or sexual assault at the hands of the clinician or others, and that the building is not likely to collapse or burn during the session. Psychological safety, which is sometimes more difficult to provide, means that the client will not perceive himself or herself to be criticized, humiliated, rejected, dramatically misunderstood, needlessly interrupted, or laughed at during the treatment process, and that psychological boundaries and therapist-client confidentiality will not be violated. It is often only when such conditions are reliably met that the client can begin to reduce his or her defenses and more openly process the thoughts, feelings, and memories associated with traumatic events. In fact, as is discussed in Chapter 8, it is critical that the client experience safety while remembering danger; only under this circumstance will the fear and distress associated with trauma in the past lose the capacity to be evoked by the present.

Unfortunately, in order to feel safe, there must not only be safety; the client must be able to perceive it. This is often a problem because, as noted earlier, trauma exposure can result in hypervigilance; many traumatized people come to expect danger, devote considerable resources to detecting impending harm, and have a tendency to misperceive even safe environments and interactions as potentially dangerous (Janoff-Bulman, 1992; Pearlman & Courtois, 2005). Even a safe therapeutic environment may appear unsafe to some traumatized clients. As a result, therapy may take considerably longer—and call more on the clinician's patience and sustained capacity for caring—than is allowed for by short-term therapies. Some multiply traumatized individuals—former child abuse victims, torture survivors, victims of political oppression, adolescent gang members, "street kids," or battered women, for example—may need to attend therapy sessions for relatively long periods of time before they can fully perceive and accept the fact that they will not be hurt if they become vulnerable in treatment. For such people, interventions such as therapeutic exposure or psychodynamic interpretation may not be appropriate until therapy has been in place for a long enough time to allow an expectation of safety. Given these concerns, it is obviously important that the therapist be able to determine the client's relative *experience* of therapeutic safety, since many clinical interventions involve the activation and processing of upsetting memory material. To the extent that such memories trigger fear and pain, those who are not aware that they are safe may be more distressed by such activations.

As noted earlier in this chapter, ensuring safety also means working to ensure that the client will be relatively free of danger outside of the therapeutic setting. Highly fearful or endangered survivors are unlikely to have sufficient psychological resources to participate in psychotherapy without being emotionally overwhelmed and/or especially avoidant. The battered woman should be as safe as possible from further battery, and the sexual abuse victim must be out of danger from his or her perpetrator, before psychological processing of symptoms is attempted. Otherwise, the client's life and physical integrity may be risked in the service of symptom relief. Although this may seem an obvious fact, many therapists fall into the trap of attempting to process traumatic memories with acutely traumatized individuals who continue to live in obviously dangerous circumstances.

This does not mean that all psychological interventions are ruled out in work with the still-at-risk—only those having as their primary focus the direct processing of traumatic memories and feelings, or those that prize insight over safety. For example, the acutely battered woman may easily gain from psychoeducational activities or cognitive interventions that provide information on increasing personal safety or that support the often daunting task of leaving an abusive partner (Jordan, Nietzel, Walker, & Logan, 2004). On the other hand, she may be placed at continued risk if the immediate focus of therapy is to emotionally process her last battery experience or to analyze what childhood issues are involved in her attraction to authoritarian men in the first place. Of course, some chronic life-endangering phenomena, such as unsafe sexual practices or intravenous substance abuse, are not threats that can be easily terminated—the individual may need some level of symptom reduction, increased coping, or psychoeducation before these behaviors can be reduced or ended. Nevertheless, when the danger is acute and potentially avoidable, the clinician's first focus must be on ensuring immediate safety.

Provide and Ensure Stability

Stability refers to an ongoing psychological and physical state whereby one is not overwhelmed by disruptive internal or external stimuli. It also implies some degree of capacity to resist the effects of such stimuli in the near future. Stability concerns are highly relevant to work with trauma survivors, since adverse events are often destabilizing and can produce conditions (for example, chaotic interpersonal or physical environments, posttraumatic stress, depression) that further increase susceptibility to stress. In addition, some trauma-related responses (for example, substance abuse, problematic personality traits, or reactive psychosis) can contribute to unstable lifestyles, such as homelessness, recurrent involvement in chaotic and intense relationships, or chronic self-destructiveness.

Life Stability

Life stability refers to generally stable living conditions. For example, those living in extreme poverty, chaotic environments, or chronically risky occupations (for example, prostitution) may have difficulty tolerating the additional distress sometimes activated by trauma therapy. Such conditions may involve hunger, fear, racial or sexual oppression, and the insecurity associated with inadequate or absent housing—none of which support emotional resilience in the face of activated distress. In fact, without sufficient security, food, and shelter, avoidance of traumatic material (for example, through numbing or substance abuse) may appear more useful to the trauma victim than the seemingly counterintuitive notion of reliving painful memories. Trauma therapy is most helpful to those who have the social and physical resources necessary to experience safety and the option of trust. As a result, the first intervention with traumatized people who have few resources is often social casework: arranging adequate and reliable food, shelter, and physical safety.

Emotional Stability

In addition to physical stability, trauma survivors should have some level of psychological homeostasis before formal trauma therapy can be initiated (Ford, Courtois, Steele, van der Hart, & Nijenhuis, 2005; Herman, 1992a). In general, this means that those with acute psychotic symptoms, high suicidality, extremely high levels of posttraumatic stress, or debilitating anxiety or depression may require other interventions before trauma therapy can be initiated. These include the appropriate use of medication (see Chapter 11), crisis intervention, and, in some cases, supportive psychotherapy. In the absence of such pretreatment, activation of trauma-related material may result not only in an exacerbation of existing symptoms (for example, renewed psychosis or posttraumatic stress) but also may overwhelm the survivor's existing capacity to regulate his or her emotional state, producing new distress and dysfunction. Exacerbated or newly activated symptoms, in turn, may result in increased avoidance behaviors, such as substance abuse or suicidality, as well as increasing the likelihood that the client will drop out of therapy.

It is not always easy to determine when symptoms are too intense to warrant trauma-specific interventions as opposed to being worthy targets of treatment. For example, when is posttraumatic stress or anxiety too severe to support cognitive-behavioral therapy, and when are these symptoms in the range that would be appropriate for such treatment? Specific assessment approaches that may shed some light on these issues were presented in Chapter 3. Most generally, the issue is whether the symptoms in question have significantly reduced the client's capacity to "handle" or regulate the almost inevitable upsurge of emotion that follows therapeutic exposure to unresolved trauma memories. If the increased activation is not overwhelming, classic trauma treatment is usually indicated. If the response to treatment would be to become flooded with negative affects, pretreatment (or solely supportive psychotherapy) is required until greater psychological stability is present.

Interestingly, some forms of disorder traditionally assumed to be synonymous with psychological instability may not always be contraindications for trauma therapy. For example, some traumatized individuals with borderline personality disorder or low-level chronic psychosis may be sufficiently stable to tolerate classic trauma treatment, whereas others with less diagnostic severity may not. Clinicians often have concerns when working with psychotic or Axis II disturbance because such disturbances are frequently associated with affect regulation problems and more extreme dysphoria. However, the critical issue is less the type of disorder, per se, than the client's relative capacity to tolerate the emotions associated with exposure to traumatic memories.

Maintain a Positive and Consistent Therapeutic Relationship

One of the most important components of successful trauma therapy is a good working relationship between client and therapist (Pearlman & Courtois, 2005). In fact, a number of studies indicate that therapeutic outcome is best predicted by the quality of the treatment relationship, as opposed to the specific techniques used (Lambert & Bergin, 1994; Orlinski, Grawe, & Parks, 1994). Although some therapeutic approaches stress relationship dynamics more than others, it is probably true that all forms of trauma therapy work better if the client feels accepted, liked, and taken seriously. Even in short-term, highly structured treatment approaches (for example, some forms of cognitive-behavioral or pharmacologic therapies), clients with good working relationships with their helpers are more likely to persevere in treatment, adhere to whatever regimen is in place, and, as a result, experience a more positive clinical outcome (Rau & Goldfried, 1994). Longer-term and more interpersonal treatment approaches, in which relational issues are more prominent, are probably even more likely to benefit from a strong therapeutic relationship.

Because trauma therapy almost always involves revisiting and processing painful memories, as well as potentially reactivating feelings of danger and vulnerability, successful treatment is especially contingent on therapeutic support and connection. Distant, uninvolved, or emotionally disconnected client-therapist relationships are, in our experience, quite often associated with less positive therapeutic outcomes (see Dalenberg 2000, for an empirically based discussion of this issue). At minimum, a positive therapeutic relationship provides a variety of benefits. These potentially include:

- Decreased treatment drop-out and more reliable session attendance (Rau & Goldfried, 1994)
- Less avoidance and greater disclosure of personal material (Farber & Hall, 2002)
- Greater treatment adherence and medication compliance (Frank & Gunderson, 1990)
- Greater openness to—and acceptance of—therapist interpretations, suggestions, and support (Horvath & Luborsky, 1993)
- More capacity to tolerate painful thoughts and feelings during therapeutic exposure to trauma memories (American Psychiatric Association, 2001)

In addition to supporting effective treatment, the therapeutic relationship is more likely to be helpful to the extent that it both (1) gently triggers memories and schemas associated with prior relational traumas, and (2) provides the opportunity to process these activations in the context of therapeutic caring, safety, and support (Briere, 2002a). As is described in more detail in Chapter 9, even the most benign client-therapist relationship may trigger at least some rejection or abandonment fears, misperception of danger, or authority issues in survivors of extended or severe trauma. When these intrusions occur at the same time that the client is feeling respect, caring, and empathy from the therapist, they may gradually lose their generalizability to current relationships and become counterconditioned by current, positive relational feelings. In this sense, a good therapeutic relationship is not only supportive of effective treatment, it is virtually integral to the resolution of major relational traumas.

Tailor the Therapy to the Client

Although a review of some currently available treatment manuals might suggest that clinical interventions are applied more or less equally and in similar ways to all mental health clients, this is almost never the case in actual clinical practice. In fact, the highly structured, sometimes manualized nature of some empirically validated therapies more directly reflects the requirements of treatment outcome research (that is, the need for treatment to be highly similar and equally applied for each client in a given study) than any clinically based intent to provide equivalent interventions for all presenting clients (Westen, Novotny, & Thompson-Brenner, 2004). In the real world of clinical practice, clients vary significantly with regard to their presenting issues, comorbid symptoms, and the extent to which they can utilize and tolerate psychological interventions. For this reason, therapy is likely to be most effective when it is tailored to the specific characteristics and concerns of the individual person (Cloitre, Koenen, Cohen, & Han, 2002). We describe next several of the more important individual variables that should be taken into account when providing mental health interventions, including trauma therapy.

Affect Regulation and Memory Intensity Issues

As noted previously, *affect regulation* refers to an individual's relative capacity to tolerate and internally reduce painful emotional states. People with limited affect regulation abilities are more likely to be overwhelmed and destabilized by negative emotional experiences—both those associated with current negative events and those triggered by painful memories. Since trauma therapy often involves activating and processing traumatic memories, individuals with less ability to internally regulate painful states are more likely to become highly distressed, if not emotionally overwhelmed, during treatment (Cloitre et al., 2002).

The idea of "affect regulation" is likely to be oversimplified, however. For example, some people are better at tolerating or regulating one type of feeling (for example, anxiety) than another (for example, anger), despite the common implication that any given person has a generalized capacity to regulate emotions. As well, some people's emotional responses may be more intense than others', as a function of having been exposed to more painful experiences. In this regard, it may take more affect regulation capacity to downregulate emotions associated with some very painful memories (for example, prolonged torture) than those associated with less intense memories (for example, of an automobile accident). It is rarely enough to decide that someone has "affect regulation difficulties" without also determining the affective load that requires regulating (Briere, in press).

Variability in affect regulation capacity—and the severity of the memory-triggered affect to be regulated—has significant clinical implications. Most generally, individuals with impaired affect regulation—especially in the context of easily triggered, highly painful memories—are more likely to experience overwhelming emotionality when exposed to upsetting memories during treatment, and to respond with increased avoidance, including "resistance" and/or dissociation. Such responses, in turn, reduce the client's exposure to traumatic material and to the healing aspects of the therapeutic relationship. As described in Chapter 7, treatment of those with impaired affect regulation capacities and/or a heavy trauma load should proceed carefully, such that traumatic memories are activated and processed in smaller increments than otherwise might be necessary. Often described as "titrated exposure" or "working within the therapeutic window" (Briere, 1996, 2002a), this usually involves adjusting treatment so that trauma processing that occurs within a given session does not exceed the capacities of the survivor to tolerate that level of distress—while, at the same time, providing as much processing as can reasonably occur (see Chapter 8). In individuals with substantially reduced affect regulation capacities (and/or especially distressing memories), this level of exposure and processing may be quite limited at any given moment. Nevertheless, over time, even seemingly small amounts of trauma processing tend to add up, ultimately leading to potentially significant symptom relief and greater emotional capacity without the negative side effect of overwhelming affect.

Preponderant Schemas

As noted in Chapter 2, trauma exposure often has effects on cognition. Depending on the type of trauma and when in development it occurred, this may include easily triggered perceptions of oneself as inadequate, bad, or helpless, expectations of others as dangerous, rejecting, or unloving, and a view of the future as hopeless. Such distortions inevitably affect the client's perception of the therapist and of therapy. For example, the survivor may expect the therapist to be critical, unloving, or even hostile or abusive.

Early child abuse and neglect may result in latent gestalts of preverbal negative cognitions (Baldwin, Fehr, Keedian, Seidel, & Thompson, 1993) and feelings that are easily evoked by reminiscent stimuli in the immediate interpersonal environment. These relational schemas, when triggered, may result in sudden, intense thoughts and feelings that were initially encoded during childhood maltreatment. As a result, the adult abuse survivor may experience sudden feelings of abandonment, rejection, or betrayal during psychotherapy.

Because the cognitive effects of trauma vary from client to client, as a function of the individual's specific history, therapy must be adjusted to take into account each client's preponderant schemas of self and others (Pearlman & Courtois, 2005). In general, this means that the clinician should do as much as possible to (1) respond in ways that specifically do not reinforce the client's negative expectations, and (2) avoid (to the extent possible) triggering under-lying cognitive-emotional gestalts related to broader themes such as interper-sonal danger or rejection. The individual with a tendency to view important interpersonal figures with distrust, for example, may require a therapist who is especially supportive and validating and who is careful not to trigger too many relational memories of maltreatment. This does not simply involve statements to the client that he or she is safe or positively valued—more important, the therapist should act and respond in such a manner that safety and caring is demonstrated and can be inferred. Because the distrustful client will be predisposed to miss such signs, and perhaps even actively misinterpret them, therapeutic interventions must be even more explicit and obvious in these areas than is the case for those without (or less of) this cognitive set.

It is important to note here that tailoring one's treatment approach to a given person's major cognitive issues does not mean that these distortions or disruptive schemas are not evoked in therapy. No matter how hard the clini-cian tries, the survivor who has been substantially maltreated in the past is likely to view some of the therapist's behaviors as punitive, critical, or abu-sive, and thus issues in this area almost unavoidably become a topic of dis-cussion during therapy. However, because the therapist is working hard to minimize the extent of these misattributions and triggered schemas, whatever emerges over time in therapy is likely to be less intense and more easily demonstrable as contextually inaccurate. The repetitive experience of fearing that one's therapist is cold and rejecting, for example, and yet finding, over time, that these perceptions are manifestly untrue is often extremely helpful.

Significantly, although the clinician works hard to communicate an absence of criticism or rejection, this does not mean that he or she does not support the client's discussion and processing of these perceptions and feel-ings as they relate to subtle client-therapist dynamics or to others in the client's environment. Ultimately, the goal is to make treatment possible for those who are especially sensitive and suspicious of the vulnerability, connec-tion, and intimacy that are part of the normal operating conditions of treat-ment. Knowledge that client X has "abandonment issues," client Y tends to perceive caring as intrusive or sexual in nature, or that client Z responds to authority figures with expectations of hostility or domination can allow the therapist to adjust his or her approach so that it does not unnecessarily trig-ger these issues and thereby interfere with the process of treatment.

Take Gender Issues Into Account

Although there is little doubt that men and women undergo many of the same traumatic events and suffer in many of the same ways, it is also clear that (1) some traumas are more common in one sex than the other, and

(2) sex role socialization affects how such injuries are experienced and expressed. These differences, in turn, have significant impacts on the content and process of trauma-focused therapy.

As noted in Chapter 1, women are more at risk for victimization in close relationships than are men, and are especially more likely to be sexually victimized. In contrast, boys are at greater risk than girls of childhood physical abuse, and men are more likely to experience nonintimate physical assaults than women. In addition to trauma exposure differences, men and women tend to experience, communicate, and process the distress associated with traumatic events in different ways. Although there is major variation among people within each sex, women are generally socialized to express more directly certain feelings, such as fear or sadness, but are taught to dampen or avoid others, such as anger (Renzetti & Curran, 2002). Men, on the other hand, are often more permitted the expression of anger, but may be socially discouraged from communicating "softer" feelings, such as sadness or fear (Cochrane, 2005). Men and women also may differ in how they act upon feelings and needs. Men are to some extent taught to externalize or cognitively suppress unpleasant feelings, and to act on the environment in order to reduce pain or distress, whereas women are generally socialized to express their distress to trusted others, and are, overall, less prone to externalizing their pain through acting on the environment (Bem, 1976; Briere, 1996; Renzetti & Curran, 2002). These sex-role-related differences in symptom expression and behavioral response often manifest themselves during trauma-focused psychotherapy. All things being equal, for example, male trauma survivors in treatment may be more prone to expressions of anger—or to denying posttraumatic distress entirely—than female survivors, whereas traumatized women may be more open to emotional expression, especially of feelings of sadness, fear, or helplessness.

Given these sociocultural influences, the therapist should be alert to ways in which trauma survivors express or inhibit their emotional reactions based on sex-role-based expectations. Often, this will involve supporting the client to express the full range of feelings and thoughts associated with a traumatic event, as opposed to only those considered socially appropriate to his or her gender. In fact, to the extent that (as described in Chapter 8) feelings and thoughts are more easily processed when fully expressed during treatment, unaddressed sex role constraints are likely to inhibit full psychological recovery.

The therapist should also be aware of sex differences in how trauma is cognitively processed. Because boys and men are often socialized to present themselves as strong and able to defend themselves, victimization may be more of a sex role violation for them than it is for girls and women (Mendelsohn & Sewell, 2004). Such social expectations can result in different responses to trauma. Victimized men, for example, may struggle with feelings of inadequacy, shame, and low self-esteem associated with the social implication that an inability to fight off maltreatment reflects lesser masculinity or competence (Mendel, 1995). In addition, many sexually assaulted or abused males have sexual orientation concerns related to their trauma. In the case of childhood sexual abuse, for example, heterosexual boys and men may fear that molestation by another male has caused them to be latently homosexual—a response that, in a homophobic culture, may result in compensatory hypermasculinity or overinvolvement in heterosexual activity (Briere, 1996). Conversely, homosexual men who were sexually abused by males as children may believe that their sexual orientation somehow caused them to be abused by men, or that their abuse caused them to be homosexual, conclusions that can lead to feelings of guilt, shame, and self-hatred (Briere, 1996).

Sex role expectations also affect, to some extent, how traumatized women view their victimization. Women who have been sexually assaulted may believe that they in some way enticed their perpetrators into raping them—a concern that reflects the traditional stereotype of females as sexual objects who are intentionally seductive (Burt, 1980). Similarly, women battered or otherwise abused by their partners may believe that their supposed lack of subservience or failure to perform as an adequate mate means that they deserved to be maltreated (Walker, 1984).

Given these gender-specific influences on trauma-related cognitions, the clinician is likely to be more helpful if he or she closely attends to concerns about unacceptability, self-blame, low self-esteem, shame, and sexual orientation as they are expressed in survivors' cognitive reactions to trauma. Traumatized men may require additional reassurance that they are not less masculine (regardless of sexual orientation) by virtue of having been victimized, and may gain from interventions that support the full range of emotional and cognitive expression without fear of stigmatization. Especially relevant, in this regard, is the need for many victimized men to process feelings of shame associated with viewing themselves as deviant and socially unacceptable. Women survivors, on the other hand, may gain especially from interventions that support self-determination and help them to reject feelings of responsibility for their abuse, including the unwarranted notion that they somehow sought out or otherwise deserved maltreatment.

Be Aware of—and Sensitive to—Sociocultural Issues

Social Maltreatment

One of the more overlooked issues in the treatment of trauma survivors is that people with lesser social status are more likely than others to be victimized

(Bassuk, Dawson, Perloff, & Weinreb, 2001; Breslau, Wilcox, Storr, Lucia, & Anthony, 2004). Social, sexual, and racial discrimination often have negative psychological effects that are, in a sense, posttraumatic (Loo et al., 2001; Root, 1996), and typically are associated with environmental conditions in which further trauma is common (Breslau et al., 1998; North, Smith, & Spitznager, 1994; Sells, Rowe, Fisk, & Davidson, 2003). Some groups in North America suffer from multigenerational trauma, including African Americans, whose ancestors were often held in slavery (Mattis, Bell, Jagers, & Jenkins, 1999), and American Indians who, as a group, have experienced extended maltreatment and cultural near-annihilation (Duran & Duran, 1995; Manson et al., 1996). Combined with the discrimination and marginalization often experienced by other non-Caucasian racial/ethnic groups, and the relatively dangerous living environments in which many are forced to live, social inequality provides a vast depot of trauma and trauma impacts in North America.

Beyond North America, individuals from some regions of the world are especially likely to be maltreated. When some of these people immigrate (or escape) to North America, they carry with them the trauma experienced in their countries of origin. Mental health centers specializing in refugee or immigrant issues regularly deal with the effects of holocausts or mass murder (for example, "ethnic cleansing"), political imprisonment, war, extended torture, "honor" killings, sexual violence, and extreme ethnic or gender discrimination (Basoglu, 1992; Marsella, Bornemann, Ekblad, & Orley, 1994; Miller & Rasco, 2004). This concatenation of social adversity and ethnic variation means that cultural and historical issues are often highly relevant to the process and content of trauma-focused psychotherapy.

Cultural Variation

Partially because ethnic and racial minorities are more likely to be traumatized, and partially due to the general multicultural mix present in North American and European societies, individuals presenting for trauma services are likely to reflect a wide range of cultures and ethnic groups. Such cultural differences are not merely a function of race: people of low socioeconomic status often have different worldviews and experiences than those of the same race or ethnicity who have more economic and social opportunities. Similarly, merely knowing that someone is, for example, "African American," "Hispanic," "Asian," or "American Indian" says little about his or her cultural context. An individual from Vietnam, for example, may be quite different in perspective, language, and emotional style than a person from Japan. The 1999 Surgeon General's report on the cultural aspects of mental health services notes that:

Asian Americans and Pacific Islanders . . . include 43 ethnic groups speaking over 100 languages and dialects. For American Indians and Alaska Natives, the Bureau of Indian Affairs currently recognizes 561 tribes. African Americans are also becoming more diverse, especially with the influx of refugees and immigrants from many countries of Africa and the Caribbean. (U.S. Surgeon General, 1999)

These wide cultural differences often translate into different trauma presentations and idioms of distress, as described in Chapter 2. In addition, above and beyond their social status in North America, people from the various cultures and subcultures of the world have widely different expectations of how clinical intervention should occur, and of the ways in which clinicians and clients should interact (Marsella et al., 1996). In one culture, for example, eye contact between clinician and client is a sign of respect; in another, it may be the complete opposite. Similarly, in some cultures, certain topics (for example, sexual issues, visible loss of dignity) are considered to be more embarrassing or shameful than in others, and thus should be raised only when relevant to treatment, and then with great sensitivity.

Although the focus of this book precludes a detailed discussion of this issue, a central point must be made: cultural awareness and sensitivity are an important part of any psychotherapeutic process—including trauma therapy. Clinicians who find themselves, for example, regularly working with Cambodian refugees, Hmong clients, or Mexican immigrants have a responsibility to learn the primary "rules" of clinical engagement with people from these counties, as well as, if possible, something of their culture, history, and language.

Monitor and Control Countertransference

A last general topic of this chapter is what is commonly referred to as *countertransference* (also described as *counteractivation* in self-trauma theory [Briere, 2005]; see Chapter 8). Although this phenomenon has many different definitions, we use it here to refer to occasions when the therapist responds to the client with cognitive-emotional processes (for example, expectations, beliefs, or emotions) that are strongly influenced by prior personal experiences. In many of these cases, these experiences involve childhood maltreatment, adult traumas, or other upsetting events. Of course, all behavior is influenced by past experience, and not all countertransference responses are negative (Dalenberg, 2000; Pearlman & Saakvitne, 1995). Even positive countertransference, however, must be monitored by the therapist, since it may produce unwanted responses such as idealization of the client, the need to normalize what are actually problematic client behaviors or symptoms, or even sexual or romantic feelings. Ultimately, the concern is that counter-transference can interfere with treatment by leading to either (1) a deleterious clinical experience for the client or (2) processes that disrupt the treatment process.

For example,

- Therapist A was raised by a critical, psychologically punitive parent. She now finds that she tends to experience angry or guilty feelings when her client complains about any aspect of the therapy.
- Clinician B was sexually assaulted slightly more than a year ago. Now—upon hearing a client's disclosure of sexual abuse—she experiences powerful feelings of fear and revulsion.
- Therapist C, who is dealing with a recent traumatic death of a loved one, finds that he is prone to feelings of extreme sadness and emptiness while treating a client whose son was killed in a fire.
- Clinician D grew up in a violent, chaotic family atmosphere, where safety and predictability were rarely in evidence; her supervisor notices that she has a strong need to control the process of therapy and tends to see certain clients as manipulative, inappropriately challenging, or engaging in therapeutic "resistance."
- As a child, Clinician E was often protected by a supportive aunt when his mother would go into angry, abusive tirades. He is now treating an older, kindly woman whom he has a difficult time seeing as psychologically disabled, despite her obvious symptomatology.

An additional form of countertransference involves therapist denial or cognitive avoidance of certain subjects or themes during the treatment process. A clinician who tends to avoid thinking about unresolved traumatic material in his or her own life may unconsciously work to prevent the client from exploring his or her own trauma-related memories and feelings. In such instances, the clinician may even become resentful of the client for restimulating his or her own avoided memories or feelings, or may reinterpret appropriate client attempts to confront the past as hysteria, self-indulgence, or attention seeking.

The primary manifestations of an unconscious desire to distance oneself from the client's distress are (1) attempts to avoid discussion of the client's trauma history and (2) a generally decreased emotional attunement to the client. In each instance, the underlying strategy is the same: reduced therapeutic contact as a way to reduce the likelihood of triggered emotional pain. When this response is especially powerful, the clinician may slow or neutralize therapy by decreasing the client's exposure to traumatic material to such a point that it is not processed. At the same time, therapist distance or lack of attunement may activate client abandonment issues, further impeding treatment.

Obviously, given the client's need for safety, stability, boundaries, positive regard, and connection, therapist countertransference can be problematic. The trauma survivor, who inherently relies on the therapist for objective data and relatively uncontaminated responses, may be triggered or misdirected by the intrusion of the clinician's trauma history.

Reducing the Negative Effects of Therapist Countertransference

As noted earlier, not all countertransference is necessarily problematic, and, in fact, all therapists experience some level of countertransference in their work. When countertransference interferes with treatment, however, steps must be taken to reduce its influence.

Generally, one of the best preventive measures against countertransference problems is regular consultation with a seasoned clinician who is familiar with trauma issues and, hopefully, the therapist (Pearlman & Courtois, 2005). Another option is to form a consultation group with one's peers. However they are structured, such meetings should allow the clinician to share the burden of his or her daily exposure to others' pain, as well as to explore ways in which his or her own issues can negatively affect therapeutic outcome. In many instances, inappropriate identification or misattribution can be prevented or remedied by the consistent availability of an objective consultant who is alert to countertransference issues in general, and the clinician's vulnerabilities in specific.

An additional intervention, for clinicians who acknowledge the impacts of trauma in their own lives, is psychotherapy. It is an ironic fact that, at least in some environments, clinicians endorse the power of psychological treatment for others yet eschew it for themselves as somehow shameful or unlikely to help. This double standard is unfortunate, since having experienced psychotherapy is usually a good thing for therapists. Therapy is not only likely to reduce the clinician's trauma-related difficulties; it can also increase the richness of his or her appreciation for human complexity, and can dramatically decrease the intrusion of his or her issues into the therapeutic process.

Suggested Reading

Bassuk, E. L., Melnick, S., & Browne, A. (1998). Responding to the needs of low-income and homeless women who are survivors of family violence. *Journal of the American Medical Women's Association, 53,* 57–64.

Courtois, C. A. (1988). *Healing the incest wound: Adult survivors in therapy.* New York: Norton.

Dalenberg, C. J. (2000). *Countertransference and the treatment of trauma.* Washington, DC: American Psychological Association.

Pearlman, L. A., & Saakvitne, K. W. (1995). *Trauma and the therapist: Countertransference and vicarious traumatization in psychotherapy with incest survivors.* New York: Norton.

Marsella, A. J., Friedman, M. J., Gerrity, E. T., & Scurfield, R. M. (Eds.). (1996). *Ethnocultural aspects of posttraumatic stress disorder: Issues, research, and clinical applications.* Washington, DC: American Psychological Association.

West, C. M. (2002). Battered, black, and blue: An overview of violence in the lives of black women. *Women and Therapy, 25,* 5–27.

5

Psychoeducation

Although much attention is paid in the treatment literature to the cognitive and emotional processing of traumatic memories, psychoeducation is also an important aspect of trauma therapy (Allen, 1991; Flack, Litz, & Keane, 1998; Friedman, 2000a; Najavits, 2002). Many survivors of interpersonal violence were victimized in the context of overwhelming emotion, narrowed or dissociated attention, and, in some cases, a relatively early stage of cognitive development; all of which may have reduced the accuracy and coherence of the survivor's understanding of these traumatic events. In addition, interpersonal violence frequently involves a more powerful figure who justifies his or her aggression by distorting objective reality—for example, by blaming victimization on the victim. These fragmented, incomplete, or inaccurate explanations of traumatic events are often carried by the survivor into adulthood, with predictable negative results.

Therapists can assist in this area by providing, when indicated, accurate information on the nature of trauma and its effects, and by working with the survivor to integrate this new information and its implications into his or her overall perspective. Although often presented relatively early in treatment (for example, Talbot et al., 1998), psychoeducational activities are helpful throughout the therapy process. For example, as the client addresses traumatic material later in treatment, he or she may gain from additional information that normalizes or provides a new perspective on traumatic memory.

Although psychoeducation is usually provided during ongoing individual treatment, it also can occur in the context of separate, clinician-led support groups, wherein a small number of people with similar trauma histories compare stories, give each other advice, and discuss interpersonal violence and its effects. An advantage of group interventions is that the survivor can learn from the similar experiences of others; a process that may be more powerful and enduring than when similar material is delivered solely by the therapist. On the other hand, by their very nature, support groups may be less efficient than face-to-face psychotherapy for the client's own processing, integration, and personal application of whatever he or she learns from such information.

Handouts

Whether it occurs in individual therapy or in a guided support group, psychoeducation sometimes includes the use of printed handouts. These materials typically present easily understood information on topics such as the prevalence and impacts of interpersonal violence, common myths about victimization, and social resources available to the survivor.

The therapist should keep at least four issues in mind when deciding what (if any) written material to make available and how it should be used:

1. *The quality of the materials.* Some handouts contain misinformation, may advocate religious or social perspectives that may indirectly blame, proselytize, or exclude, or may be written at a level that is not easily understood by the survivor.

2. *The language of the materials.* For example, a person whose primary language is Spanish may gain little from a pamphlet written in English.

3. *The cultural appropriateness of the information or depictions.* For example, materials may reflect more middle-class concerns, or visual depictions may be limited to Caucasian figures.

4. *The risk of insufficient cognitive-emotional integration.* Merely offering educational materials is not the same as providing effective psychoeducation, especially if the materials are distributed without sufficient discussion or application to the client's own history or current situation.

Most important, handouts should be considered tools in the psychoeducation process, not stand-alone sources of information. The public health literature, for example, suggests that didactic material alone may not be especially effective in changing the beliefs or behaviors of victimized individuals (Becker, Rankin, & Rickel, 1998; Briere, 2003). Instead, the clinician should ensure that the information is as personally relevant to the survivor as possible, so that whatever is contained in the handout or media is directly applicable to his or her life, and thus has greater implicit meaning.

Client-oriented brochures and information sheets can be obtained from a number of organizations, either via the Web or by requesting materials by mail. At the time of this writing, three Web sites that include especially useful consumer information are:

International Society for Traumatic Stress Studies
http://www.istss.org/resources/index.htm

Office for Victims of Crime (U.S. Department of Justice)
http://www.ojp.usdoj.gov/ovc/help/welcome.html

David Baldwin's Trauma Pages
http://www.trauma-pages.com/pg4.htm

Books

Clinicians may also refer clients to readily available books that are "survivor-friendly," such as Judith Herman's *Trauma and Recovery* (1992a). Although obviously limited to individuals with adequate reading skills, such books allow clients to "read up" on traumas similar to their own. Other books are specifically written for the survivor or interested layperson (one of the best being Jon Allen's [2005] *Coping With Trauma*) and contain advice as well as information. Some may be too emotionally activating for some survivors with unresolved posttraumatic difficulties, however—at least those individuals early in their recovery or treatment process. Other books may contain erroneous information or suggest self-help strategies that are not, in fact, helpful. For these reasons, we recommend that the clinician personally read any book before recommending it to a client; not only to make sure that it is appropriate to the client's needs and is factually accurate, but to gauge its potential to activate significant posttraumatic distress in those unprepared for such emotional exposure.

Verbal Information During Therapy

Although written psychoeducational materials can be helpful, more typically information is provided verbally by the clinician during the ongoing process of psychotherapy. Because the educational process is directly imbedded in the therapeutic context, it is often more directly relevant to the client's experience, and thus more easily integrated into his or her ongoing understanding. (Briere, 2003) Additionally, psychoeducation provided in this manner allows the therapist to more easily monitor the client's responses to the material and to clear up any misunderstandings that might be present. As noted at the end of this chapter, however, over- or misapplication of psychoeducation during treatment can also impede therapy progress; as with many aspects of good therapy, the issue is often the correct balance of content versus process and sufficient attunement to the client's clinical response.

General Focus

Whether through written or verbal means, clinicians in the trauma field often focus on several major topics during psychoeducation. These include:

- *The prevalence of the trauma.* Data on the prevalence of interpersonal violence tends to contradict the common belief that the client was specifically selected by the perpetrator by virtue of weakness, badness, or unconscious provocation, or that the client is virtually alone in having experienced the trauma. For example, knowing that approximately 1 in 5 women in the general population have been raped at some point in their lives, or that 20 percent of men have been sexually abused as children, may be a meaningful antidote to the survivor's fear that he or she alone has experienced such events and that something specific to him or her caused the event to occur.
- *Common myths associated with the trauma.* As noted at various points in this book, interpersonal violence often occurs within a broader social context that, to some extent, blames victims for their experiences and/or supports perpetrators for their behaviors. For example, rape victims are often believed to have been seductive or otherwise to have "asked for" their victimization (Burt, 1980); domestic violence may be justified as appropriate and rightful dominance of wives by husbands (Walker, 1984); and it may be assumed that individuals, in general, frequently lie about having been abused or assaulted in the service of manipulation or retribution. When the client subscribes to these myths, he or she is more likely to, in fact, blame himself or herself for the victimization or explain away the trauma as something not worthy of treatment (Resick & Schnicke, 1993). For this reason, it can be helpful to discuss "rape myths" or "common myths about wife battering" in a way that makes it clear that such beliefs are not accurate.
- *The usual reasons why perpetrators engage in interpersonal violence.* This may include describing the often compulsive, multivictim nature of many perpetrator behaviors, and the psychology driving the perpetrator's actions—including the offender's frequent need for power and dominance in the face of insecurity and feelings of inadequacy. Such information can reduce the client's self-focused

explanations for the assault and increase his or her awareness of the perpetrator's dysfunctional or malignant characteristics. This shift in attribution may make self-blame appear less logical to the survivor. In addition, knowledge that the client was "one of many" for the perpetrator may further decrease his or her tendency to take personal responsibility for what was done to him or her.

- *Typical immediate responses to trauma.* Among other victim reactions to adverse events, this may include peritraumatic dissociation (for example, "spacing out," out of body experiences, or experiencing time distortion at the time of the trauma), occasional sexual responses associated with sexual traumas (as opposed to, in many cases, positive psychological feelings), relief at not being injured or killed when others have been, and "Stockholm effects," wherein the victim becomes attached or somehow bonded with the perpetrator. Because these are all relatively normal responses to trauma, despite their apparent negative qualities, the client may eventually experience relief, as well as decreased guilt and self-blame, upon receiving and integrating such information.

- *The lasting posttraumatic responses to victimization.* Information on the commonness and logical nature of posttraumatic stress symptoms (for example, flashbacks, numbing, or hyperarousal responses) and other trauma-related responses (for example, substance abuse, panic attacks, or intimacy fears)—as described in Chapter 2—are an important part of most good trauma therapy. As the client comes to understand that posttraumatic symptoms are normal (in the sense that such symptoms are logical and relatively common) responses to abnormal or toxic circumstances, he or she is less likely to experience himself or herself as damaged or mentally ill and may feel less out of control. Similarly, it is almost always preferable to view oneself as suffering from a well-understood cluster of typical responses to traumatic events (for example, posttraumatic stress disorder [PTSD]) than it is to see oneself as besieged by a variety of bizarre, unrelated symptoms. In addition, psychoeducation may prepare the client for symptoms that arise in the future. By describing symptoms before they occur, the clinician can provide a sense of predictability. This, in itself, may significantly reduce posttrauma anxiety. And successfully predicting potential symptoms enhances the overall credibility of the therapist especially in terms of his or her nonpathologizing analysis of what symptoms mean and do not mean.

- *Reframing symptoms as trauma processing.* Psychoeducation can involve reframing certain posttraumatic symptoms more positively, even as evidence that recovery is occurring. This is a somewhat more active process than the normalization of symptoms described earlier. Not all symptoms can be reframed, of course, nor should they be. Depression, panic attacks, suicidality, or psychosis, for example, are generally what they appear to be: evidence of psychological disturbance of some form or another. On the other hand, as described in Chapter 8, posttraumatic reliving symptoms are often signs of attempted psychological processing (even when unsuccessful), and posttraumatic avoidance is frequently an adaptive attempt to reduce the overwhelming aspects of reactivated distress. By reframing posttraumatic symptoms as potentially adaptive, the clinician may counter some of the helplessness, perceived loss of control, and stigmatization that often accompanies flashbacks, activated trauma memories, or psychological numbing. In fact, clients who accept the reframing of flashbacks as trauma processing may even come to welcome some reexperiencing responses as evidence of movement toward recovery.

- *Safety plans.* Women who are at risk for ongoing domestic violence may need to learn about "safety plans" that other women have used successfully in similar circumstances. Typically, this involves developing a detailed strategy for exiting the home (for example, prepacked suitcases, escape routes) and finding a new, safer, environment, whether it be a friend's home or a local women's shelter (Jordan, Nietzel, Walker, & Logan, 2004). Other clients may benefit from concrete information on how to access medical or social services, a child protection worker, or police assistance (Briere & Jordan, 2004). The goal of such interventions is to increase the power of victims to ensure their own safety, and thus to decrease not only the likelihood of continued victimization, but also some of the helplessness often associated with exposure to chronic interpersonal violence.

Constraints

Despite its generally salutatory effect, psychoeducation can backfire if not carefully adapted for the individual client, or if the conclusions that the client draws from the information are not monitored. For example, while information on the commonness of interpersonal violence may reduce the client's sense of being the only one who has been victimized, it may also reinforce the client's overestimation of the amount of danger in the interpersonal environment, leading to increased fear and avoidance of others. Similarly, too much focus on perpetrator dynamics may reinforce the client's need to excuse his or her perpetrator, and information on standard posttraumatic reactions may inadvertently cause the client to feel disordered or dysfunctional or to take on a trauma "sick-role."

Ultimately, psychoeducation should not occur in a vacuum. Information is often helpful, and may be antidotal to distorted beliefs and maladaptive responses, but it must occur in the context of ongoing therapeutic discussion and evaluation (Najavits, 2002). Specifically, the clinician should attend carefully to how clients integrate new information into their worldviews and how they apply such information in their daily lives. Simply teaching (let alone lecturing) clients about what to do or not do, or suggesting how they should think about trauma and its effects, is rarely helpful in and of itself (Neuner, Schauer, Klaschik, Karunakara, & Ebert, 2004). Instead, psychoeducation is most useful when it is integrated into the ongoing therapeutic process.

Suggested Reading

Allen, J. G. (2005). *Coping with trauma: Hope through understanding.* Washington, DC: American Psychiatric Press.

Briere, J. (2003). Integrating HIV/AIDS prevention activities into psychotherapy for child sexual abuse survivors. In L. Koenig, A. O'Leary, L. Doll, & W. Pequenat (Eds), *From child sexual abuse to adult sexual risk: Trauma, revictimization, and intervention* (pp. 219–232). Washington, DC: American Psychological Association.

Herman, J. L. (1992). *Trauma and recovery: The aftermath of violence—from domestic abuse to political terror.* New York: Basic Books.

Najavits, L. M. (2002). *Seeking safety: A treatment manual for PTSD and substance abuse.* New York: Guilford.

Resick, P. A., & Schnicke, M. K. (1993). *Cognitive processing therapy for rape victims: A treatment manual.* Newbury Park: Sage.

6

Distress Reduction and Affect Regulation Training

A s described in Chapter 2, treatment-seeking trauma survivors often experience chronic levels of anxiety and posttraumatic arousal. Many also describe extremely negative emotional responses to trauma-related stimuli and memories—feeling states that are easily triggered and hard to accommodate internally. When faced with overwhelming arousal, dysphoria, and/or emotionally laden memories, the survivor is often forced to rely on emotional avoidance strategies such as dissociation, substance abuse, or external tension reduction activities. Unfortunately, as described in Chapter 8, excessive avoidance often inhibits psychological recovery from the effects of traumatic events. In the worst case, the need to avoid additional posttraumatic distress may lead the hyperaroused or emotionally dysregulated client to avoid threatening or destabilizing material during therapy, or to drop out of treatment altogether. As well, emotional states that are aversive enough to overwhelm available affect regulation resources may negatively affect the client's perception of the treatment process and the psychotherapist.

This chapter describes two sets of interventions: those intended to reduce acute, destabilizing emotions and symptoms that emerge during the treatment process, and those focused on the client's more general capacity to regulate negative emotional states. This material is presented early in the treatment part of the book because, in some cases, high anxiety and/or low affect regulation capacity must be addressed before more classic trauma therapy (for example, emotional processing) can be fully accomplished (Chu, 1998; Cloitre, Koenen, Cohen, & Han, 2002; Courtois, 1988; Ford, Courtois, Steele, van der Hart, & Nijenhuis 2005). The interventions outlined here can be used at any point during therapy, however. For example, although the relaxation techniques described in this chapter may be initiated early in treatment, these and other approaches to affect regulation may be relevant whenever the survivor experiences escalating or intrusive negative internal states. In addition, the intrinsic development of affect regulation skills described at the end of this chapter usually occurs in the context of repeated exposure to—and processing of—trauma-related emotions, a phenomenon that progressively unfolds as treatment continues.

The techniques presented here are variously described in the trauma and anxiety literature as forms of "grounding," relaxation training, cognitive therapy, stress inoculation, and anxiety management. However labeled, these approaches all focus on the client's increased capacity to tolerate and down-regulate painful emotional states, both during treatment and in his or her ongoing life.

Dealing With Acute Intrusion: Grounding

Although much of this chapter is devoted to increasing trauma survivors' affect regulation skills, there are occasions when the clinician may have to intervene more directly in a client's emotional dysregulation. For example, in response to some triggering stimulus or memory, the client may experience sudden panic, flashbacks, intrusive negative thoughts, dissociative states, or even transient psychotic symptoms during therapy. These internal processes can be frightening—if not destabilizing—to the client, and can diminish the client's moment-to-moment psychological contact with the therapist. At such times, it may be necessary to refocus the survivor's attention onto the immediate therapeutic environment (with its implicit safety and predictability) and the therapist-client connection.

This intervention, often referred to as "grounding," can be quite helpful in acute situations. It is also, by its very nature, potentially disruptive. Grounding techniques tend to alter the immediate narrative/relational stream of psychotherapy, and run the risk of implying that something is going awry, such that a sudden, "emergency" procedure is required. For this reason, grounding should only be used when clearly indicated, should be adjusted to the minimal level necessary to reduce the client's internal escalation, and should be framed in such a way that it does not stigmatize the client or over-dramatize the experience. In some cases, other therapeutic interventions may be just as effective, such as gently moving the client's narrative into more cognitive or less emotionally intense aspects of whatever is under discussion (see Chapter 8), or by engaging in some other intervention that does not involve an obvious change in focus.

If, despite these concerns, grounding is indicated (that is, the client is acutely overwhelmed by intrusive symptoms or escalating trauma memories, and psychological contact with the therapist is diminishing), we suggest the following general steps.

1. *Attempt to focus the client's attention onto the therapist and therapy,* as opposed to whatever internal processes are occurring. This may involve shifting one's chair slightly closer to the client, carefully moving into the client's visual field, or slightly changing one's voice so that it compels attention. This does not mean, of course, that the therapist yells at the client or behaves in an unduly intrusive manner. In addition, it may not mean that the therapist touches the client, since physical contact can intensify the client's fear or sense of invasion. In other cases, however, gentle physical touch is an effective attention-focusing device. Whether to touch or not is contingent on the specifics of the situation, including, for example, the nature of the trauma, and whether the therapist is well known to the client and trusted by him or her. In general, however, we recommend verbal, as opposed to physical, therapist interventions in this regard.

2. *Ask the client to* briefly *describe his or her internal experience.* For example, "Susan, is something going on/upsetting you/happening right now?" If the client is clearly frightened or responding to distressing internal stimuli, but can't or won't describe them, go to Step 3. If the client is able to talk about the internal experience, however, it is often helpful for him or her to generally label or broadly describe it. This does not mean the survivor should necessarily go into great detail—detailed description of the flashback or dissociative state may increase its intensity, thereby reinforcing the response rather than lessening it.

3. *Orient the client to the immediate, external environment.* This often involves two, related messages: (a) that the client is safe and is not, in fact, in danger, and (b) that he or she is *here* (that is, in the room, in the session, with the therapist) and *now* (that is, not in the past, reexperiencing the trauma). In some cases, the client can be oriented by reassuring statements, typically using the client's name as an additional orienting device (for example, "Susan, you're okay. You're here in the room with me. You're safe"). In others, grounding may involve asking the client to describe the room or other aspects of the immediate environment (for example, "Susan, let's try to bring you back to the room, okay? Where are we?/What time is it?/Can you describe the room?"). The client might be asked to focus his or her attention on the feeling of the chair or couch underneath him or her, or of his or her feet on the floor. However accomplished, the client's reorientation to the here and now may occur relatively quickly (for example, in a few seconds) or may take substantially longer (for example, a number of minutes).

4. *If indicated, focus on breathing or other methods of relaxation.* This is an example of when breath or relaxation training (as described later in this chapter) can be especially helpful. Take the client through the relaxation or breathing exercise for as long as is necessary (typically for several minutes or longer), reminding the client of his or her safety and presence in the here-and-now.

5. Repeat Step 2, and assess the client's ability and willingness to return to the therapeutic process. Repeat Steps 3 and 4 as needed.

If it is possible for therapy to return to its earlier focus, normalize the traumatic intrusion (for example, as a not-unexpected part of trauma processing) and the grounding activity (for example, as a simple procedure for focusing attention away from intrusive events), and continue trauma treatment. It is important that the client's temporary reexperiencing or symptom exacerbation be neither stigmatized nor given greater meaning than appropriate. The overall message should be that trauma processing sometimes involves the intrusion of (and distraction by) potentially upsetting memories, thoughts, and/or feelings, but that such events are part of the healing process, as opposed to evidence of psychopathology (see Chapter 4).

Intervening in Chronic Affect Dysregulation

In contrast to grounding, which addresses relatively acute emotional intrusions or activations, this section describes psychological interventions in the sustained hyperarousal and anxiety experienced by many survivors of major, chronic trauma.

A Note on Medication

When dysphoria or posttraumatic arousal is of sufficient intensity that it interferes with treatment and recovery, psychoactive medications may be indicated. As described in Chapter 11, pharmacologic agents that target anxiety and/or hyperarousal can be helpful in reducing such symptoms during trauma-focused psychotherapy. As also noted, however, such medications are not a cure-all for dysregulated emotional states; their efficacy is variable from case to case and may be counterindicated in some instances because of significant side effects. Often, the best approach to high pretreatment arousal and anxiety is to use psychiatric medication, if appropriate, but also to apply psychological interventions that reduce anxiety and increase affect regulation skills, as described in this chapter.

Relaxation and Breath Control

One of the most basic forms of arousal reduction during therapy is learned relaxation. Strategically induced relaxation can facilitate the processing of traumatic material during the therapy session by reducing the client's overall level of anxiety. Reduced anxiety during trauma processing both lessens the likelihood the client will feel overwhelmed by trauma-related distress, and probably serves to countercondition traumatic material, as described in Chapter 8. In addition, relaxation can be used by the survivor outside of treatment as a way to reduce the effects of triggered traumatic memories. For individuals with especially easily activated anxiety or intrusive reexperiencing, the benefits of calling upon an internal relaxation mechanism cannot be overstated.

There are two general approaches to relaxation training, *breath training* and *progressive relaxation,* both of which are described only briefly here. For more detailed information, the reader should consult the Suggested Reading at the end of this chapter.

Progressive Relaxation

This technique involves clenching and then releasing muscles, sequentially from head to toe, until the entire body reaches a relaxed state (Jacobson, 1938; Rimm & Masters, 1979). As clients practice progressive relaxation on a regular basis, most are eventually able to enter a relaxed state relatively quickly, if not automatically. Some practitioners begin each session with relaxation exercises; others teach it initially in treatment, then utilize it only when specifically indicated, for example, when discussion of traumatic material results in a high state of anxiety. Two points should be made about the use of relaxation training in the treatment of posttraumatic stress: (1) use of this technique alone (that is, in the absence of coexisting trauma-processing activities) is unlikely to significantly reduce trauma-related symptoms, per se (Rothbaum, Meadows, Resick, & Foy, 2000), and (2) clinical experience suggests that a minority of traumatized individuals may have unexpected anxious or dissociative reactions to induced relaxation (for example, Allen, 2001; Fitzgerald & Gonzalez, 1994) or may not be able to successfully self-induce a relaxed state. Those who are chronically flooded with flashbacks and other reexperiencing symptoms may be less likely to gain from relaxation training (Taylor, 2003). In our experience, progressive relaxation can be quite helpful, when indicated, but the client should be monitored for possible, seemingly paradoxical, increases in arousal during this procedure.

Breath Training

Although progressive relaxation is successfully used by some clinicians, our preference—all other things being equal—is to teach breathing techniques. When stressed, many individuals breath in a more shallow manner, hyperventilate, or, in some cases, temporarily stop breathing altogether. Teaching the client "how to breathe" during stress can help restore more normal respiration, and thus adequate oxygenation of the brain. Equally important, as the client learns to breathe in ways that are more efficient and more aligned with normal, nonstressed inhalation and exhalation, there is usually a calming effect on the body and the autonomic nervous system.

Breath training generally involves guided breathing exercises that teach the client to be more aware of his or her breathing—especially the ways in which it is inadvertently constrained by tension and adaptation to trauma—and to adjust his or her musculature, posture, and thinking so that more effective and calming respiration can occur (Best & Ribbe, 1995). There are a number of manuals that include information on breath training during trauma treatment (for example, Foa & Rothbaum, 1998; Rimm & Masters, 1979). Presented in Appendix 3 is a version of the protocol used in the trauma program at Los Angeles County + University of Southern California Medical Center.

Learned relaxation—however initiated—can be employed by the client to down-regulate stress responses as they occur. In many cases, relaxation can be cued by repetitively associating it with a calming word during relaxation training, so that later use of the word releases a conditioned relaxation response (Best & Ribbe, 1995). For example, the emotionally activated trauma survivor might say the word *relax* to himself or herself during progressive relaxation activities. Similarly, as presented in Appendix 3, counting during inhalation and exhalation can both focus awareness and produce a cue (counting) that eventually can come to trigger a relaxation response.

Once the client is able to induce relaxation, the therapist can call on this skill during the processing of traumatic memories. As described in Chapter 8, for example, the therapist may either ask the client to induce relaxation prior to memory exposure activities or may suggest relaxation when the client specifically appears to need it, for example when trauma-related anxiety or distress emerges during the session. In many instances, the client may only have to focus on breathing, or relaxing muscle groups for a short while (for example, less than a minute), using the cue word (or counting breaths), before relaxation is sufficient to allow further trauma processing. In some cases, of course, it may take longer.

It should be reiterated that although relaxation training is often a helpful component of trauma therapy, it is not always necessary or indicated. Some clients are neither so hyperaroused nor so anxious that they require special intervention in this area. Other clients (and therapists) find relaxation training too mechanistic, or a distraction from the relational process of psychotherapy. Like some other techniques presented in this book, relaxation training is an option, not a requirement, for trauma treatment.

Increasing General Affect Regulation Capacity

Above and beyond immediate methods of distress reduction, such as grounding and relaxation, there are a number of suggestions in the literature for increasing the general affect regulation abilities of trauma clients. All are focused on increasing the survivor's overall capacity to tolerate and down-regulate negative feeling states, thereby reducing the likelihood that he or she will be overwhelmed by activated emotionality. In some cases, such affect regulation "training" may be necessary before any significant memory processing can be accomplished (Cloitre et al., 2002).

Identifying and Discriminating Emotions

One of the most important components of successful affect regulation is the ability to correctly perceive and label emotions as they are experienced (Linehan, 1993a). Many survivors of early, chronic trauma have trouble knowing exactly what they feel when activated into an emotional state, beyond, perhaps, a sense of feeling "bad" or "upset" (Briere, 1996; Luterek, Orsillo, & Marx, 2005). In a similar vein, some individuals may not be able to accurately differentiate feelings of anger, for example, from anxiety or sadness. Although this sometimes reflects dissociative disconnection from emotion, in other cases it represents a basic inability to "know about" one's emotions. As a result, the survivor may perceive his or her internal state as consisting of chaotic, intense, but undifferentiated emotionality that is not logical or predictable. For example, the survivor triggered into a seemingly undifferentiated negative emotional state will not be able to say, "I am anxious," let alone infer that "I am anxious because I feel threatened." Instead, the experience may be of overwhelming and unexplainable negative emotion that comes "out of the blue."

The clinician can assist the client in this area by regularly facilitating exploration and discussion of the client's emotional experience. Often, the client will become more able to identify feelings just by being asked about them on an ongoing basis. On other occasions, the therapist can encourage the client to "emotional detective work," involving attempts to hypothesize an emotional state based on the events surrounding it (for example, the client guessing that a feeling is anxiety because it follows a frightening stimulus, or anger because it is associated with resentful cognitions or angry behaviors). Affect identification and discrimination also may be fostered by the therapist's direct feedback, such as "It looks like you're feeling angry. Are you?" or "You look scared." This last option should be approached with care, however. There is a certain risk of labeling a client's affect as feeling A when, in fact, the client is experiencing feeling B—thereby fostering confusion rather than effective emotional identification. For this reason, we recommend that, in all but the most obvious instances, the therapist facilitate the client's exploration and hypothesis testing of his or her feeling state, rather than telling the client what he or she is feeling. The critical issue here is not, in most cases, whether the client (or therapist) correctly identifies a particular emotional state, but rather that the client explores and attempts to label his or her feelings on a regular basis. In our experience, the more this is done as a general part of therapy, the better the survivor eventually becomes at accurate feeling identification and discrimination.

Identifying and Countering Thoughts That Antecede Intrusive Experiences

It is not only feelings that should be identified—in many cases, it is also thoughts. This is most relevant when a given cognition triggers a strong emotional reaction, but the thought is somehow unknown to the survivor. As suggested by some clinicians (for example, Cloitre et al., 2002; Linehan, 1993a), affect regulation capacities often can be improved by encouraging the client to identify and counter the cognitions that exacerbate or trigger trauma-related emotions. Beyond the more general cognitive interventions described in Chapter 7, this involves the client monitoring whatever thoughts mediate between a triggered traumatic memory and a subsequent negative emotional reaction. For example, upon having child abuse memories triggered by an authority figure, the survivor may have the unconscious or partially suppressed thought, "He is going to hurt me," and may then react with extreme anxiety or distress. Or, the survivor of sexual abuse might think, "She wants to have sex with me," when interacting with an older woman, and then may experience revulsion, rage, or terror. In such cases, although the memory itself is likely to produce negative emotionality (conditioned emotional responses, or CERs; see Chapter 8), the associated cognitions often exacerbate these responses to produce more extreme emotional states. In other instances, thoughts may be less directly trauma related, yet still increase the intensity of the client's emotional response. For example, in a stressful situation the client may have thoughts such as "I'm out of control," or "I'm making a fool of myself" that produce panic or fears of being overwhelmed or inundated.

Unfortunately, because triggered thoughts may be out of superficial aware-ness, their role in subsequent emotionality may not be observed by the survivor (Beck, 1995). As the client is made more aware of the cognitive antecedents to overwhelming emotionality, he or she can learn to lessen the impact of such thoughts. In many cases, this is done by explicitly disagreeing with the cogni-tion (for example, "Nobody's out to get me," or "I can handle this"), or merely by labeling such cognitions as "old tapes" rather than accurate perceptions (Briere, 1996). In this regard, one of the benefits of what is referred to as *insight* in psychodynamic therapy is often the self-developed realization that one is act-ing in a certain way by virtue of erroneous, "old" (for example, trauma- or abuse-related) beliefs or perceptions—an understanding that often reduces the power of those cognitions to produce distress or motivate dysfunctional behav-ior (see Chapter 7).

When the thoughts that underlie extremely powerful and overwhelming emotional states are triggered by trauma-related memories, the therapist can focus on these intermediate responses by asking questions such as "What happened just before you got scared/angry/upset?" or "Did you have a thought or memory?" If the client reports that, for example, a given strong emotion was triggered by a trauma memory, the therapist may ask him or her to describe the memory (if that is tolerable), and to discuss what thoughts the memory triggered. Ultimately, this may involve exploration and discussion of four separate phenomena:

1. The environmental stimulus that triggered the memory (for example, one's lover's angry expression)

2. The memory itself (for example, of maltreatment by an angry parent)

3. The current thought associated with the memory (for example, "He/She hates me," "I must have done something wrong," or "He/She is blaming me for something I didn't do")

4. The current feeling (for example, anger or fear)

These triggered, often "catastrophizing" cognitions (that is, expectations of extremely negative outcomes) can then be discussed as to their relevance to the current situation. In such instances, the client is generally asked to explore the accuracy of such thoughts, their possible etiology (often involving child-hood abuse, neglect, or other maltreatment), and what he or she could do to counter such thoughts (for example, remind himself or herself that the thought is not accurate or that it is "just my childhood talking"). As the client becomes better able to identify these cognitions, place them in some realistic context, and counter them with other, more positive thoughts, he or she often develops greater capacity to forestall extreme emotional reactivity, and thereby better regulate the emotional experience.

Trigger Awareness and Intervention

There is another cognitive intervention that can help the survivor maintain internal equilibrium in his or her daily life: the clinician can help the survivor to learn to identify and address triggers in the environment that activate unwanted posttraumatic reliving, such as flashbacks or intrusive negative feeling states. Although, as noted in Chapter 2, activated memories of trauma are not intrinsically negative phenomena, they can be disruptive and induce feelings of helplessness when they intrude without warning, especially in contexts where attention or adaptive functioning is required. Successful trigger identification may facilitate a greater sense of control and better interpersonal functioning by allowing the client to alter those situations in which these triggers might occur. Although avoiding all interpersonal conflict in one's life as a way to reduced triggered flashbacks is likely be maladaptive, it is often helpful to identify such triggers at work, in close relationships, or other contexts where reexperiencing may lead to unwanted behaviors or interfere with ongoing functioning.

Trigger identification can be taught as a series of tasks:

1. *Identify a given thought, feeling, or intrusive sensation as posttraumatic.* This is relatively easy in some cases. For example, it may not be difficult to recognize an intrusive sensory flashback of a gunshot as posttraumatic. In others, however, the reexperiencing may be more subtle, such as feelings of anger or fear, or intrusive feelings of helplessness that emerge during relational interaction. Typical questions the client can learn to ask himself or herself include:
   - Does this thought/feeling/sensation "make sense" in terms of what is happening around me right now?
   - Are these thoughts or feelings too intense, based on the current context?
   - Does this thought or feeling carry with it memories of a past trauma?
   - Am I experiencing any unexpected alteration in awareness (for example, depersonalization or derealization) as these thoughts/feelings/sensations occur?
   - Is this a situation where I usually get triggered?

2. *Evaluate the stimuli present in the triggering environment, and identify which are trauma reminiscent* (that is, "find the trigger"). This typically involves a certain level of detective work, as the client learns to objectively evaluate the environment to see what might be trauma reminiscent, and thus potentially a trigger. Examples of triggers the client might learn to recognize, depending on his or her trauma history, include:
   - Interpersonal conflict
   - Sexual situations or stimuli
   - Interactions with an authority figure

- People with physical or psychological characteristics that are in some way similar to the client's past perpetrator(s)
- Boundary violations
- Sirens, helicopters, gunshots
- The sound of crying

In some cases, the trigger will be obvious, and easily recognized. In others, the client may have to work hard to identify what may be triggering him or her.

3. *Construct an adaptive strategy.* This usually involves some version of "improving the moment" (Linehan, 1993a, p. 148), whereby the survivor reduces the likelihood of an extreme emotional response. Examples include:
   - Intentional avoidance or "time outs" during especially stressful moments (for example, leaving a party when others become intoxicated; intentionally minimizing arguments with authority figures; learning how to discourage unwanted flirtatious behavior from others)
   - Analyzing the triggering stimulus or situation until a greater understanding changes one's perception and thus terminates the trigger (for example, carefully examining the behavior of an individual who is triggering posttraumatic fear, and eventually becoming more aware of the fact that he or she is not acting in a threatening manner; or coming to understand that a given individual's seemingly dismissive style does not indicate a desire to reject or ignore as much as it does interpersonal awkwardness)
   - Increasing support systems (for example, bringing a friend to a party where one might feel threatened, or calling a friend to "debrief" an upsetting situation)
   - Positive self-talk (for example, working out beforehand what to say to oneself when triggered, such as "I am safe," "I don't have to do anything I don't want to do," or "This is just my past talking, this isn't really what I think it is")
   - Relaxation induction or breath control, as described earlier in this chapter
   - Strategic distraction, such as starting a conversation with a safe person, reading a book, or going for a walk, as a way to pull attention away from escalating internal responses such as panic, flashbacks, or catastrophizing cognitions

Counseling Resistance to Tension Reduction Behavior

Another way in which affect regulation skills can be learned is by intentionally forestalling tension reduction behaviors (TRBs). In general, this involves encouraging the client to "hold off," as long as possible, on behaviors that he or she normally would use to down-regulate distress (for example, self-mutilation, impulsive sexual behavior, or binging/purging), and then, if the behavior must be engaged in, doing so to the minimal extent possible. Although preventing TRBs entirely would obviously be the best course, in reality the clinician's ability to stop such behavior may be limited, short of hospitalizing the client. It is an unavoidable fact of clinical life that tension reduction and other avoidance behaviors are survival based and are therefore not easily given up by the survivor.

In general, we recommend that the therapist take a clear stand on the harmfulness of certain behaviors, and work with the client to terminate or at least decrease their frequency, intensity, and injuriousness. It is important that the therapist not appear to judge the client regarding TRBs: Value judgments about the wrongness or immorality of a given behavior—other than activities that harm others—are rarely helpful. Such statements not only increase guilt and shame, they often "drive the therapy underground" by forcing the client to keep things (in this case, continued tension reduction) from the therapist.

Because TRBs serve to reduce distress, client attempts to delay their use provide opportunities to develop affect tolerance. For example, if a survivor is able to promise to *try* to not binge eat or act on a sexual compulsion, if only for a few minutes beyond when he or she would otherwise engage in such activity, two things may happen:

1. The client may be exposed to a brief period of sustained (but temporarily manageable) distress, during which time he or she can learn a small amount of distress tolerance.

2. The impulse to engage in the TRB may fade, because the emotionality associated with the urge to TRB often lessens if not immediately acted upon.

With continued practice, the period between the initial urge to tension reduce and the actual TRB may be lengthened, the TRB itself may be decreased in severity, and affect tolerance may be increased. An added benefit of this approach is that the goal of decreasing (and then ending) TRBs is seen as not stopping "bad" behavior, but rather as a way for the client to learn affect regulation and get his or her behavior under greater personal control.

Affect Regulation Learning During Trauma Processing

Finally, it appears that affect regulation and tolerance can be learned implicitly during longer-term exposure-based trauma therapy. Because, as discussed in later chapters, trauma-focused interventions involve the repeated activation, processing, and resolution of distressing but non-overwhelming distress, such treatment slowly teaches the survivor to become more "at home" with some level of painful emotional experience and to develop whatever skills are necessary to deescalate moderate levels of emotional arousal. As the client repetitively experiences titrated (that is, not overwhelming or destabilizing) levels of distress during exposure to trauma memories, he or she may slowly develop the ability to self-soothe, reframe upsetting thoughts, and call upon relational support. In addition, by working with the client to deescalate distress associated with activated CERs, the therapist often models affect regulation strategies, especially those involving normalization, soothing, and validation. However developed, this growing ability to move in and out of strong affective states, in turn, fosters an increased sense of emotional control and reduced fear of negative affect.

Suggested Reading

Cloitre, M., Koenen, K. C., Cohen, L. R., & Han, H. (2002). Skills training in affective and interpersonal regulation followed by exposure: A phase-based treatment for PTSD related to childhood abuse. *Journal of Consulting and Clinical Psychology, 70,* 1067–1074.

Jacobson, E. (1938). *Progressive relaxation.* Chicago: University of Chicago Press.

Linehan, M. M. (1993). *Cognitive-behavioral treatment of borderline personality disorder.* New York: Guilford.

Schore, A. N. (2003). *Affect regulation and the repair of the self.* New York: Norton.

7

Cognitive Interventions

As noted in Chapter 2, trauma survivors—especially victims of interpersonal violence—are prone to self-blame, guilt, shame, low self-esteem, overestimation of danger, and other negative beliefs and perceptions. The rape victim may believe she somehow "asked for it" or otherwise caused herself to be assaulted, and the battered woman may assume that she deserved to be beaten. Individuals who have been repeatedly exposed to situations in which they were helpless to escape or otherwise reduce their trauma exposure often develop a sense of having little power to affect future potentially negative events. Some survivors view their posttraumatic symptoms as evidence of being defective or "crazy." Victims of sexual trauma often feel ashamed and isolated by their experiences.

In general, cognitive therapy of posttraumatic disturbance involves the guided reconsideration of negative perceptions and beliefs about self, others, and the environment that arose from the trauma. As these negative assumptions are reevaluated, a more affirming and empowering model of self and others frequently takes its place. At the same time, the client may develop a more detailed and coherent understanding of the traumatic event, a process that is associated with clinical improvement (Foa, Molnar, & Cashman, 1995).

Cognitive Processing

In most cases, trauma-related cognitive disturbance is addressed through detailed verbal exploration of the traumatic event and its surrounding circumstances. As the client repeatedly describes the trauma in the context of treatment, he or she, in a sense, relives the past while viewing it from the perspective of the present. By verbally recounting the traumatic event, the client (often with the assistance of the therapist) has the opportunity to "hear" the assumptions, beliefs, and perceptions that were encoded at the time of the trauma, understand the reasons they arose, and compare them with what he or she now knows. Together, the client and therapist can then work to create a more accurate cognitive model of what occurred.

This interactive process frequently fosters more positive self-perceptions as the client comes to reinterpret former "bad" behaviors, deservingness of maltreatment, and presumed inadequacies in a more accurate light. For example, the client who has always interpreted her behavior just prior to a rape as "sluttish" or "asking for it" may gain from the opportunity to relive and review what actually happened and to see if her judgments about herself seem valid. Exploration of the events prior to the rape may reveal that she was not behaving in a "seductive" manner, nor is she likely to recall wanting to be abused or otherwise hurt. It is important to acknowledge that such exploration typically does not suggest that this early perception was "irrational," but rather that it logically arose from the context of the trauma.

A growing awareness of what one could reasonably have done at the time of the trauma—that is, what one's options actually were—can be antidotal to inappropriate feelings of responsibility, self-blame, or self-criticism. For example, describing memories of childhood abuse—while at the same time listening to them from the perspective of an adult—may lead to the realization that one had few options other than subservience or accommodation at the time of the abuse. The notion that "I should have done something to stop it," for example, might be countered by a greater experiential understanding of the size and power differentials inherent in an adult forcing his or her will (and body) on a 7-year-old child.

Finally, blaming or shaming statements made by an assailant may gradually lose their power when examined in the context of a safe environment. Many victims of interpersonal violence tend to internalize or otherwise accept rationalizations used by the perpetrator at the time of the assault (Salter, 1995). These include batterer statements that the victim deserved violence for failing to be a good spouse, rapist statements that the victim was asking to be sexually assaulted, and child abuser statements that physical abuse was merely appropriate punishment for bad behavior. For example, a refugee may have partially accepted statements made by his torturers that he was responsible for his family's death by virtue of being a "traitor," when, in fact, (1) he did nothing to justify such horrible events, and (2) the deaths were committed by the government, not by him. The childhood trauma survivor may internalize more general perpetrator comments that he or she is bad, fat, ugly, or worthless. As the client and therapist discuss the circumstances of the event and consider perpetrator statements in the absence of danger or coercion, the objective lack of support for these statements may become more apparent to the client.

Because he or she is often more able to see these cognitive distortions than is the client, the clinician may feel pressed to voice an opinion regarding the lack of culpability of the victim or the obvious cruelty of the perpetrator. This is understandable, and, in small doses, is usually appropriate. But such statements should be presented as a form of "going on the record" regarding the therapist's clear understanding that the victim was, in fact, victimized. Rarely will such statements, in and of themselves, actually change the client's opinion. In fact, clinical experience suggests that cognitive therapy is rarely helpful when the clinician merely disagrees (or argues) with the client about his or her cognitions or memories, or makes definitive statements about what reality actually is or was. Rather, cognitive interventions are most effective when they provide opportunities for the client to experience the original trauma-related thoughts and self-perceptions (for example, feelings of responsibility and guilt when recalling being beaten by a spouse), while at the same time considering a more contemporary and logical perspective (for example, that the beatings were, ultimately, about the spouse's chronic anger, alcoholism, and feelings of inadequacy, and not due to the client's failure to wash the dishes or provide sex on demand).

As suggested by Resick and Schnicke (1992), the reworking of trauma-related assumptions or perceptions is probably most effective when it occurs while the client is actively remembering the trauma and reexperiencing the thoughts and feelings he or she had at the time. In other words, merely discussing a traumatic event without some level of emotional memory activation is less likely to allow the client to change the cognitions related to the memory. In contrast, active recall and description of a traumatic event probably trigger two parallel processes: (1) observation of one's own trauma-related attributions regarding the specifics of the event, and (2) activation of the emotions associated with the event. The second component of this response is covered in detail in the next chapter. However, it is important to acknowledge it here because emotional activation allows the client to more directly relive the traumatic event, such that any cognitive interventions are more directly linked to specific memories of the trauma.

There are two major ways that the client can remember and, to some extent, reexperience traumatic events during the process of treatment: (1) by describing them in detail, and (2) by writing about them. In the first instance, the therapist encourages the client to describe the traumatic event or events in as much verbal detail as is tolerable, including feelings he or she experienced during and after the victimization experience. As noted in the next chapter, this is an important component of emotional processing. It also facilitates cognitive processing to the extent that it includes discussion of conclusions or beliefs the survivor formed from the experience. In response to the client's description, the therapist generally asks open-ended questions that are intended to make apparent any cognitive distortions that might be present regarding blame, deservingness, or responsibility. As the client responds to these questions, the therapist provides support and encouragement, and, when appropriate, offers information that counters the negative implications or self-perceptions that emerge in the client's responses. The client might then have responses that lead to further questions from the therapist. Or, the topic might shift to the client's emotional processing of the implications of any new information, insights, or feelings that arose from the discussion process.

The second major form of cognitive processing involves the use of "homework," wherein the client is asked to write about a specific topic related to the trauma, bring it to the next session, and read it aloud in the presence of the clinician. In this way, the client has the opportunity to continue therapeutic activities outside of the session, including desensitization of traumatic memories (see Chapter 8) and continued cognitive reconsideration of trauma-related assumptions and perceptions. In addition, research suggests that the mere act of writing about an upsetting event, especially if done on multiple occasions, can reduce psychological distress over time (Pennebaker & Campbell, 2000). (See pages 131–132 in Chapter 8 for an example of trauma processing homework, adapted from Resick and Schnicke, 1992.)

The goal of such activities, whether verbal or written, is to activate the client's memories of the traumatic event and to cognitively process them in subsequent discussions. The initiation and maintenance of such discussions often center on what is known as the *Socratic method:* a series of gentle, often open-ended inquiries that allow the client to progressively examine the assumptions and interpretations he or she has made about the victimization experience.

Typical questions, in this regard, include (but are not limited to):

- "Did you have any thoughts while it was happening? What were they?"
- "Given the situation, do you think there was anything else you could have done?"
- "So, that made you feel that you were to blame/responsible/bad/stupid/seductive. Can we go over what happened and see what made you think that?"
- "Did you want him/her/them to rape/beat/abuse/hurt you? Do you remember ever wanting that?"

- "You say that you were hurt/raped/beaten because you asked for it/were seductive/didn't lock the door/were out late. Can we go over the evidence for that conclusion? Maybe it's more complicated than that?"
- "If this happened to someone else, would you come to the same conclusions?"
- "It sounds like you believe what he/she said about that. Was he/she the kind of person you would believe when he/she said something?"
- "Why do you think he/she did that? Did he/she get anything out of it?"

The goal here is for the client to update his or her trauma-based understanding—not merely to incorporate the therapist's statements about the true state of reality or the client's "thinking errors." In this regard, although therapist statements about the presumed reality of things may sometimes be helpful, much of the knowledge the client acquires in therapy is best learned from him- or herself. By repeatedly comparing "old" trauma-based versions of reality with newer understandings that arise in the context of a detailed examination of past events, the client can often revise his or her personal history—not in the sense of making things up, but by updating assumptions and beliefs that were made under duress and were never revisited in detail.

This approach also can be used to examine distorted beliefs about future events, not just feelings of responsibility or self-blame. Most typically, these thoughts involve beliefs such as:

- I am broken and will never get better/be loved/get what I want.
- The environment is dangerous and I will be hurt again.
- I am helpless to avoid additional traumas.
- People/men/women/authority figures are predatory and can't be trusted.
- The future is hopeless.

Cognitive interventions for such trauma-related assumptions are much like those used to address self-blame, except that they focus more on an analysis of future outcomes. Among the general questions the therapist might ask, rephrased for better attunement, as necessary, are the following:

- "What are the chances that something like that would happen again in the future?"
- "What makes you believe that your assumption is/would be true?"
- "Can you think of any examples that wouldn't fit your belief? Could there be exceptions to the rule?" (For example, any men who probably wouldn't rape you, any places where you would be safe, any things you could do to avoid potential exposure to the trauma, at least one person you can probably trust)

- "Is there any way in which you might be underestimating your abilities when you say that?"
- "Can you think of something you might be able to do if that happened/looked like it might happen again?"

The therapist may ask such questions, which obviously will vary from client to client and session to session, as the description of the trauma unfolds or after the client's rendition is completed. We tend to favor the latter approach: encouraging the client to describe the trauma in detail, and then following up with questions. In doing so, the client is more able to more fully expose herself or himself to the story, with its attendant emotional triggers, and the therapist has a better chance of determining what the client thinks about the trauma without the rendition being affected by therapist responses.

However accomplished, the central goal of cognitive therapy in this area is to assist the client to more fully and accurately explore his or her beliefs or assumptions, and the context in which they arose, without lecturing, arguing, or labeling such beliefs as "wrong." Instead, such cognitions should be viewed (and reflected back to the client) as entirely understandable reactions to overwhelming events that involved extreme anxiety and distress, incomplete information, coercion, confusion, and, in many cases, the need for survival defenses. Trauma-related cognitions should be treated not as the product of client error or of inherent neurosis, but rather as initial perceptions and assumptions that require updating in the context of safety and support. The reader is referred to Resick and Schnicke (1992) and Chard, Weaver, and Resick (1997) for more detailed and programmatic discussions of the cognitive processing of traumatic experiences both conversational and written.

While addressing cognitive distortions about the event and what it means to the client, the clinician also may encounter distortions the client has formed regarding the meaning of symptoms he or she is experiencing. In general, these involve beliefs that the intrusive-reliving, numbing/avoidance, and hyperarousal components of traumatic stress represent loss of control or major psychopathology. In the style outlined earlier for trauma-related cognitions, the therapist can facilitate cognitive processing of these perceptions or beliefs by asking the client—especially after some level of psychoeducation has transpired—about (1) what might be a nonpathologizing explanation for the symptom (for example, the survival value of hypervigilance, or the self-medicating aspects of substance abuse), (2) whether the symptoms actually indicate psychosis or mental illness (for example, whether flashbacks are the same thing as hallucinations, or whether it is really "paranoid" to be fearful about trauma-reminiscent situations), and (3) whether it is better to actively experience posttraumatic stress (especially reexperiencing) than to "shut down" or otherwise avoid trauma memories. Each of these (and similar) questions may stimulate lively and clinically useful conversations, the goal of which is not for the clinician's view to prevail, but for the client to explore the basis for (and meaning of) his or her internal experience.

Developing a Coherent Narrative

In addition to the cognitive processing of traumatic memories, therapy can provide broader meaning and context. Clinical experience suggests that client descriptions of past traumatic events often become more detailed, organized, and causally structured as they are repeatedly discussed and explored in therapy. Research (for example, Amir, Stafford, Freshman, & Foa, 1998) indicates that such increased coherence is directly associated with a reduction in posttraumatic symptoms. Although it is likely that narrative coherence is a sign of clinical improvement, it also appears that the development of an integrated version of one's trauma has a positive effect on recovery (Pennebaker, 1993). As the client is increasingly able to describe chronologically and analytically what happened, and to place it in a larger context, he or she often experiences an increased sense of perspective, reduced feelings of chaos, and a greater sense that the universe is predictable and orderly, if not entirely benign (Meichenbaum & Fong, 1993). Further, creating meaning out of one's experiences (including conclusions about cause and effect) may provide some degree of closure, in that the experiences "make sense" and thus may not require further rumination or preoccupation. Finally, a more coherent trauma narrative, by virtue of its organization and complexity, may support more efficient and complete emotional and cognitive processing (Amir et al., 1998). In contrast, fragmented recollections of traumatic events that do not have an explicit chronological order and do not have obvious cause-effect linkages can easily lead to additional anxiety, insecurity, and confusion—phenomena that inhibit effective trauma processing.

The development of a coherent narrative usually occurs naturally during effective trauma-focused therapy. As the traumatic event (or events) is discussed repetitively and in detail, a process sometimes referred to as *context reinstatement* (Anderson & Bower, 1972) may occur. Specifically, a detailed trauma description may increase the survivor's access to more aspects of the memory that, in turn, may trigger recall of additional details. For example, a client might initially report that "he hit me on the head, and there was yelling and blood." In the moment of making this statement, the reference to blood might activate more specific memories of blood on the carpet, which, in turn, might trigger additional recollection of the location or, perhaps, the feeling of pain associated with a scalp laceration. Further discussion might then provide the context for a chronological sequence. For example:

> Okay, he was yelling at me, saying I was lazy, and then he hit me with an ash-tray, a green one, and it cut my head. I bled all over the carpet in the living room, I remember some part of me thinking I'd never get that stain out.

As the sequence and details of the event become clearer, there is more material to cognitively process, and a greater sense of stability associated with "knowing what happened." Further, as described earlier, greater detail often provides information that is antidotal to cognitive distortions. For example, a client might state:

> I was thinking about all the weird stuff he used to say to me and my friends, like, before he did it to me. I'm starting to get that I didn't do anything that caused it—he was already looking to get me.

Or, in a date rape scenario:

> I just remembered, I told him to stop, when it started to get too heavy. I tried to stop him. It's not like I wanted it to happen. The kissing, maybe. But not the other things.

Although a more coherent narrative often arises naturally from repeatedly revisiting the trauma in therapy, the clinician can work to further increase the likelihood of this happening. This generally involves gentle, nonintrusive questions regarding the details of the trauma, and support for the client's general exploration of his or her thoughts and feelings regarding the event—in the same manner described earlier for cognitive processing. In partial contrast to cognitive processing interventions, however, narrative interventions support the development of broader explanations and an overbridging "story" of the traumatic event, its antecedents, and its effects. In addition to its obviously clinical effects, an integrated version of adverse experiences may lead to a broader overall perspective on life, and, perhaps, greater personal wisdom, as described in Chapter 4.

Cognitive Changes Arising From Non-Overwhelming Emotional Activation

As emphasized by Foa and Rothbaum (1998), not all cognitive effects of trauma therapy involve verbal reconsideration or "restructuring" of traumatically altered thinking patterns—it is also possible for the survivor's beliefs to change during the process of remembering and processing upsetting memories during treatment. Summarizing a cognitive component of Foa and Kozak's (1986) emotional processing model, Rogers and Silver (2002) note that

> individuals with anxiety disorders also have erroneous beliefs about the nature of anxiety. They tend to see anxiety as something that will persist until they escape the feared situation, that anxiety is physically or psychologically damaging, and that the consequences of being anxious are very aversive. (p. 45)

In the context of processing traumatic memories in therapy, the client repetitively experiences three things: (1) anxiety that is conditioned to the trauma memory (that is, as a conditioned emotional response, or CER), (2) the expectation that such anxiety signals danger and/or is, itself, a dangerous state and must be avoided, and yet (3) an absence of actual negative outcome—he or she does not actually experience physical or psychological harm from anxiety or what it might presage. This repetitive *disparity* (a technical term that is discussed in greater detail in Chapter 8) between the expectation of anxiety as signaling danger and yet, the subsequent experience of non-danger probably changes the expectation over time (in Foa & Kozak's [1986] parlance, it modifies the attendant "fear structure"). Beyond its cognitive effects on beliefs and assumptions associated with the specific trauma memory, the repetitive experience of feeling anxious during trauma therapy—in the context of therapeutic safety—probably lessens the negative valence of anxiety, per se. In many cases, this appears to mean that the client is less anxious about anxiety; coming to see it as merely an emotion and not necessarily as a harbinger of danger, loss of control, or psychological disability. Viewed in this context, the interconnection between trauma processing and affect regulation training, as described in the previous chapter, becomes clear: increased ability to experience negative affect without the associated catastrophizing cognitions reduces the likelihood that such emotion will be overwhelming.

Cognitive Interventions and Insight

As noted earlier in this chapter, one of the major goals of cognitive interventions is to change how the client views himself or herself, his or her prior life experiences, and others in his or her interpersonal environment. Such cognitive reconsideration is often equivalent to the psychodynamic notion of *insight*. For example, when the client understands (has insight into the fact) that there really wasn't much that he or she could do in the face of one or more uncontrollable traumatic events, self-blame for having experienced or deserved the trauma—or for not having avoided it—is actively contradicted. Although, as noted, such newer cognitive understanding may not have immediate salutary effects, over time (and upon repeatedly revisiting this fact in treatment and out) the disparity between old assumptions and perceptions versus more recent, more accurate appraisals can serve to neutralize or "overwrite" distorted trauma-related cognitions.

In addition, a greater understanding of the past—and insight into the various ways in which it differs from the present—may reduce the capacity of stimuli in the current environment to trigger posttraumatic responses. For example, "realizing" (that is, through cognitive reconsideration and/or ongoing interactions with a benign therapist) that interpersonal closeness is not always dangerous may reduce the amount of distrust, fear, or anger triggered by relationships in one's adult environment. In a sense, what would otherwise be a trigger for memories of previous interpersonal violence can be changed. An understanding that one can be vulnerable around some people and not be hurt means that, on average, fewer directly reminiscent or trauma-similar stimuli are likely to be experienced during current intimate interactions. In other words, if people, as a group, are not immediately equated with one's abusive parent, batterer, or rapist, close relations with people—in general— are less likely to trigger trauma-related memories and associated distress. Similarly, the realization (experience) that one can be anxious without being annihilated may result in an increased sense of security and, in some cases, better interpersonal functioning.

There are, of course, theoretical differences in how psychodynamic and cognitive clinicians seek to change cognitive distortions. Whereas the cognitive therapist generally works to identify irrational thinking and to supplant it with more accurate perceptions and beliefs, the psychodynamic clinician is especially invested in helping the client understand the original basis for such distortions. As Goin (1997) notes, "The cognitive therapist battles the illogic with logic, while the psychodynamic therapist searches for the logic in the illogical" (p. 308). In trauma therapy (and some forms of modern cognitive-behavioral therapy), both phenomena ideally occur: the client is provided with opportunities to identify prior inaccurate thoughts about self, others, and the future (that is, through cognitive reconsideration), and is supported in finding more accurate models of reality, but also learns the logical basis for these distortions, given the parameters of the trauma and the client's initial need to adapt to them. In the latter instance, this greater understanding of the "whys" of cognitive distortion allows a more coherent narrative of the past, its logical effects on the survivor, and, ultimately, the greater validity of more recent (that is, less trauma-influenced) understandings.

The similarity and confluence between the notion of "insight" and cognitive interventions is emblematic of the hidden similarities between many supposedly different therapeutic approaches. In this regard, most of the best therapies provide new information and the opportunity for new learning, often in the context of a supportive therapeutic relationship. Frequently, the issue is less what specific treatment is involved in this process than it is how well the client's access to—and integration of—new information is accomplished. The heavy-handed "cognitive" confrontation of "thinking errors" is probably as likely to be unsuccessful as is the ill-timed or disattuned use of depth "interpretation" in psychodynamic treatment. On the other hand, a therapeutic approach that facilitates the client's growing knowledge (and coherent narrative) of himself or herself, both now and in the past, can have substantial impacts on his or her psychological recovery.

Suggested Reading

Beck, J. S. (1995). *Cognitive therapy: Basics and beyond.* New York: Guilford.

Chard, K. M., Weaver, T. L., & Resick, P. A. (1997). Adapting cognitive processing therapy for child sexual abuse survivors. *Cognitive and Behavioral Practice, 4,* 31–52.

Follette, V. M., Ruzek, J. I., & Abueg, F. R. (Eds.). (1998). *Cognitive-behavioral therapies for trauma.* New York: Guilford.

Janoff-Bulman, B. (1992). *Shattered assumptions: Towards a new psychology of trauma.* New York: Free Press.

Kubany, E. S., & Watson, S. B. (2002). Cognitive trauma therapy for formerly battered women with PTSD: Conceptual bases and treatment outlines. *Cognitive and Behavioral Practice, 9,* 111–127.

Resick, P. A., & Schnicke, M. K. (1993). *Cognitive processing therapy for rape victims: A treatment manual.* Newbury Park: Sage.

8

Emotional Processing

In addition to the cognitive interventions described in the previous chapter, most trauma therapies include some form of *emotional processing*. However, the definitions of this term vary considerably. A commonly cited perspective is that emotional processing occurs when erroneous perceptions, beliefs, and expectations ("pathological fear structures") associated with trauma-related fears are activated and habituated in the context of new, more accurate information (Foa & Kozak, 1986). Although implicitly cognitive, this model is referred to as *emotional* because it requires the evocation and eventual diminution of fear responses.

The perspective on emotional processing used in this book (the self-trauma model; Briere, 1996, 2002a), is more directly emotion focused, albeit not especially antithetic to Foa and Kozak's view. It holds that emotional processing occurs when exposure to trauma-reminiscent stimuli (either in the environment or as a result of thinking about or describing a traumatic event) (1) triggers associated implicit and/or explicit memories, which then (2) activate emotional responses initially co-encoded with (and conditioned to) these memories; and, yet, (3) the activated emotional responses are not reinforced in the external environment, or they are, in fact, (4) counterconditioned by opposite emotional experiences, leading to (5) extinction of the original memory-emotion association. For example, talking about a trauma in treatment requires access to explicit (narrative) trauma memories that—through context reinstatement and the cuing aspects of reminiscent stimuli—often activate conditioned emotional responses (CERs; for example, fear, horror) that are conspicuously not reinforced within the safety of good psychotherapy and that may be counterconditioned, over time, by the positive feelings engendered by the therapeutic relationship. As a result, after sufficient trauma processing, exposure to trauma triggers and memories no longer activates posttraumatic distress.

This model further assumes, however, that things are not always this simple—any given "trauma memory" is likely to encompass a collection of many separate and discrete memories of that traumatic event. Further, evocation of these memories (and associated CERs, which can, themselves, be considered memories of a sort) may trigger recollections of other traumas and other conditioned responses—leading to a highly complicated cascade of internal associations and activated states or experiences. In fact, as is noted later in this chapter, thoughts and expectations also may be activated by trauma memories. Specifically, we suggest that—similar to CERs—triggered trauma memories may activate simple cognitive material (for example, assumptions or expectations) that was encoded at the time of the event and became conditioned to the memory (see Olsen & Fazio, 2002, for a discussion of implicit, classically conditioned "attitudes"). Such activated cognitions do not necessarily represent "fear structures," because they do not inevitably produce fear (for example, they may be associated with anger or shame) and they may not, in fact, always lead to distressing emotions at all.

It is important to note that the self-trauma model does not necessarily require that cognitions be verbally addressed or altered in order for memories to be processed. For example, a reminiscent event in the environment (for example, a critical comment by a loved one) may trigger a memory or cluster of memories of earlier, traumatic experiences (for example, physical and verbal abuse by a parent), which may directly activate emotional or cognitive responses (for example, expectations of danger, intrusive fear, or anger) without the contribution of cortical processes (that is, "thinking" about what happened). If these responses are not reinforced in the environment (for example, the loved one is reliably not abusive or dangerous), or a similar process occurs in therapy (for example, the therapist's appearance or behavior repeatedly triggers memories of abuse, though he or she is not abusive), these responses may diminish without ever being discussed or even explicitly "thought about."

In this regard, LeDoux (1998) and others suggest that emotional (and perhaps simple cognitive) responses can be triggered "without the involvement of the higher processing systems of the brain, systems believed to be involved in thinking, reasoning, and consciousness" (LeDoux, 1998, p. 161). LeDoux has demonstrated that this "subcortical" route transmits sensory information directly from the thalamus to the amygdala, as opposed to the slower, "cortical" route that transmits from the thalamus to both the cortex and the hippocampus—where it is integrated with more contextual and often verbal information—and then sent to the amygdala.

In other words, trauma memories may be processed on noncognitive as well as cognitive levels, and thus may not inevitably require the modification of "fear structures" in order to reduce their emotional properties. On the other hand, similar to Foa and Kozak's view of habituation as partially cognitive (for example, the client learns that sustained fear is not intrinsically dangerous), extinction can involve nonverbal learning that certain responses are no longer relevant to formerly triggering stimuli. This may be a "cognitive" conclusion, but it is not a verbal (or even necessarily conscious) one. As is seen throughout this book, although much emphasis is placed on the cognitions of trauma survivors as they seek to understand and resolve traumatic experiences, it is also true that much of trauma activation and processing occurs at implicit, nonverbal, often relational, levels.

Reexperiencing as Trauma Processing

Before we can proceed with a description of how trauma memories can be addressed during treatment, we must first introduce the notion of *intrinsic processing* through reexperiencing. We, like some others, suggest that intrusive reexperiencing is an inherent form of trauma processing, wherein the mind's repeated presentation of upsetting memories to itself (through flashbacks, nightmares, or other intrusive memories) represents an evolutionally derived attempt to prompt cognitive accommodation to the reality of the traumatic event (Horowitz, 1978) and to systematically desensitize or extinguish emotions (CERs) and conditioned expectations associated with trauma memories (Briere, 1996, 2002a). This mechanism may, in part, explain why many people recover from posttraumatic stress within months of the trauma (Bryant & Harvey, 2000; Norris et al., 2002; Rothbaum, Foa, Riggs, Murdock, & Walsh, 1992), even in the absence of therapy. In fact, many early traumatic stress responses may represent attempts at self-healing as much as symptoms of an emerging stress disorder.

However, some traumatic memories are so upsetting (for example, those associated with extended abuse, torture, rape, or concentration camp experiences) that they cannot be easily accommodated or desensitized. In addition, some traumatized people are sufficiently compromised by other psychological phenomena (for example, psychosis, comorbid depression or anxiety, or preexisting posttraumatic stress), neurological dysregulation (for example, traumatic brain injury or an altered hypothalamic-pituitary-adrenal [HPA] axis), distressing cognitions (for example, guilt or shame), or insufficient affect regulation skills (see Chapter 6) that they are unable to experience "normal" trauma reliving without being overwhelmed by the attendant emotionality. The resultant distress may motivate the various avoidance responses described in Chapter 2, which then interfere with exposure to traumatic memory and reduce further processing. For example, the individual whose negative emotional responses (CERs) to a triggered trauma memory exceed his or her capacities to tolerate such feelings may be forced to use dissociation, substance abuse, thought suppression, distraction, and other avoidance responses to maintain internal equilibrium. In such a case, the intrusion-extinction process is likely to be ineffective, resulting in continuing reexperiencing without recovery.

The self-trauma model has significant implications for the process of trauma therapy. It suggests that avoidance may be adaptive, even necessary, for individuals who have especially aversive trauma memories or significant difficulties in regulating the associated negative emotions. It also implies that overly enthusiastic or heavy-handed attempts by the therapist to prematurely remove such avoidance, resistance, denial, or dissociative symptoms may represent a threat to the client's internal equilibrium.

This presents a therapeutic conundrum—some individuals (especially chronic trauma survivors) are unable to tolerate the emotional (CER) activation associated with remembering trauma in therapy, and thus cannot easily process such material (Ford, Courtois, Steele, van der Hart, & Nijenhuis, 2005). The solution lies in finding a way to monitor and control the level of the client's emotional activation yet still provide sufficient exposure to some extent to trauma memories—to provide enough therapeutic exposure that extinction or counterconditioning can eventually occur, but not so much that the client becomes overwhelmed and has to invoke avoidance strategies that block processing. In this regard, part of the therapist's role in treatment may be to take on the "job" of intrinsic trauma exposure, to some extent replacing intrusive reexperiencing with careful therapeutic exploration of trauma memories. In contrast to naturally occurring trauma processing, however, therapy provides a relatively controlled environment in which the therapist can adjust or *titrate* the level of memory exposure (and subsequent emotional activation) within the session in order to accommodate the reduced emotional capacities or excessively upsetting memories of some trauma survivors.

It should be noted that not all trauma specialists accept the validity of titrated exposure, as it is described here. Clinician-researchers such as Foa and Rothbaum (1998) advocate, instead, *prolonged exposure,* wherein the client is encouraged to experience the full extent of trauma-related emotionality while recounting the experiences in the first person, present tense, for up to an hour at a time. Although we do not deny the effectiveness (and efficiency) of prolonged exposure in some cases, the current model reflects concerns that such activities can exceed the affect regulation capacities of individuals with more severe or complex posttraumatic symptomatology. Instead, we suggest that treatment generally occur within the *therapeutic window* (Briere, 1996, 2002a), as described following.

The Therapeutic Window

The *therapeutic window* refers to a psychological midpoint between inadequate and overwhelming activation of trauma-related emotion during treatment: it is a hypothetical "place" where therapeutic interventions are thought to be most helpful. Interventions within the therapeutic window are neither so trivial or nonevocative that they provide inadequate memory exposure and processing, nor so intense that the client's balance between acceptable memory activation and overwhelming emotion is tipped toward the latter. In other words, interventions that take the therapeutic window into account are those that trigger trauma memories and promote processing but do not overwhelm internal protective systems and thereby motivate unwanted avoidance responses.

Interventions that "undershoot" the therapeutic window are those that either completely and consistently avoid traumatic material, or are focused primarily on support and validation with a client who could tolerate greater exposure and processing. Undershooting is rarely dangerous; it can, however, waste time and resources in instances when more effective therapeutic interventions are possible.

"Overshooting" the window, on the other hand, occurs when the clinician inadvertently provides too much memory exposure and emotional activation relative to the client's existing affect regulation resources or is unable to prevent the client from flooding him- or herself with overwhelming traumatic distress. Interventions that are too fast-paced may overshoot the window because they do not allow the client to adequately accommodate and desensitize previously activated material before triggering new memories. When therapy consistently overshoots the window, the survivor must engage in avoidance maneuvers in order to keep from being overwhelmed by the therapy process. Most often, the client will increase his or her level of dissociation (for example, through disengagement or "spacing out") during the session, or will interrupt the focus or pace of therapy with arguments, by "not getting" obvious therapeutic points, distracting the therapist with various behaviors, or by changing the subject to something less threatening. In the worst case, he or she may drop out of treatment.

Although therapists may interpret these behaviors as "resistance," such avoidance often represents appropriate protective responses to therapist process errors. Unfortunately, the need for avoidance can easily impede treatment by decreasing the client's exposure to memory material and the ameliorative aspects of therapy.

In contrast, effective trauma therapy provides titrated exposure to traumatic material while maintaining the safety necessary to eventually extinguish conditioned emotional responses. By carefully adjusting the amount of therapeutic exposure so that the associated emotional activation does not exceed the survivor's emotional capacities, treatment within the therapeutic window allows the client to slowly process trauma memories without being retraumatized and needing to "shut down" the process.

Intensity Control

Intensity control refers to the therapist's awareness and relative control of the level of emotional activation occurring within the session. We recommend that—especially for those clients with impaired affect regulation capacities—emotional intensity be highest at around (or slightly before) mid-session, whereas the beginning and end of the session should be at the lowest intensity (see Figure 8.1). Ideally, at the beginning of the session, the client gradually enters the process of psychotherapy; by the middle of the session, the focus has shifted to relatively more intense processing and activation; at the end of the session the client is sufficiently dearoused that she or he can reenter the outside world without needing later avoidance activities. The relative safety of psychotherapy sessions may allow some clients to become more affectively aroused than they would outside of the therapeutic environment. As a result, it should be the therapist's goal to leave the client in as calm an affective state as is possible—ideally no more emotionally aroused than he or she was at the beginning of the session.

The need for the client to experience upsetting feelings and thoughts during trauma-focused treatment requires that the therapist carefully titrate the level of emotional activation the client experiences, at least to the extent that this is under the therapist's control. From the therapeutic window perspective, intense affect during treatment pushes the client toward the outer edge of the window (that is, toward an increased possibility of being overwhelmed), whereas less intensity (or a more cognitive focus) moves the client toward the inner edge (that is, toward reduced exposure and processing). The goal is to keep the client near the "middle" of the window—to feel neither too little (for example, to dissociate or otherwise avoid to the point that abuse-related CERs and cognitions cannot be processed) nor too much (for example, to become flooded with previously avoided emotionality that overwhelms available affect regulation resources and is retraumatizing).

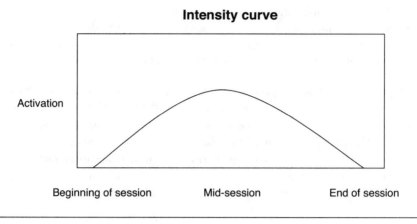

Figure 8.1   Therapeutic Intensity Over Time During Session

Constraints on Trauma Processing

As noted throughout this book, exposure to trauma memories and the attendant distress can be quite challenging. In most instances, trauma processing is tolerable to the extent that it occurs within the therapeutic window. In some relatively rare cases, however, almost any level of memory processing "overshoots the window," irrespective of the clinician's efforts. When this occurs, it is usually because (1) the trauma is so recent or severe that CER activation is inherently overwhelming; (2) the client has insufficient affect regulation capacities; and/or (3) he or she generally suffers from such high levels of comorbid emotional distress or negative cognitive preoccupation that the additional (especially trauma-related) distress is incapacitating.

For these reasons, exploration of traumatic material is not always appropriate. As noted by various authors (for example, Bryant & Harvey, 2000; Cloitre, Koenen, Cohen, & Han, 2002; Najavits, 2002; Pitman et al., 1991), therapeutic exposure to trauma memories may be contraindicated for clients experiencing:

- Very high anxiety (including easily triggered panic attacks)
- Severe depression
- Acute psychosis
- Major suicidality (that is, high risk of suicide attempts)
- Overwhelming guilt and shame associated with the traumatic event
- Especially impaired affect regulation capacity

- Very recent and substantial trauma exposure
- Substance intoxication or some instances of substance dependence (specific recommendations regarding exposure-based treatment of substance addicted trauma survivors are presented later in this chapter)

When these conditions preclude exposure therapy, the clinician is advised to focus on the various other interventions outlined in this book, including affect regulation (Chapter 6), cognitive (as opposed to emotion-based) interventions (Chapter 7), psychiatric mediation (Chapter 11), and/or psychiatric hospitalization. In many cases, repeated use of these other interventions will eventually set the stage for more classic emotional processing and thus more efficient trauma desensitization.

The Components of Trauma Processing

Assuming that none of the constraining conditions presented here are in force, or that they have been sufficiently diminished, formal trauma processing can be initiated. For the purposes of this book, the processing of traumatic memory within the therapeutic window will be divided into five components: *exposure, activation, disparity, counterconditioning*, and *desensitization/ resolution* (Briere, 2002a). These components do not always follow a linear progression. In fact, in some cases, interventions at a "later" stage may lead to further work at an "earlier" stage. In other instances, certain components (for example, counterconditioning) may be less important than others (for example, disparity). And, finally, as described in Chapter 6, the therapy process may require the client to learn (or invoke previously learned) affect regulation techniques to down-regulate distress when emotional responses inadvertently become overwhelming.

Exposure

In the current context, *exposure* refers to any activity engaged in by the therapist or the client that provokes or triggers client memories of traumatic events. Therapeutic exposure has been described, for example, as "repeated or extended exposure, either in vivo or in imagination, to objectively harmless but feared stimuli for the purpose of reducing anxiety" (Abueg & Fairbank, 1992, p. 127). From the trauma perspective, the "objectively harmless" stimuli are memories of prior trauma that are, by definition, not currently occurring; the "anxiety" is the triggered emotional response to these trauma memories.

Several types of exposure-based therapies are used to treat traumatic stress, one of which—prolonged exposure—has been shown to be relatively effective in treating adult traumas, most notably sexual assault (Foa & Rothbaum, 1998). As noted earlier, this approach typically eschews titrated or graduated access to traumatic memories and, instead, involves extended exposure to the full force of traumatic memories (for example, the moment-to-moment experience of a rape) until the associated anxiety is habituated. In contrast, the exposure approach we suggest here is a variant of *systematic desensitization* (Wolpe, 1958), wherein the client is asked to recall non-overwhelming but moderately distressing traumatic experiences in the context of a safe therapeutic environment. The exposure is generally (but not inevitably) graduated according to the intensity of the recalled material, with less upsetting memories being recalled and verbalized before more upsetting ones. However, this approach usually does not adhere to a strict, preplanned (that is, hierarchical) series of extended exposure activities. This is because the client's ability to tolerate exposure may be quite compromised and may vary considerably as a function of outside life stressors, level of support from friends, relatives, and others, and, most important, the extent of affect regulation capacities available to him or her at any given point in time. In self-trauma parlance, the "size" of the therapeutic window may change within and across sessions.

In general, exposure involves the client recalling and discussing traumatic events with the therapist, or writing about them and then reading them to the therapist. Although some forms of trauma therapy focus on memories of a single trauma (for example, of a motor vehicle accident or physical assault) and discourage much discussion of other traumas, the approach we advocate is considerably more permissive. It is quite common for trauma survivors to "jump" from one memory to another, often making associations that are not immediately apparent to the therapist—or even, in some cases, to the client. Especially for survivors of multiple, complex, and extended traumas, the focus of a given session may move from a rape experience to earlier childhood maltreatment, and then, perhaps, to an experience of domestic violence. For example, a war veteran may begin the session with a memory of hand-to-hand combat, and find himself, 20 minutes later, describing being physically abused by his father when he was a child.

The broader exposure activities of the therapy described here reflect the complexity of many trauma presentations. Although a client may come to treatment in order to address a recent assault experience, it may soon become apparent that either (1) an earlier trauma is actually more relevant to his or her ongoing distress, or (2) the distress is due to the interacting effects of multiple traumas. A woman engaged in prostitution, for example, might seek treatment for the effects of a violent rape by a customer, and soon discover that this rape activates memories of the vast collection of other distressing experiences she undergoes on a regular basis, as well as the childhood incest experiences that may have partially determined her involvement in prostitution in the first place (Farley, 2003). In such instances, insisting that the client focus exclusively on a single trauma during therapy, or even on just one trauma at a time, may be contraindicated and not well appreciated by the client. As well, recollections of early trauma are often fragmented and incomplete (Williams, 1994), and, in many cases, preverbal (Berliner & Briere, 1998), precluding the client's exposure to a discrete, coherent, describable memory. Instead of being constrained to a single trauma, we suggest that the trauma survivor be allowed to discuss—and thereby expose him- or herself to—whatever trauma seems important at a given time, or whatever memory—or part of a memory—is triggered by any other memory. There is little doubt that this approach is less efficient, in terms of addressing any given single (especially adult) trauma. It is, however, more appropriate when the multitrauma client presents for treatment.

Explaining the Value of Therapeutic Exposure

Although therapeutic exposure is widely understood by clinicians to be a powerful treatment methodology, the trauma survivor can be forgiven for initially responding more negatively to the idea. Prior to therapy, the survivor may have devoted considerable time and effort to controlling his or her symptoms by avoiding people, places, and conversations that trigger posttraumatic intrusion. In fact, avoidance of reminders of the trauma is a central aspect of posttraumatic stress disorder (PTSD) and other stress responses. As a result, exposure techniques, wherein the client is asked to intentionally experience events that he or she has been avoiding, may seem—at best—counterintuitive.

For this reason, an important aspect of trauma therapy is *prebriefing*: explaining the rationale for exposure, and its general methodology, prior to the onset of formal treatment. Without sufficient explanation, the process and immediate effects of exposure may seem so illogical and stressful that the client will automatically resist and avoid. On the other hand, if exposure can be explained so that the client understands the reasons for this sometimes distressing procedure, it usually is not hard to form a positive client-therapist alliance and a shared appreciation for the process.

Although the way in which exposure is introduced may vary from instance to instance, the clinician should attempt to address most of the following content when preparing clients for exposure work:

- Explain that reexperiencing is not only a source of upsetting symptoms but, also, evidence of the mind's attempt to heal itself.
- Emphasize that unresolved memories of the trauma usually have to be talked about and reexperienced, or else they may not be processed and will be more likely to keep coming back as symptoms.
- Indicate that although the client understandably would like to not think about what happened, and may have been avoiding upsetting feelings about the trauma, such avoidance often serves to keep the symptoms alive.
- Suggest that if the client can talk enough about what happened, the pain and fear associated with the trauma is likely to decrease. Do not, however, promise recovery.
- Note that, by its nature, exposure is associated with some level of distress. In addition, warn the client that some people who undergo exposure experience a slight increase in flashbacks, nightmares, and distressing feelings between sessions, but that this is normal and usually not a bad sign. At the same time, ask the client to tell you if and when this occurs, so that you can monitor whether exposure has been too intense.
- Emphasize that you will work to keep the discussion of these memories from overwhelming the client, and that he or she can stop talking about any given memory if it becomes too upsetting. Reassure the client that he or she only needs to talk about as much as he or she is comfortable with. But stress that the more the client can remember, think, feel, and talk about the memories, the more likely it will be that significant improvement will occur.

Homework

As noted in the previous chapter, trauma therapy sometimes includes "homework" assignments. This typically involves the client writing about the traumatic event outside of therapy and then reading aloud what he or she has written in next session. Along with providing additional opportunities to examine and process cognitions initially associated with the event (see Chapter 7), this activity requires that the client access the original trauma memory in order to write about it, and thus provides significant therapeutic exposure. This exposure is then repeated when the client reads the narrative aloud to the therapist.

Adapting from Resick and Schnicke's (1992) assignment for a rape victim, the therapist might say something like:

Try to write a page or two about the rape/shooting/abuse incident/car accident. Include as much detail about it as you can remember, and be as specific as possible—for instance, what happened, what feelings you had, what you thought when it happened, what anyone else said, and what you did right afterward. You don't have to do all of this at once; sometimes people take several tries to get it all down. After you're done writing, read it to yourself at least once before our next session. If it is too upsetting to read all at once, try reading as much as you can, and then read the rest when you are able.

Typically, the client is asked to repeat this writing exercise on several different occasions over the course of treatment, and to read his or her writing each time to the therapist. The specific timing of these writing and reading exercises may vary according to (1) the client's current capacity for written expression, (2) his or her readiness to directly confront the trauma, and (3) his or her immediate stability and affect regulation capacity. The therapist's response to hearing the client's story should be characterized by support, validation, and appreciation for the client's willingness to engage in such a potentially difficult task.

Obviously, this approach is not possible for those who are unable to read and write fluently or who are too cognitively debilitated (for example, by psychosis or severe depression) to accomplish such activities. In cases where literacy and comorbidity are not issues, however, this exercise can be initiated at some point after the first few sessions and then repeated several times at intervals. The total number of times this exercise is done may increase if there are several different traumas in need of emotional processing. In general, the clinician will find that these written renditions become more detailed and emotionally descriptive upon repetition, and that the client's emotional responses when reading the assignment aloud become less extreme over time.

Activation

If treatment is to be effective, some degree of activation must take place during exposure. *Activation* refers to conditioned emotional responses (such as fear, sadness, or horror) that are triggered by trauma memories, and trauma-specific cognitive reactions (such as intrusive negative self-perceptions or sudden feelings of helplessness). Other related memories and their associated affects and cognitions may be triggered as well. A woman who is asked to describe a childhood sexual abuse experience, for example, undergoes therapeutic exposure to the extent that she recalls aspects of that event during the therapy session. If these memories trigger emotional responses conditioned to the original abuse stimuli (for example, fear, disgust, or horror), or associated cognitive intrusions (for example, "I am such a slut"), or stimulate further memories (for example, of other traumas or other aspect of the abuse triggered by remembering certain aspects of it), therapeutic activation can be said to have taken place.

Activation is usually critical to trauma processing; in order to extinguish emotional-cognitive associations to a given traumatic memory, they must be

(1) activated, (2) not reinforced, and, ideally, (3) counterconditioned. As a result, therapeutic interventions that consist solely of the narration of trauma-related memories without emotional activation will not necessarily produce symptom relief (Foa & Kozak, 1986; Samoilov & Goldfried, 2000). In order for optimal activation to occur, there should be as little avoidance as is reasonably possible during the exposure process. The dissociated client, for example, may experience very little activation during treatment, despite giving what may be quite detailed renditions of a specific trauma memory. On the other hand, as noted throughout this book, too much activation is also problematic, because it generates high levels of distress (thereby linking memory to emotional pain rather than to safety or positive feelings) and motivates avoidance (thereby reducing further exposure and processing).

Because activated cognitive-emotional responses are, to some extent, the crux of trauma work, we describe in the following sections several interventions aimed at controlling the level of activation during treatment. The goal, in each case, is to work within the therapeutic window—to support emotional and cognitive activation that is neither too little nor too much for optimal processing.

Increasing Activation

The therapist typically seeks to increase activation in instances when, despite available affect regulation capacity, the client unnecessarily blocks some portion of his or her emotional responses to the traumatic material. It is not uncommon for avoidance responses to become so overlearned that they automatically, but unnecessarily, emerge during exposure to stress. In other instances, gender roles or occupational socialization may discourage emotional expression in an individual who could otherwise tolerate it, as described in Chapter 4. In such cases, a reduction in avoidance during treatment is not only likely to be reasonably safe; it is usually necessary for significant desensitization to occur. When avoidance is not required for continued emotional homeostasis, yet appears to be blocking trauma processing, several interventions may be appropriate. In each case, the goal is increased awareness and, thus, increased activation—not criticism or, necessarily, even symptom identification.

First, the therapist may ask questions that can only be answered in a relatively less avoidant state. These include, for example:

- "What were you feeling/how did it feel when that happened?"
- "What are you feeling now?"
- "Are you aware of any thoughts or feelings when you describe the trauma?"

In such cases, the avoidance may decrease, yet never be acknowledged—an outcome that is entirely appropriate, since the primary intent is to keep activation at a reasonable level, not to label the client's reaction as problematic.

Second, the clinician can indirectly draw attention to the avoidance, without stigmatizing it, and ask the client to increase his or her level of contact during the process of activation. This is often most effective when the client's avoidance, or the power of the CERs to overwhelm, has previously been identified as an issue in therapy. This may involve encouraging suggestions such as:

- "You're doing well. Try to stay with the feelings."
- "Don't go away now. You're doing great. Stay with it."
- "I can see it's upsetting. Can you stay with the memory for just a few more minutes? We can always stop if you need to."

In other cases, however, for example, when dissociation is just one possibility, or when the client is more prone to a defensive response, the therapist may intervene with a question-statement combination, such as:

- "How are you doing? It looks like maybe you're spacing out a little bit."
- "It looks like you're going away a little bit, right now. Are you?"

Although calling direct attention to avoidance is sometimes appropriate, it tends to break the process of exposure/activation, and probably should be used only when less direct methods of encouraging activation (and thus reducing avoidance) have not been effective.

The clinician can increase activation not only by discouraging cognitive or emotional avoidance but also by increasing the emotional experience. Often, this involves requesting more details about the traumatic event and responding in ways that focus the client on emotional issues. As the client provides more details, the opportunity for greater activation increases—both because greater details often include more emotionally arousing material, and because greater detail reinstates more of the original context in the client's mind, thereby increasing the experience of emotions that occurred at the time of the trauma. The following is an example of a discussion that evoked greater levels of emotional activation in the client without specifically addressing avoidance.

THERAPIST: Can you tell me what happened?

CLIENT: [*flattened voice*] A drive-by.

THERAPIST: A drive-by shooting? Did anyone get hurt?

CLIENT: [*pause*] Yeah. A neighbor got shot.

THERAPIST: A neighbor? Who was it?

CLIENT: A lady I sorta knew. She was nice.

THERAPIST: *Was* nice? Is she okay?

CLIENT: [*slight increase in volume, face slightly reddened*] She's dead.

THERAPIST: [*pause*] Man . . . What happened? It sounds bad.

CLIENT: Yeah, it was [*voice lower, looking away*].

THERAPIST: So, she was shot. Were you there? When she got hit?

CLIENT: Yeah, she got shot in the chest [*voice wavering, throat sounding constricted*]. She was bleeding all over the place. I hit the ground. I had to, because the guy was still shooting, but I could hear her screaming. I couldn't help her. I had to protect myself [*hand covering face*].

In this case, the client is reluctant to describe the event, but does not indicate dramatic signs of emotional dysregulation. His avoidance responses (initially reduced emotional response, looking away, covering his face with his hand) are minor, suggesting that he can tolerate some further emotional activation and processing without becoming overwhelmed. Cognitive intervention is probably also indicated, at some point, to address what appears to be guilt or shame at not being able to help the woman.

Decreasing Activation

In general, the intensity of activation is determined by (1) the level of exposure, (2) the aversiveness of the trauma memory (that is, the extent of negative emotionality conditioned to it), and (3) the amount of affect regulation capacity available to the client. If the therapist encourages too much activation, or is unsuccessful in keeping the client's emotional activation to a tolerable level, the therapeutic window will be exceeded. Those with reduced affect regulation capacities typically should not be exposed to especially upsetting memories until their ability to regulate negative emotions improves (Chu, 1998; Cloitre et al., 2002). This may mean that the therapist redirects the client to less upsetting material when the client becomes too activated, focuses the client on relaxation, or directs the conversation to less emotionally charged aspects of the event. In such cases, affect skill development (see Chapter 6) may receive priority over especially intense trauma processing, and supportive interventions and responses may predominate over exploratory ones. When avoidance is more extreme, for example, when the client becomes highly dissociated in the session, the therapist will generally stop the exposure/activation process and focus stabilizing interventions on whatever is producing the avoidance.

This general approach might appear to deprive the client of the opportunity to address major traumas. We believe, however, that such restraint is one of the responsibilities of the therapist. If the clinician suspects—based on observation of the client—that activation is likely to exceed the therapeutic window in any given circumstance, it is important that he or she ensure safety by reducing the intensity and pace of the therapeutic process. This does not mean that the clinician necessarily avoids trauma processing altogether; only that processing should proceed slowly and carefully, or be temporarily delayed. Fortunately, the need for such a conservative approach is usually transient. As the traumatic material is slowly and carefully processed, progressively fewer trauma memories will have the potential to activate overwhelming affect, and, as described in Chapter 6, the client's overall capacity to tolerate distress will grow. The primary issue, overall, is one of time: the individual with good affect regulation capacities, less than extremely distressing trauma memories, and no interfering comorbidities may be able to tolerate higher levels of activation without exceeding the therapeutic window, and thus may respond relatively quickly to treatment. Those with difficulties in one or more of these areas, however, may require titration to lower levels of activation during trauma processing, and thus may have to be in therapy for a considerably longer period of time before major symptom improvement occurs.

Unfortunately, not all activation is visible to the therapist. There may be occasions when the client "overshoots" the therapeutic window during treatment yet does not appear to be especially overwhelmed. This may occur because (1) the client feels relatively safe in the controlled environment of the therapist's office and does not fully experience the overwhelming nature of the exposure until he or she leaves the session; (2) he or she is concerned about therapist approval and does not show distress in the session so as to appear strong, healthy, or in control; or (3) the client is dissociating or cognitively suppressing upsetting internal processes. Such unapparent overshooting of the therapeutic window, whether or not it is acknowledged by the client, may cause elevated anxiety, despondence, or shame after the session ends—distress that may then result in tension reduction behaviors (for example, self-injurious or impulsive behavior), substance abuse, or other avoidance activities. In some cases, the client may make emergency calls to the therapist, may miss the next therapy session, or may arrive late to it.

In trauma work, missed sessions and lateness sometimes represent avoidance of the distress associated with previous therapeutic exposure to traumatic material. In such instances, the client's behavior may reflect his or her fear of further emotional activation in subsequent sessions. Once a session is missed, further missed sessions may follow. When a client repeatedly misses appointments, we recommend that the therapist explore this issue with him or her in a nonjudgmental manner, assessing what aspects of the therapeutic process or content is motivating avoidance and assuring the client that the therapist is not angry and will not be punitive. Often, a permissive attitude toward "no-shows" is more necessary in trauma work than in other forms of psychotherapy. By accepting and discussing the underlying motivation for nonattendance—as opposed to confronting and criticizing it—the therapist has a better chance of decreasing the likelihood of future missed sessions.

Remediating Window Errors

Obviously, it is important to avoid exceeding the therapeutic window whenever possible. Given the delicate nature of exposure work, however, and the sometimes obscuring effects of client emotional avoidance, it is often impossible to entirely avoid overactivation. As a result, part of the clinician's job in therapy is to intervene when overactivation occurs and to work to repair the effects of such experiences.

When it is apparent that the therapeutic window has been significantly exceeded, the therapist is advised to consider:

- Reducing the duration and intensity of the current activation, through relaxation or breathing exercises, cognitive (as opposed to emotional) interventions, and, generally, a shift in focus away from overly activating topics
- Taking some responsibility for the client's overactivation while, at the same time, not disparaging one's own work or abilities
- Supporting and validating the client's expression of distress, including suggesting that emotional reactivity is indicative of doing "good work" (as opposed to engaging in avoidance)
- Discussing and reframing major activation after it occurs, so that the client understands his or her reactions as a normal reaction to the power of the triggering memory, and does not pathologize them
- Problem-solving with the client ways in which (1) the therapist can detect the client's escalating distress (this is especially relevant if the client habitually uses emotional avoidance defenses in the session), (2) the client can communicate distress at the time it occurs, and (3) the therapist and client can work to bring the activation level back into the therapeutic window
- Making nondefensive, supportive, and validating statements that convey cautious optimism that the "emotional rollercoaster" of early trauma sessions may gradually abate over time

Disparity

Exposure and activation are not, in and of themselves, sufficient in trauma treatment. As noted in Chapter 7, there also must be a *disparity* between what the client is feeling (for example, activated fear associated with a trauma memory) and the current state of reality (for example, the manifest absence of immediate danger). For CERs to traumatic memories to be diminished or extinguished over time, they must consistently not be reinforced by similar danger (physical or emotional) in the current environment.

As we have described earlier, safety should be manifest in at least two ways. First, the client should have the opportunity to realize that he or she is safe in the presence of the therapist. This means safety not only from physical injury and sexual exploitation, but also from harsh criticism, punitiveness, boundary violation, or underappreciation of the client's experience. Because the survivor of interpersonal violence, maltreatment, or exploitation tends to overidentify danger in interpersonal situations (Janoff-Bulman, 1992), the absence of danger in the session must be experienced directly, not just promised. In other words, for the client's anxious associations to trauma memories to lose their power, they must consistently not be reinforced by current danger or maltreatment in the session, however subtle.

Second, safety in treatment includes protection from overwhelming internal experience. The client whose trauma memories produce destabilizing emotions during treatment may not find therapy to be substantially disparate from the original experience. As noted earlier, such overwhelming affect may occur because one or both of two things are present: (1) the memory is so traumatic and has so much painful affect (for example, anxiety, rage) or cognitions (for example, guilt or shame) associated with it that untitrated exposure produces considerable psychic pain; or (2) the survivor's affect regulation capacities are sufficiently compromised that any major reexperiencing is overwhelming. In each instance, safety—and therefore disparity—can only be provided within the context of the therapeutic window. Because processing within the window means, by definition, that exposure to memories does not exceed the client's ability to tolerate those memories, reexperiencing trauma in this context is not associated with overwhelming negative affect, identity fragmentation, or feelings of loss of control.

The processing of CERs to trauma memories operates in a manner similar to the processing of fear in behavioral treatments for phobias. The ongoing activation of fear and other negative emotional responses during the repetitive recounting of traumatic material in the absence of any discernable, "real" reason for such responses in the session means that such emotionality goes unreinforced. Eventually, responses that are not reinforced tend to fade.

Possible reasons for this phenomenon range from traditional extinction theories (Wolpe, 1958) to newer cognitive models involving the experience-based modification of cognitive "fear structures" (Foa & Kozak, 1986). Regardless of the underlying mechanisms, the role of disparity in trauma recovery is clear—the environment in which trauma activation occurs must reliably not reinforce the original danger-fear association. Otherwise the client's fear response to the memory will remain strong, if not increase.

Counterconditioning

Not only is it important that there be a manifest absence of danger during trauma processing; in the best circumstances there also should be *counterconditioning*—the presence of positive phenomena that are antithetic to physical or psychological danger. Thus, for example, a woman in therapy for problems related to long-standing domestic violence may expect her therapist to be critical or rejecting. When her fears not only are met with the absence of those things in treatment (the disparity associated with therapeutic safety), but occur in fact in the presence of acceptance, validation, and nurturing, the activated distress may diminish in intensity because it is incompatible with the positive feelings that arise in therapy. As a result, the emotional associations to memories of being battered are not only not reinforced, they are weakened by contradictory, positive feeling states. A similar (although often less powerful) process may ensue for the client who recounts other types of traumatic material (including noninterpersonal events) in the presence of therapist support, understanding, and caring—the negative emotions associated with trauma activation are countered by simultaneous positive feelings associated with the treatment environment. Like many aspects of cognitive-behavioral therapy, the contribution of counterconditioning to trauma resolution is debated, with some arguing that it is probably not an active ingredient of treatment. However, the primary counterconditioning state examined thus far has been relaxation during exposure therapy (Foa, Keane, & Friedman, 2000)—a considerably less powerful experience, we believe, than the sustained positive emotions stimulated by a positive therapeutic relationship.

A second form of counterconditioning may be the experience of emotional release. Crying or other forms of emotional expression in response to upsetting events typically produces relatively positive emotional states (for example, relief) that can countercondition the fear and related affects initially associated with the traumatic memory. In other words, the common suggestion that someone "have a good cry" or "get it off of your chest" may reflect cultural support for emotional activities that naturally countercondition trauma-related CERs. From this perspective, just as traditional systematic desensitization often pairs a formerly distressing stimulus to a relaxed, anxiety-incompatible state in an attempt to neutralize the anxious response over time, repeated emotional release during exposure to painful memories may pair the traumatic stimuli to the relatively positive internal states associated with emotional expression. For this reason, optimal trauma therapy typically provides gentle support for—and reinforcement of—expressed emotionality during exposure activities. The level of emotional response in such circumstances will vary from person to person, partially as a function of the client's affect regulation capacity, personal history, and socialization. As a result, the therapist should not "push" for emotional expression when the client is unable or unwilling to engage in such activity, but should support it when it occurs.

Desensitization/Resolution

Together, the process of remembering painful (but not overwhelming) events in the context of safety, positive relatedness, emotional expression, and minimal avoidance can serve to break the connection between traumatic memories and associated negative emotional responses. As this *desensitization* occurs, environmental and internal events that trigger memories of traumatic experiences no longer produce the same level of negative emotion. Once they are processed, traumatic memories become, simply, memories; their ability to produce great distress is significantly diminished. In the case of the multiply trauma-exposed person, however, the process does not end with the resolution of a given memory or set of memories. Instead, other memories, often those that are associated with even greater distress, tend to become more available for discussion—at which point the process continues with this new material. In our experience, however, later memories often desensitize more quickly than memories addressed earlier in therapy. This may be due to the increased affect regulation abilities associated with the successful processing of traumatic material (see Chapter 6), as well as the possibility that the extinction of CERs to one traumatic memory may partially generalize to CERs related to other trauma memories.

Processing "Hot Spots"

It may become apparent during a given session that certain memories are especially powerful activators of negative CERs and intrusive cognitions. These memories may respond less well to the titrated exposure methodologies that have been presented thus far in this chapter. Such "hot spots" (Foa &

Rothbaum, 1998) may require more concentrated attention in order to produce significant symptom relief. Examples of hot spots include:

- A client describes a rape in which she was forced to engage in an especially abhorrent act. Whenever she recalls this aspect of her assault, she becomes increasingly upset and cognitively disorganized. In addition, although other memories of the rape experience are becoming desensitized over time, this memory continues to produce the same level of distress.
- A survivor of the terrorist attacks of September 11, 2001, "can't get one thing out of my mind," despite otherwise successful treatment for what he experienced and witnessed on that day. He continues to have intrusive flashbacks of people jumping out of the windows of the World Trade Center, and perseverates on these images whenever discussing the attacks.
- A woman who accidentally ran over a homeless man on a crowded city street becomes especially upset when describing the sound of her tires traveling over his body. This specific memory produces obsessional thoughts and repetitive nightmares, and she continues to hear her tires making a bumping sound whenever she drives.

In cases when such intrusive memory fragments are part of a general presentation of multiple traumatic events and reduced affect regulation capacities, the therapist may find it helpful to focus on less evocative and distressing memories with the client, at least until he or she builds a more effective affect regulation repertoire. In other instances, however, such hot spots may occur in someone who could reasonably be expected to tolerate more direct processing of aversive memories. In the latter case, the clinician may choose to induce—with the client's permission—more highly focused and circumscribed exposure and activation. As opposed to the general approach outlined in this volume, this therapeutic activity more directly parallels the "prolonged exposure" methodology advocated by Foa and her colleagues (Foa & Rothbaum, 1998), except that the entire process is usually limited to a shorter period of time.

We suggest the following general procedure with regard to hot spot processing:

- *Thoroughly explain the procedure, and gain consent before initiating it.* Indicate that some memories occasionally need more concentrated attention than others if they are to lose their painful qualities. Describe the procedure, especially the idea that the client will be asked to describe the "hot spot" in greater detail, perhaps repetitively, and that the process is likely to be somewhat more challenging emotionally. Note that the client can always stop the process at any time if it becomes overwhelming. Nevertheless, note that the longer he or she can tolerate the exposure, the more benefits may accrue.

- *Encourage the client to become as relaxed as possible.* If the client appears especially anxious, suggest slow, even breathing, and/or some level of focused muscle relaxation, as described in Chapter 6. When the client indicates that he or she is in a relatively relaxed state, move on to the next step. Repeat this step whenever needed during the process, in order to keep the experience within the therapeutic window.

- *Ask the client to close his or her eyes (if tolerable) and describe the upsetting memory slowly and in detail, using the present tense.* Tell him or her to try to "go back" to the event, and relive it as much as possible while talking about it. Present-tense processing involves statements like "The car is coming right at me, it's not going to stop," as opposed to "The car was coming right at me, I was thinking it wasn't going to stop." This grammatical shift tends to increase activation, since it frames the event as though it were happening at the present moment. If present tense processing appears to be too stressful, allow the client to use past tense for a time, until using the present tense becomes possible again. When appropriate, ask (in the present tense) about how he or she felt when the trauma happened, what it looked, smelled, or sounded like, what other objects or people were present at the time, and what his or her specific thoughts were at the time. Generally, the greater the detail, the more effective the processing— but only if it occurs within the therapeutic window. Although some clients will be able to close their eyes to increase the intensity of the exposure and activation, others (for example, some survivors of interpersonal violence) may feel safer with their eyes open.

- *Encourage emotional expression whenever it appears to emerge* (for example, tears or anger), but do not put pressure on the client to express emotion if he or she appears resistant to it. The more emotional access the client has to the CERs, the more direct and potentially effective the eventual extinction of this response may be. Note, again, that emotional activation should not exceed the therapeutic window. If there is significant evidence of affect dysregulation, such as emotional lability, cognitive disorganization, dramatically increased dissociation, or seemingly overwhelming distress, hot spot processing should be carefully discontinued—while congratulating the client on how far he or she was able to go in the process. Early termination of hot spot processing should not be framed as a failure, but rather as partial completion of a task that can be taken up again at a later time.

- *Feel free to interrupt,* gently, to focus the client on the topic, to keep him or her in the present tense, to invite him or her to relax or focus on breathing, or to move his or her attention away from overwhelming material.

- *Whenever necessary, orient the client to the here-and-now.* If the client appears to be experiencing potentially overwhelming activation, remind the client that, although he or she is remembering the past, it is just a memory—he or she is actually safe in the room with the therapist. For example, the clinician might say, "Remember, even though you are remembering the [trauma] in your mind, it is not really happening right now. This is a very important point: the [trauma] is in the past. You are here, safe with me. These are just memories." If further orientation is needed, consider using the grounding techniques described in Chapter 6.

- *Repeat these steps* over as many sessions as indicated. Hot spot processing is typically limited to one episode per session, however, and generally should not exceed 20 minutes in duration. This time limit is based on clinical experience with survivors of more complex trauma, who typically require significant time after hot spot processing for relational support and deescalation of potential trauma-related distress. Proponents of prolonged exposure, however, typically prescribe considerably longer exposure/activation periods.

Hot spot processing can be an efficient way of addressing especially symptom-producing material while still providing ongoing, relational psychotherapy. The extent to which such processing is needed—and tolerable to the client—varies from case to case. When trauma memories are especially upsetting, or affect regulation capacity is notably low, this procedure is rarely appropriate until later in treatment. On the other hand, hot spot processing may be a regular part of trauma therapy for relatively uncomplicated traumatic material in a client who has reasonably good affect regulation skills.

An Example of Hot Spot Processing

We present a brief example of this technique following. The client has followed the instructions described in this chapter, and is recounting an especially problematic part of his trauma in the present tense, with eyes closed. He is at midpoint in a 20-minute processing period.

CLIENT: There's fire everywhere, the car's on fire, and I can't get to them. The door's stuck. And it's too hot. I'm pulling and pulling, and all I can hear is the screaming. . . . I know they're burning up in there! I think I was crying, pulling at the door handle, that's how I got burned.

THERAPIST: You're doing really well, Paul. Remember, stay with the present tense. You are pulling on the door handle. . . .

CLIENT: Yeah, okay . . . I'm yanking at the handle, but the doors are super-hot, I can't hold on. . . . I can feel my hands are burning. I have to let go, because it hurts so bad, but they're screaming and I have to do something, but there's nothing I can do! [*begins to hyperventilate slightly*]

THERAPIST: You're okay, Paul, you're doing fine. Take a deep breath, hold it, and then let it out slowly.

CLIENT: Okay. [*deep breath and release*] Alright. [*appears somewhat calmer*] I'm okay. It's just so real.

THERAPIST: Right, well, that's good, it's good that you're able to do this. Okay, so, your hands are burning, and the door's stuck. . . .

CLIENT: The worst part is the screams, even with the windows up. [*begins crying*]

Emotional Processing and Substance Dependence

Most of the cognitive-behavioral principles called upon in modern trauma therapy were developed in the context of treatment-outcome research that excluded substance abusing or dependent participants (Bradley, Greene, Russ, Dutra, & Westen, 2005; Spinazzola, Blaustein, & van der Kolk, 2005). As a result, there is less known about using exposure and other emotional processing approaches with those who suffer from both posttraumatic stress and involvement in substance abuse (Ouimette, Moos, & Brown, 2003). This is unfortunate, since, as described in Chapter 2, a substantial number of substance abusers have trauma histories, and many experience significant posttraumatic stress.

The usual suggestion for treating comorbid trauma symptoms and substance use disorders (SUDs) is to first treat the chemical dependency and then, after abstinence has occurred, treat trauma-related symptoms (Chu, 1988; Keane, 1995). The primary rationale for this treatment sequence is that premature exposure to trauma memories may intensify substance abuse, trigger relapses, or otherwise challenge the diminished affect regulation capacities and coping skills of many substance abusing trauma survivors. Perhaps apropos of these reasonable concerns, one of the best known and most effective treatment approaches to comorbid PTSD and SUD ("Seeking Safety"; Najavits, 2002) eschews any form of therapeutic exposure to, or exploration of, trauma memories.

Despite these concerns, however, there are several problems with using an "abstinence first" approach in general clinical practice. These include (1) the fact that a high proportion of those presenting for trauma treatment have significant substance abuse issues—blocking their access to treatment would mean underserving the majority of treatment-seeking trauma survivors; (2) in most urban mental health contexts, competent and readily available chemical dependency services are rarely immediately available—waiting lists are often many months long, and specialized programs for substance abusing trauma survivors are exceedingly rare; and (3) research indicates that SUD treatment is considerably less effective for those who also experience major posttraumatic stress (Ouimette et al., 2003)—in other words, successful SUD "pretreatment" before trauma treatment may in some cases be empirically, if not logically, inconsistent.

Given these problems, some clinicians and researchers advocate combined trauma and SUD treatment (for example, Abueg & Fairbanks, 1991; Expert Consensus Guideline Series, 1999). Further, recent studies suggest that classic trauma therapy, including therapeutic exposure, can be effective with some substance dependent trauma survivors (see Coffey, Dansky, & Brady, 2003, for a review). In basic agreement with this perspective, we suggest that the most useful and inclusive approach to trauma-SUD comorbidity is to treat posttraumatic stress in abusing or addicted survivors generally as outlined for others in this book. Given what is known about PTSD-SUD comorbidity, however, and the problems associated with substance abuse in general, we suggest several potential modifications to regular trauma processing:

1. Many substance abusing trauma survivors are noteworthy for their diminished affect regulation skills and coping capacities (Khantzian, 1997). For this reason, the clinician should consider delaying emotional (or even cognitive) processing of trauma memories until the emotionally unstable client has benefited from the stress reduction and affect regulation interventions outlined in Chapter 6.

2. If some level of trauma processing is possible, either because affect regulation is adequate or as a result of successful intervention in this area, therapeutic exposure and activation should be approached with caution. Specifically, the clinician should especially ensure that processing occurs within the therapeutic window when SUD is present. Most important, exposure to traumatic memory should follow the dictum, "Start low and go slow." Traumatic material should be explored and processed in small increments, and exposure should be terminated if it appears to overly challenge existing affect regulation capacities (that is, if it exceeds the therapeutic window).

3. Trauma therapy generally should not take place if the survivor comes to treatment in an intoxicated state. Instead, the focus should be on client safety (for example, did he or she drive to the session, and can he or she get home safely?), and on managing any clinical issues that might be present (for example, suicidality, aggression, intoxication-related "decompensation"). Further, the next session should include discussion of the client's reason for previously coming to treatment intoxicated, reiteration that intoxication automatically means that therapy is not possible, and exploration of ways in which the client can regain abstinence or at least ensure sobriety at the time of future sessions. Although therapists may vary on this point, typically we do not require substance abstinence in trauma clients (although we recommend it).

We do, however, require that the client not abuse substances close enough to his or her session that he or she arrives in an altered state.

4. Whenever possible, the client should be involved in some sort of outside group, self-help or clinician-guided, that focuses on substance abuse issues. Alcoholics Anonymous or other "12-step" programs may serve this purpose, to the extent that their precepts are psychologically and spiritually acceptable to the client.

5. Trauma treatment, as outlined in this book, should be augmented, when possible, with effective substance abuse treatment techniques. The reader is referred to Najavits's (2002) treatment manual and Ouimette and Brown's (2003) edited volume for excellent coverage of specific PTSD-SUD approaches.

Emotional Processing From Another Perspective: EMDR

In addition to classic cognitive-behavioral and psychodynamic approaches to emotional processing, a growing number of therapists use an additional model, Eye Movement Desensitization and Reprocessing (EMDR). This approach, developed by Shapiro (1995), involves asking the client to recall a traumatic event, and then to focus on visual images, negative beliefs, bodily sensations, and emotional responses associated with the memory. At the same time, the client visually tracks the therapist's finger as it moves back and forth across his or her visual field, or the client is exposed to tapping, auditory tones, or moving or flashing lights. This is repeated on multiple occasions during a given session.

Several meta-analyses suggest that EMDR is relatively effective, generally reducing posttraumatic stress symptoms to the same degree demonstrated for therapeutic exposure methods (for example, Bradley et al., 2005; Van Etten & Taylor, 1998). Interestingly, the eye movement component of EMDR appears to have little effect on outcome, and may be superfluous (Davidson & Parker, 2001). EMDR clinicians and researchers generally disagree with this interpretation, however (Shapiro, 2002).

Our own conclusion is that EMDR is a form of cognitive-behavioral therapy that can be about as effective as other brief therapies in treating PTSD. Whether EMDR offers more or less than classic cognitive-behavioral therapy remains an open question. EMDR may be most helpful in treating relatively discrete, less complex trauma effects, or in providing "hot spot" processing during more long-term, relational therapy. As noted by the EMDR Institute, this procedure, like other exposure therapies, is not recommended unless "the client has adequate methods of handling emotional distress and good coping skills, and . . . the client is in a relatively stable state. If further stabilization is required, or if additional skills are needed, therapy focuses on providing these" (EMDR Institute, 2004).

Sequence and Session-Level Structure of Memory Processing

The current and previous chapters have described various techniques and approaches for the cognitive and emotional processing of traumatic memory. In this last section we suggest an overall context in which these interventions might best occur. Although the actual processing and desensitization of traumatic memory will vary in degree from session to session, generally all such sessions should adhere to a basic structure. This framework allows the therapist to assess the client's current needs, provide relevant processing activities as needed, reassess the client's current state, deescalate session-level arousal if needed, and provide end-of-session closure. We suggest some version of the following in a 50-minute session:

- Opening (5–15 minutes):
  1. Inquire about any changes in the client's life since the last session.
     - Have there been any new traumas or victimizations?
     - Has the client engaged in dysfunctional or self-destructive behaviors?
     - If any of the foregoing is of concern, work to assure or increase the client's ongoing physical safety. Do this before (or instead of) formal trauma processing.

  2. Check with the client regarding his or her internal experience since the last session. Have intrusive or avoidance symptoms increased significantly since the last meeting? If yes, normalize the experience and validate symptoms as intrinsic trauma processing. If the intrusions or avoidance responses are substantial, consider decreasing the intensity of exposure and activation in the current session.

- Mid-session (20–30 minutes):
  1. Provide emotional and cognitive memory processing, staying within the therapeutic window whenever possible.
  2. If significant processing is contraindicated, revert to psychoeducation, general discussion, or a focus on less upsetting events in the client's life.

- Later in session (15–25 minutes):
  1. Debrief, normalize, and validate any memory processing that occurred, as necessary.

2. Inquire about the client's subjective experience during processing, as well as any thoughts or feeling he or she had while it was occurring.
3. Provide cognitive therapy as needed for additional cognitive distortions that emerged during processing (see Chapter 7).
4. If the client's level of activation remains high, work to deescalate his or her emotional arousal. This may include an increasing focus on nonemotional issues, further cognitive (but not emotional) processing, and/or grounding per Chapter 6.

- Ending (final 5–10 minutes):
  1. Remind the client (as necessary) of the potential delayed effects of trauma processing, including occasionally increased flashbacks, nightmares, and a desire to engage in avoidance activities such as substance abuse or tension reduction behaviors.
  2. Provide safety planning (if necessary) regarding dangers identified in the session, or any possible self- (or other-) destructive behavior.
  3. Provide closure statements (for example, summing up the session) and encouragement.
  4. Explicitly refer to the time and date of the next session.

Suggested Reading

Briere, J. (2002). Treating adult survivors of severe childhood abuse and neglect: Further development of an integrative model. In J. E. B. Myers et al. (Eds.), *The APSAC handbook on child maltreatment* (2nd ed.; pp. 175–202). Thousand Oaks, CA: Sage.

Cloitre, M., Koenen, K. C., Cohen, L. R., & Han, H. (2002). Skills training in affective and interpersonal regulation followed by exposure: A phase-based treatment for PTSD related to childhood abuse. *Journal of Consulting and Clinical Psychology, 70,* 1067–1074.

Foa, E. B., & Rothbaum, B. O. (1998). *Treating the trauma of rape: Cognitive-behavioral therapy for PTSD.* New York: Guilford.

Follette, V. M., Ruzek, J. I., & Abueg, F. R. (Eds.) (1998). *Cognitive-behavioral therapy for trauma.* New York: Guilford.

Ouimette, P., & Brown, P. J. (2003). *Trauma and substance abuse: Causes, consequences, and treatment of comorbid disorders.* Washington, DC: American Psychological Association.

9

Increasing Identity and Relational Functioning

As noted in Chapter 2, trauma can produce chronic problems in identity and interpersonal relatedness, above and beyond posttraumatic stress, cognitive distortions, and affect dysregulation. Most typically associated with a history of ongoing and severe childhood abuse and neglect (Cole & Putnam, 1992; Pearlman & Courtois, 2005; Schore, 2003), identity and relational disturbance is often viewed by clinicians as evidence of a personality (especially "borderline") disorder. Although there is a significant link between trauma and some forms of enduring psychological disturbance, not all problems in this area necessarily relate to a dysfunctional personality, per se. In many cases, they represent reactions, accommodations, or coping strategies developed in the face of chronic childhood maltreatment.

With the exception of models developed by Cloitre, Koenen, Cohen, and Han (2002), Linehan (1993a), Najavits (2002), and a few others, most cognitive-behavioral trauma therapies focus solely on treating cognitive or posttraumatic stress symptoms. However, many survivors of multiple, complex traumas present with significant—often highly distressing—difficulties in identity and interpersonal functioning. As a result, we recommend interventions that address these areas as well.

Identity Problems

Survivors of early and severe childhood trauma often complain of problems associated with an inability to access, and gain from, an internal sense of self. This may present, for example, as problems in:

- Determining one's own needs or entitlements
- Maintaining a consistent sense of self or identity in the context of strong emotions or the presence of compelling others
- Having an internal reference point at times of stress
- Predicting one's own reactions or behavior in various situations
- Being one's "own best friend," that is, having direct access to a positive sense of self

Many of these difficulties are thought to develop in the first years of life, when the parent-child attachment relationship is disrupted by caretaker aggression or, somewhat paradoxically, neglect (Allen, 2001; Hesse, Main, Abrams, & Rifkin, 2003). In addition to possible negative impacts on the developing child's psychobiology (for example, reducing the orbitofrontal cortex's capacity to regulate cortical and autonomic processes; Schore, 1994, 1996; Siegel, 1999), childhood abuse and neglect can motivate the development of adaptations and defenses that, in turn, reduce the child's development of a coherent sense of self.

Although the reasons for identity disturbance in survivors of childhood trauma are no doubt complex, probable etiologies include early dissociation, other-directedness, and the absence of benign interactions with others (Briere, 2002a). Dissociating or otherwise avoiding trauma-related distress early in life is likely to block the survivor's awareness of his or her internal state at the very time that a sense of self is thought to develop in children. Further, the hypervigilance needed by the endangered child in order to ensure survival means that much of his or her attention is directed outward, a process that detracts from internal awareness. In this context, when introspection (which is probably necessary for the development of an internal model of self; Stern, 1985) occurs, it is punished, since (1) such inward focus takes attention away from the environment and, therefore, increases danger, and (2) greater internal awareness means—in the context of ongoing trauma—greater emotional pain. Finally, most theories of self-capacities stress the role of benign others in the child's development of an internal model of self (Bowlby, 1988). One may have to interact with positive others in order to form a coherent and positive sense of oneself. This is thought to occur when the loving and attuned parent or caretaker reflects back to the child what the child appears to be feeling or experiencing (for example, smiling when the infant smiles, or appearing concerned when the infant cries), responds to the child's needs in a way that reinforces the child's legitimacy, and treats the child in such a manner that he or she can infer positive self-characteristics. As the child develops into an adolescent, and then an adult, the growing complexity of his or her interactions with the social environment ideally bestows a growing sense of self in the context of others. Unfortunately, this progression into increasingly coherent identity may be less possible for those who were deprived of positive parenting.

Intervention

Because much of self-development appears to involve interactions with caring others, the therapeutic relationship can be a powerful environment in which the client's sense of identity may evolve. In this context, the clinician works to provide safety, support self-validity, and encourage self-exploration.

Providing Safety

Introspection is, ultimately, a luxury that can only occur when the external environment does not require hypervigilance. For this reason, the clinical setting should promulgate those aspects of safety previously outlined in this book. Not only should the client feel physically safe, that is, from the therapist and (at least temporarily) from the world, he or she should experience psychological safety—the clinician should be psychologically noninvasive, careful to honor the client's boundaries (regardless of whether the client is yet aware of them), and reliable enough to communicate stability and security. When these conditions are met, the client is more likely to trust the environment enough to explore his or her internal thoughts, feelings, and experiences and, as noted later in this chapter, form a more positive attachment to the therapist. The process of actually discovering that one is safe in treatment, however, may be protracted—as noted earlier, many survivors of severe childhood or adult trauma experiences may have to be in treatment for some time before they are able to accurately perceive the safety inherent in the session (Allen, 2001). Even then, this sense of relative safety may wax and wane throughout therapy.

Supporting Self-Validity

Also helpful is the therapist's visible acceptance of the client's needs and perceptions as intrinsically valid, and the therapist's communication to the client regarding the client's basic relational entitlements (Herman, 1992a). To some extent, this might appear to contradict the need to challenge the client's negative self-perceptions and other cognitive distortions. However, the approach advocated in this book is not to argue with the client regarding his or her "thinking errors" about self, but rather to work with the client in such a way that the he or she is able to perceive incorrect assumptions and reconsider them in light of his or her current (therapy-based) relational experience. Although the therapist typically will not validate the client's self-rejection (for example, the belief that one does not have entitlement to respectful and caring treatment by others), he or she will provide a therapeutic experience that contradicts such thoughts. This is, in some ways, a form of the disparity described in Chapter 7: although the client may view himself or herself as not having rights to self-determination, these self-perceptions will be contrary to the experience of acceptance and positive regard experienced in the therapeutic session. Such cognitions, when not reinforced by the clinician, are likely to decrease over time. Equally important, as the message of self-as-valid is repeatedly communicated to the client by the therapist's behavior, client notions of undeservingness and unacceptability are relationally contradicted.

This general focus on the client's entitlements can help to reverse the other-directness the survivor learned in the context of abuse or neglect (Briere, 1996). During most childhood abuse, attention is typically focused on the abuser's needs, the likelihood that he or she will be violent, and, ultimately, on the abuser's view of reality. In such a context, the child's needs or reality are irrelevant, if not dangerous when asserted. In a client-focused environment, however, reality becomes more what the client needs or perceives than what the therapist demands or expects. In such an environment, the client is more able to identify internal states, perceptions, and needs, and discover how to "hang on to" these aspects of self even when in the presence of meaningful others (that is, the therapist). By stressing to the client that his or her experience is the ultimate focus, and by helping the client to identify and label his or her internal feelings and needs, the therapist helps the client to build a coherent and positive model of self—much in the way parents would have, had the client's childhood been more safe, attuned, and supportive.

Encouraging Self-Exploration

By facilitating self-exploration and self-reference (as opposed to defining self primarily in terms of others'—including the therapist's—expectations or reactions), therapy can allow the survivor to gain a greater sense of his or her internal topography. Increased self-awareness may be fostered particularly when the client is repeatedly asked about his or her ongoing internal experience throughout the course of treatment. This may include (as described in Chapter 7) multiple, gentle inquiries about the client's early perceptions and experiences, his or her feelings and reactions during and after victimization experiences, and what his or her thoughts and conclusions are regarding the ongoing process of treatment. Equally important, however, is the need for the client to discover, quite literally, what he or she thinks and feels about current things, both trauma related and otherwise. Because the external-directedness necessary to survive victimization generally works against self-understanding and identity, the survivor should be encouraged to explore his or her own likes and dislikes, views regarding self and others, entitlements and obligations, and related phenomena in the context of therapeutic support and acceptance. This more broad, less specifically trauma-focused intervention is, to some extent, "identity training": providing the survivor with the opportunity to discover what he or she thinks and feels, as distinct from what others think and feel.

The therapist's consistent and ongoing support for introspection, self-exploration, and self-identification allows the client to develop a more articulated and accessible internal sense of self. Ultimately, the therapist takes on the role of the supportive, engaged, helpful attachment figure whose primary interest—beyond symptom resolution—is the development of the client's internal life and self-determinism. This process, although less anchored in specific therapeutic techniques or protocols, can be one of the more important aspects of treatment.

Relational Disturbance

The perspective offered in this book is that many of the relationship problems experienced by traumatized people arise from early learning about—and accommodation to—a harsh interpersonal world. Although such difficulties may occur as a result of chronic interpersonal traumas in adulthood (for example, ongoing domestic violence, torture, or living in a chronically dangerous environment), they are seen far more often in the context of earlier childhood maltreatment (Pearlman & Courtois, 2005). One of the earliest impacts of abuse and neglect is thought to be on the child's internal representations of self and others (Allen, 2001), based on how he or she is treated by his or her caretakers. In the case of abuse or neglect, these inferences are likely to be especially negative. For example, the child who is being maltreated may conclude that he or she must be intrinsically unacceptable or malignant to deserve such punishment or disregard, or may come to see himself or herself as helpless, inadequate, or weak. As well, this negative context may mean that the abused or neglected child comes to view others as inherently dangerous, rejecting, or unavailable.

These early inferences about self and others often form a generalized set of expectations and assumptions, sometimes described as *internal working models* (Bowlby, 1982) or *relational schemas* (Baldwin, Fehr, Keedian, Seidel, & Thompson, 1993). Such core understandings are often relatively nonresponsive to verbal information or the expressed views of others later in life, since they are encoded in the first years of life, and thus are preverbal in nature. For example, the individual who believes, based on early learning, that he or she is unlikable or unattractive to others, or that others are not to be trusted, will not easily change such views based on other people's declarations that the person is valued by them or that they can be relied upon.

Such memory is often referred to as *implicit,* involving largely nonverbal and nonautobiographical memories that cannot be recalled, per se, but can be triggered by reminiscent stimuli in the current environment (see Siegel, 1999, for a discussion). As a result, most people have "infantile amnesia" for these early relational memories—although such memories can trigger cognitions and conditioned emotional responses (CERs), they cannot be consciously recalled as part of the past.

The quality and valence of these core schemas are thought to affect the individual's later capacity to form and maintain meaningful connections and attachments with other people (Bowlby, 1988). As a result, formerly abused or neglected individuals may find themselves in conflictual or chaotic relationships later in life, may have problems with forming intimate adult attachments, and may engage in behaviors that are likely to threaten or disrupt close relationships (Allen, 2001). These core schemas are often referred to as *attachment styles.* The reader is encouraged to read modern texts on attachment theory (for example, Collins & Read, 1990; Simpson & Rholes, 1998; Solomon & Siegel, 2003), since the lessons learned by the child during early parent-child attachment are clearly relevant to dysfunctional interpersonal behavior in traumatized adolescents and adults (Alexander, 1992; Carlson, 1998; Coe, Dalenberg, Aransky, & Reto, 1995).

Because relational schema (or internal working models) are typically encoded at the implicit, nonverbal level, and are primarily based in safety and attachment needs, they may not be evident except in situations where the survivor perceives interpersonal threats similar to the abuse, such as rejection, abandonment, criticism, or physical danger. When this occurs, these underlying cognitions may be triggered with resultant negative affect and interpersonal difficulties (Simpson & Rholes, 1994). For example, an individual who experienced early separation or abandonment may relate relatively well in a given occupational or intimate context until he or she encounters stimuli that suggest (or are in some way reminiscent of) rejection, empathic disattunement, or abandonment. These perceived experiences, by virtue of their similarity to early trauma, may then trigger memories, emotions (CERs), and cognitions that, although excessive or out of proportion in the immediate context, are appropriate to the feelings and thoughts of an abused or neglected child (Briere, 2002a). This activation may then motivate behavior that, although intended to ensure proximity and to maintain the relationship, is so characterized by "primitive" (that is, child-level) responses and demands, and so affectively laden that it challenges or even destroys that relationship.

The most dramatic example of chronic relational trauma activations may be what is referred to as "borderline personality disorder." As noted in Chapter 2, those individuals with borderline personality features are often described as prone to (1) sudden emotional outbursts in response to minor or imagined interpersonal provocation, (2) self-defeating cognitions, (3) feelings of emptiness and intense dysphoria, and (4) impulsive, tension-reducing behaviors that are triggered by perceptions of having been abandoned, rejected, or maltreated by another person (American Psychiatric Association, 2000). A fair portion of such behavior and symptomatology can be seen as arising from triggered relational memories and CERs associated with early abuse, abandonment, rejection, or lack of parental responsiveness, generally in the context of reduced affect regulation capacities. The "borderline" individual, upon having abuse memories triggered by stimuli in adult relational contexts, may then attempt to avoid the associated distress by engaging in activities such as substance abuse, inappropriate proximity seeking (for example, neediness or attempts to forestall abandonment), or involvement in distracting, tension-reducing behaviors.

Intervention

The interventions for relational disturbance parallel, to some extent, those outlined in Chapters 7 and 8. In the relational context, however, the various components of trauma processing occur more directly as a function of the therapeutic relationship. Because most disturbed relatedness appears to arise from maltreatment early in life, and is often triggered by later interpersonal stimuli, it is not surprising that the most effective interventions for relational problems are, in fact, relational as well. As stated by a trauma survivor in Kohlenberg and Tsai (1998), "If bad relationships messed me up, then it follows that I need good relationships to help me heal" (p. 305). Far from being the nonspecific placebo effect or inert ingredient suggested by some advocates of short-term therapy, the relationship between client and therapist can be seen as directly and specifically curative.

Among other things, the therapeutic relationship is a powerful source of interpersonal triggers. As the connection between client and therapist grows, the client's increasing attachment to the therapist can increasingly trigger implicit (nonverbal, sensory, or experiential) memories of attachment experiences in childhood. For many clients, these early attachment memories include considerable abuse or neglect, which may be reexperienced in the form of maltreatment-related thoughts and feelings during therapy. Such emergent, largely implicit "relational flashbacks" do not contain contextual information that they represent the past (Siegel, 1999), and thus are often misperceived as being feelings related to the current therapist-client relationship (what cognitive theorists sometimes call a "source attribution error"). Once activated and expressed, such cognitions and emotions can be discussed and processed in the context of the safety, soothing, and support associated with a positive therapeutic relationship.

As in work with more "simple" traumatic memories, the therapeutic processing of relational memories and their associations (for example, CERs and attachment-level cognitions) can be seen as involving the exposure, activation, disparity, and counterconditioning described in the previous chapter.

Exposure

In the session, the client reexperiences implicit memories of earlier interpersonal traumas in response to therapeutic stimuli that are in some way similar to those early experiences.

Therapy stimuli that can trigger exposure to relational memories, by virtue of their similarity to the original trauma, include the clinician's physical appearance, his or her age, sex, or race, and the power differential between client and therapist (including client feelings of vulnerability). Even positive feelings associated with the therapeutic relationship can trigger distress—the client's loving feelings toward the therapist (or perception of similar feelings from the clinician) can activate sexual feelings or fears, and perceptions of therapist caring and acceptance can trigger fears of losing such experiences (that is, of abandonment by an attachment figure). As well, therapists are inevitably prey to the vagaries of normal human experience, including momentary lapses in empathic attunement, distraction by personal problems, fatigue, or, as described in Chapter 4, the triggering of their own issues by some aspect of the client's presentation—any of which may inadvertently expose the client to memories of earlier maltreatment or neglect.

Beyond these discrete triggers, the therapeutic relationship itself—by virtue of its ongoing nature and importance to the client—may replicate stimulus conditions similar to those of early important relationships, including the client's childhood need for attachment. To the extent that the earlier relationship was characterized by trauma, the current therapeutic relationship is likely to trigger negative relational memories.

Just as noted in previous chapters for more simple trauma processing, exposure must occur within the context of the therapeutic window. In this regard, the clinician may have to work actively, and pay careful attention, to ensure that his or her stimulus value or the characteristics of the therapeutic relationship do not produce so much exposure to negative relational memories that the client becomes overwhelmed. Just as the therapist treating PTSD may titrate the amount of exposure the client undergoes regarding a traumatic memory, the clinician treating relational traumas ideally seeks to ensure that reminiscent aspects of the therapeutic environment are not overwhelming.

For example, as noted in Chapter 4, clients with easy accessible schemas arising from punitive parenting may require treatment that especially avoids any sense of therapist judgment. Similarly, the client who has been physically or sexually assaulted may require (1) special, visible attention to safety issues, (2) therapist responses that stress boundary awareness and respect, or even (3) a greater-than-normal physical distance between the client's chair and the therapist's. A client with abandonment issues arising from early psychological neglect, on the other hand, may be more comfortable when the clinician is especially attuned and psychologically available to the client. On a more general level, therapists of chronically traumatized clients may need to devote even greater attention than usual to avoiding behaviors that in some way appear to involve intrusion, control, or narcissism.

Unfortunately, some characteristics of the therapist may be such powerful triggers that useful therapy is not always possible. Probably the best example of this is therapist gender. Many women who have been recently sexually assaulted by a man or men have considerable difficulty working in therapy with a male clinician. In some cases, regardless of the therapist's personal qualities and best intentions, his masculine stimulus value may trigger overwhelming exposure to trauma memories of assault by a male, thereby exceeding the therapeutic window and negating the possibility of meaningful intervention (Briere, 1996). In such cases, the best solution is usually to refer the client to a woman therapist. Similar scenarios may occur when the therapist's ethnic or racial identity is the same as the client's perpetrator, or where the therapy location (for example, a hospital) overwhelmingly triggers trauma memories in the client (for example, of being tortured in a similar facility in his or her country of origin).

More typically, however, therapeutic stimuli are titratable, and therefore the relationship is more able to be helpful. Such adjustment does not mean that the therapist generally undershoots the therapeutic window with regard to interpersonal trauma. It is almost inevitable that the therapeutic relationship will trigger the client's relational memories, if only because of the importance that therapy has for him or her, and because such treatment regularly involves themes of shared experience, attachment, intimacy, and vulnerability.

Activation

As a result of therapeutic exposure, the client experiences emotions and thoughts that occurred at the time of the relational trauma.

Activated emotional responses to early relational memories are often notable for the suddenness of their emergence, their intensity, and their seeming contextual inappropriateness. Intrusive negative cognitions about self or the therapist may be activated, or attachment-related schema involving submission, childlike perceptions, or dependency may suddenly appear. In some cases, such activation may also trigger sensory flashbacks and dissociative responses.

Cognitive-emotional activation can be easily understood by both client and therapist when it occurs in the context of discrete trauma memories, such as those of an assault or disaster. When activation occurs in the context of triggered relational stimuli, however, the actual "reason" behind the client's thoughts and feelings may be far less clear. Because the original trauma memory may have been formed in the first years of life, and therefore is not available to conscious (explicit) awareness, neither client not therapist may know why the client is feeling especially anxious or angry, or why he or she is suddenly so distrustful of the clinician. In fact, in instances where such activations are dramatic, they may appear so irrational and contextually inappropriate that they are seen by some as evidence of significant psychopathology, perhaps even psychosis. Ultimately, however, these activations are logical, in the sense that they represent conditioned cognitive-emotional responses to triggered relational memories.

Cognitive-emotional activation is especially relevant to longer-term, more intensive psychotherapy, wherein the triggering of client attachment responses (both positive and negative) is more likely. An example of the activation of relational trauma memories and associated negative schema is presented in Briere (2002a):

[A] 24-year-old woman with a long history of emotional abuse by her narcissistic father . . . enters therapy with an older male clinician. Although the client initially views her therapist as supportive and caring, she soon comes to feel increasing distrust toward [him], begins to see subtle "put-downs" in his remarks, and eventually finds herself angry at the therapist's perceived lack of empathy, lapses in attunement and caring, and judgmental behavior. (p. 194)

In this example, the seemingly benign relationship between client and clinician contains stimuli (for example, the growing feeling of emotional intimacy as treatment progresses) that trigger childhood abuse memories and activate trauma-specific cognitive-emotional responses. In agreement with many psychodynamic theorists, we suggest that such activation of relational memories and feelings should be expected when treating those with childhood (and extended adult) traumas and is, in fact, often necessary for the successful resolution of chronic interpersonal problems. Absent such relational activation, therapy might be easier to conduct but would be unlikely to activate the very material that has to be processed before the client's relational life can significantly improve.

Disparity

Although the client thinks and feels as if maltreatment or abandonment is either happening or is about to happen during treatment, in reality, the session is safe and the therapist is not abusive, rejecting, or otherwise dangerous.

Although this component is often critical to trauma processing, those who have been victimized interpersonally—especially if that victimization was chronic—may find disparity difficult to fully accept at first, let alone trust. There are a number of reasons for this. First, those exposed to chronic danger often come to assume that such danger is inevitable. The battered woman, combat veteran, or prostitute, for example, may find it very difficult to accept that the rules have suddenly changed and that he or she is safe—especially in situations that bear some similarity to the original (dangerous) context, such as in a relationship with a powerful other. Second, in many cases, the original perpetrator(s) of violence promised safety, caring, or support as a way to gain access to the victim. As a result, reassurance or declarations of safety may seem like just "more of the same," if not a warning of impending danger. Finally, therapy implicitly requires some level of intimacy, or at least vulnerability from the client; a requirement that—from the survivor's perspective—can be a recapitulation of past experience of intimate demands and subsequent injuries.

For these and related reasons, not only must disparity/safety be present, but the client must be able to perceive it. Although occasionally frustrating for the therapist, this sometimes means that considerable time in therapy is necessary before sufficient trust is present to allow true relational processing.

For example, the survivor of extended political torture, warfare, or gang violence may require months of weekly therapy before "letting down his or her guard" enough to fully participate in trauma therapy. Similarly, the therapist should be prepared in such cases for client disbelief or immediate rejection of statements like "You are safe here" or "I won't go away." This does not mean that the clinician shouldn't make such statements (when they are accurate, and expressed in a nonintrusive, nondemanding way), but rather should understand that such declarations rarely alter cognitions that have been repeatedly reinforced by prior adversity and may be nonverbally encoded.

In fact, for those hypervigilant to danger in interpersonal situations, disparity cannot be communicated; it must be demonstrated. As noted earlier, therapist statements that he or she should be trusted can have the opposite effect on traumatized clients—because they have heard similar promises or protestations from ill-meaning people in the past, such statements may make them feel less safe, not more. Instead, when working with chronic relational trauma survivors, the therapist typically must behave in a reliably safe and nonexploitive way over time, until the client can truly extrapolate safety into the future and imagine disparity.

The exposure/activation/disparity process may proceed in a stepwise fashion for the relational trauma survivor: early in therapy, he or she may occasionally (and often inadvertently) reveal some small degree of vulnerability or suffering to the therapist, and then reflexively expect a negative consequence. When this vulnerability is not, in fact, punished by the therapist and (as noted in the next section) is met with support and some carefully titrated level of visible caring, the client may slowly lower his or her psychological barriers (including his or her avoidance strategies) and express more thoughts or feelings. As these responses are likewise supported, and not exploited or punished, the client's willingness to process pain in "real time" (that is, directly, in the presence of the therapist) generally increases. It should be stressed that this may take time, and therapist expressions of impatience may, ironically, subvert the process by communicating criticism, rejection, or even naccissism.

In other cases—for example, when the client has experienced less extreme or less chronic relational trauma, when the conditions surrounding the victimization are clearly quite different (and perceivable as such by the client) than the current ones in therapy, or when there were supportive people in the client's environment in addition to the perpetrator(s)—disparity may be considerably easier to establish and trauma processing may be more immediately possible. In any case, however, this is an assessment issue, as opposed to something that can be automatically assumed. Failing accurate assessment, the hypervigilant or otherwise overly fearful client will not gain from full exposure-activation activities; in fact, exposure may be counterindicated until disparity has been reliably demonstrated.

Counterconditioning

Not only is the client able to perceive safety in the therapy session, he or she experiences fear-diminishing emotional states in the context of the therapeutic relationship.

When counterconditioning was described in Chapter 8, the healing aspect of this phenomenon was described as the simultaneous presence of both (1) the activated distress associated with traumatic memory exposure and (2) the positive feelings engendered by a supportive, caring therapy environment. When relational trauma is being processed, counterconditioning is potentially even more important. In this regard, activated negative relational cognitions (for example, "He/She doesn't like me," "He/She will hurt/abandon me," or "I'll be taken advantage of if I become vulnerable") and feelings (for example, associated fear of authority figures or intimacy) are directly—and, therefore, potentially more efficiently—contradicted by positive relational experiences. In other words, there may be something especially helpful about having fears and expectations of maltreatment in the specific context of nurturance and acceptance. In the language of earlier psychodynamic theory, such real-time contradiction of activated schemas and feelings may provide a *corrective emotional experience* (Alexander et al., 1946).

There is also a potential downside to the juxtaposition of negative expectations and positive experiences in therapy, however. Just as positive experiences in therapy may contradict earlier held beliefs about close relationships, it is also true that activated, negative relational cognitions can prevent the client from identifying and accessing the positive relational phenomena that occur in therapy. Fortunately, this is rarely an all-or-none experience; in most cases, even distrustful or hypervigilant clients will slowly come to reevaluate negative relational cognitions when therapist support and validation are visibly and reliably present. As is the case for client difficulties in perceiving therapeutic safety, the incremental process of "letting in" therapeutic caring and positive regard (and, thereby, positive attachment experiences) may require considerable time in treatment.

Clients involved in longer-term psychotherapy may experience an even more powerful form of counterconditioning than therapist support and caring. This is often described as a sense of deeper warmth and connectedness between client and therapist: an affective state that seems to be especially supportive of trauma processing. Although this phenomenon is difficult to quantify or identify empirically, we, like others (for example, Siegel, 2003), suspect that such responses represent the activation of relatively inborn, attachment-level emotions and cognitions.

Beginning relatively soon after the birth of a child—in the absence of intervening problems—both parent and infant typically experience very positive emotions toward one another. These feelings and their associated cognitions are likely to constitute an evolutionarily derived survival function (Bowlby, 1982). Not only does the child seek proximity to the parent in order to avoid the pain of separation, but also, we suggest, to activate biologically based positive feelings triggered by parent-child relatedness and intimacy. Similarly, the parent maintains attachment to the child because, among other reasons, separation from the child hurts, while proximity to the child produces positive emotions. This mutual desire for parent-child proximity maximizes the likelihood that the child will be fed and protected, thereby supporting the ongoing survival of the species.

Although the notion of an inborn reward system for attachment is somewhat speculative, recent research indicates that positive attachment experiences appear to activate dopaminergic and beta-endorphin reward systems (Schore, 2003). It is likely that these physiologic systems of reward for intimacy and connectedness are available to humans throughout their lives, and can be triggered in contexts where there is sustained proximity to a caring and nurturing person. When activated in parent-child dyads, major friendship, or sexual relationships, this phenomenon is usually called *love*. A similar feeling may be present when such activation occurs in nurturing, longer-term psychotherapy—something that psychoanalysts consider a form of transference, and that we will refer to, for lack of a better phrase, as *attachment activation*.

To the extent that attachment activation occurs during the process of ongoing psychotherapy, several outcomes are likely. First, the positive and sustained feelings engendered by triggered inborn attachment responses are likely to be especially effective in counterconditioning negative thoughts and feelings associated with previous traumatic experiences. Second, attachment activation may produce other kinds of child-parent thoughts, feelings, and behaviors in the client—responses that must be monitored carefully for their impacts on treatment. For example, the client may become more dependent and "childlike" as the therapeutic relationship continues and deepens. He or she may begin to request more contact with the therapist, make more phone calls to him or her, and in other ways seek greater proximity. Third, those clients whose early attachment experiences were especially insecure or otherwise problematic may find that the therapeutic relationship becomes a powerful trigger for reliving of these early relational traumas.

In some cases, this type of transformation may appear problematic, as the client "regresses" to a more basic level of relational functioning with the therapist. However, it is important that the therapist understand this as attachment-level reliving, in the same way as emotionally processing an assault in the session is reliving. As described earlier, the goal is to work within the therapeutic window—providing sufficient relational contact, support, and positive regard that the client has the opportunity to reexperience implicit childhood memories in the context of a distress-diminishing, nurturative state. At the same time, however, the clinician must not provide so much quasi-parental support that early trauma-related distress is too strongly activated, or the client's dependency needs are reinforced in a way that is detrimental to growth. The latter is probably best prevented by the therapist's continuous examination of his or her own needs to protect and/or rescue the client. In addition, obviously, the possible emergence of attachment-level feelings in the therapist requires special vigilance to the possibility of inappropriate sexualization or romanticization of the client, or exploitation of the client to meet the therapist's unmet attachment (including parenting) needs (Chu, 1992; Herman, 1992a). Any such "countertransference" (referred to as *counteractivation* in the self-trauma model), if acted upon, both destroys disparity (that is, eliminates safety) and reinforces or augments trauma-related CERs and cognitions.

Desensitization

The client's repeated exposure to relational trauma memories, triggered by his or her relationship with the therapist, in combination with the reliable nonreinforcement and counterconditioning of his or her negative expectation and feelings by the therapeutic relationship, leads to a disruption of the learned connection between relatedness and danger.

As described in Chapter 8, the process of exposure, activation, disparity, and counterconditioning, when repeated sufficiently in the context of the therapeutic window, often leads to the desensitization of trauma memories. This probably involves a series of processes, including (1) extinction of nonreinforced emotional responses (for example, CERs), via disparity, (2) counterconditioning effects, involving some form of "overwriting" the association between memory and emotional pain with new connections between memory and more positive feelings (for example, those associated with support and caring), and (3) an alteration in the capacity of relational stimuli to trigger trauma memories (that is, insight or new information that changes the client's interpretation of interpersonal events). Regarding the last point, positive therapeutic experiences may change the ability of relationships or interpersonal intimacy to automatically trigger early abuse memories, since relationship, per se, is no longer perceived as necessarily dangerous and therefore is less reminiscent of childhood abuse or neglect.

However this occurs, the overall effect of the progressive activation and processing of implicit relational memories and their cognitive and emotional associations is to change the client's reaction to his or her interpersonal world. Successful therapy, in this regard, means that the client is more able to enter into and sustain positive interpersonal relationships, because connection with others no longer triggers the same levels of fear, anger, distrust, and negative or avoidant behaviors. As a result, the client's interpersonal life can become more fulfilling and less chaotic—a source of support rather than of continuing stress or pain.

Suggested Reading

Allen, J. (2001). *Traumatic relationships and serious mental disorder.* Chichester, UK: Wiley.

Linehan, M. M. (1993). *Cognitive-behavioral treatment of borderline personality disorder.* New York: Guilford.

McCann, I. L., & Pearlman, L. A. (1990). *Psychological trauma and the adult survivor: Theory, therapy, and transformation.* New York: Brunner/Mazel.

Pearlman , L. A., & Courtois, C. A. (2005). Clinical application of the attachment framework: Relational treatment of complex trauma. *Journal of Traumatic Stress, 18,* 449–459.

Simpson, J. A., & Rholes, W. S. (Eds.). (1998). *Attachment theory and close relationships.* New York: Guilford.

Solomon, M. F., & Siegel, D. (2003). *Healing trauma: Attachment, mind, body, and brain.* New York: Norton.

10

Treating the Effects
of Acute Trauma

Catherine Scott, Janelle Jones, and John Briere

A lthough much of this book has been concerned with the treatment of chronic trauma-related distress, also important are the needs of those who have been exposed to relatively recent traumatic events. Yet, we know less about treating symptomatic trauma survivors immediately after the event than we do about helping them months or years later, when some of them have developed posttraumatic stress disorder (PTSD) or other chronic syndromes. This is unfortunate, since acute posttraumatic stress can be painful and debilitating, whether or not it transforms into an enduring psychological disorder.

As we discuss in this chapter, there are fewer well-validated treatment strategies for acute stress disorder (ASD) than for chronic posttraumatic presentations. In fact, most interventions for acute traumatic stress are modifications of treatments for PTSD, based on the assumption that what is helpful when posttraumatic stress has become chronic will also be helpful for more acute responses. Although this approach is generally valid, there are significant differences in how most people experience acute, as opposed to sustained, traumatic stress. These differences often require a somewhat different intervention strategy.

This chapter reviews the literature on acute stress, and provides an overview of how treatment should be modified to take into account the special needs of the acute trauma victim. The reader may wish to review Chapter 4, which discusses a philosophical approach to this work. In addition, the reader is referred to Chapters 7 and 8 on cognitive and exposure-based treatment, since the current chapter draws heavily from the strategies presented earlier in this book.

In the context of PTSD, the term *acute* generally refers to symptoms emerging in the first 3 months following a traumatic event. Since the introduction of the diagnosis of ASD in 1994, however, it is also used to describe reactions within the first month of a traumatic event. In this chapter, we use the term in its broadest sense, to refer to responses that occur within the first several days, weeks, or months following trauma exposure.

Research on Acute Traumatic Stress

Since the introduction of the diagnosis of ASD to *Diagnostic and Statistical Manual of Mental Disorder* (*DSM-IV-TR;* American Psychiatric Association, 2000) there has been growing interest in acute traumatic stress. Most published articles in this area discuss the phenomenology of ASD and risk factors associated with the development of PTSD, however, rather than intervention strategies or approaches.

Acute Symptoms and Risk for PTSD

As noted in earlier chapters, many acute trauma victims who present initially to mental health professionals recover "naturally"; their posttraumatic symptoms decrease over time, even in the absence of treatment (for example, Norris et al., 2002; Rothbaum, Foa, Riggs, Murdock, & Walsh, 1992). Nevertheless, data from several different sources indicate that about 80 percent of those whose symptoms are initially severe enough to meet criteria for ASD will have PTSD 6 months later; in fact, 60–70 percent will have PTSD 2 years following the event (Bryant & Harvey, 2000).

The high risk of lasting distress for those trauma survivors who develop ASD—as well as the acute distress and dysfunction associated with most ASD presentations—underscores the potential benefit of early intervention in posttraumatic symptomatology. Unfortunately, despite ongoing research, the specific nature of these interventions, as well as their ideal timing, is not entirely clear. For example, as noted in Chapter 11, the few studies of medications used in the initial days and hours after a trauma to prevent PTSD have to this point been equivocal. Similarly, as discussed following, the widespread use of psychological "debriefing" techniques has not been shown to be especially helpful in treating acute stress or preventing PTSD. Fortunately, a growing body of literature suggests that other approaches can be beneficial in the treatment of ASD and may decrease the likelihood of later PTSD.

The Literature on Interventions for Acute Stress

Debriefing

Psychological debriefing was initially developed as a way to intervene with large numbers of trauma survivors in circumstances where individual evaluation and treatment is not possible, such as during war or after terrorist attacks or natural disasters. As early as World War II, debriefing was described as a method of helping soldiers to "purge" themselves of the distress related to battle experiences (Bisson, McFarlane, & Rose, 2000).

Critical Incident Stress Debriefing. There are several models of debriefing; the most commonly used is Critical Incident Stress Debriefing (CISD), a structured protocol developed by Mitchell (1983). CISD is used quite frequently with rescuers, first responders, and law enforcement personnel after major traumatic events. For example, after the terrorist attacks of September 11, 2001, CISD was widely applied to groups of people who were directly exposed to the disaster, who lived or worked nearby, or who were otherwise affected by the attacks but did not witness or experience the event itself.

CISD is typically conducted in a group setting with 10 to 20 people, although there also are protocols for individual debriefing. Sessions last anywhere from 1 to 3 hours, and are usually conducted within a week of the trauma. Participants are asked to describe in detail their experiences of the trauma, to formulate a cognitive appraisal and interpretation of the event, and to express their emotional reactions. Group sharing is encouraged, with the intention of normalizing stress reactions as well as providing social support. Sessions end with a discussion of coping strategies and psychoeducation regarding possible future consequences of the event (Mitchell, 1983).

Unfortunately, despite anecdotal reports of its effectiveness in providing education and assistance to survivors, no clear benefit has been demonstrated for CISD. Two recent meta-analyses indicated that single-session debriefing does not protect against the development of PTSD (Rose, Bisson, & Wesley, 2002; van Emmerik, Kamphuis, Hulsbosch, & Emmelkamp, 2002). Non-CISD interventions—and no intervention at all—were both often associated with better outcomes than was CISD. In fact, in several studies, debriefing was found to have a potentially detrimental effect, with higher rates of PTSD at long-term follow-up (Mayou, Ehlers, & Hobbs, 2000).

There are several possible reasons why CISD might occasionally have deleterious effects. First, CISD in group settings often involves individuals with different trauma exposure histories, levels of distress, symptomatology, and risk for PTSD. In such situations, some individuals may be retraumatized or additionally distressed by hearing the experiences of others before they have processed and integrated their own reactions. Second, although CISD is intended to normalize and validate emotional responses, in some cases it may lead to stigmatization, for example, when certain individuals have visibly more extreme reactions to the traumatic event than others, and, as a result, perceive themselves (or are perceived by others in the group) as psychologically disturbed. Third, in some group settings—especially those in which members work closely together or depend upon each other for safety (such as in law enforcement)—expressing one's feelings and demonstrating fear and vulnerability may lead to group rejection and other interpersonal difficulties that decrease social support and lead to future job-related difficulties. Finally, to the extent that CISD is administered to all individuals in a unit or squad who were exposed to a potentially traumatic event, there are likely to be individuals who were not traumatized by the event, and who may therefore have negative reactions to being treated.

Proximity, Immediacy, and Expectancy. Another form of debriefing—Proximity, Immediacy, and Expectancy (PIE, also referred to as "Frontline Treatment"; Ritchie, Watson, & Friedman, in press)—is used in military settings, with the goal of returning injured soldiers to the front lines of war. PIE emphasizes the need to intervene with injured survivors as close to the front lines as possible (proximity), as promptly as possible (immediacy), and with the expectation of recovery upon return to the military unit (expectancy) (Jones & Wessely, 2003; Solomon & Benbenishty, 1986). This intervention also includes attention to basic needs and medical care, along with the opportunity for emotional ventilation and expression. The PIE model was used with Israeli soldiers in the 1982 Lebanon War with some apparent success (Solomon & Benbenishty, 1986). The concept of return to duty, which implies a return to the situation and circumstances of the original trauma, as well as to the possibility of further trauma exposure, is somewhat controversial, however. In the Vietnam War, for example, rapid return to duty was not associated with better mental health outcomes (Shalev, 2002). For some individuals, particularly those who are less traumatized, who have a more resilient underlying biology, or who are otherwise at low risk for posttraumatic symptomatology, it may be true that immediate reexposure hastens psychological recovery. However, for those who are overwhelmed by events, who lack sufficient affect regulation skills, or who have a biological vulnerability to stress, such reexposure may in fact be retraumatizing and harmful. The reader is referred to Jones and Wessely (2003) for a detailed and, ultimately, negative review of PIE in combat environments, including the suggestion that early estimates of its effectiveness were significantly overstated.

Other Acute Interventions

Defusing. Another, less common form of acute trauma intervention is referred to as "defusing." Defusing is a brief (typically 10–30 minute) "conversational" intervention, intended to provide support, reassurance, and information to trauma-exposed individuals in informal contexts (Ritchie et al., in press; Young, Ford, Ruzek, Friedman, & Gusman, 1998). Although little research data are available on this approach, one study of Swedish peacekeepers in Bosnia found that, in combination with peer support, defusing was associated with greater postservice mental health. This improvement did not occur, however, for those with the worst preservice psychological functioning. Although the results of this study are encouraging, further research is required to evaluate the efficacy of defusing, especially independent of the effects of peer support.

Psychological First Aid. Psychological First Aid (PFA) was developed by the Terrorism Disaster Branch of the National Child Traumatic Stress Network (NCTSN) and the National Center for PTSD (NCP). The *PFA Field Operations Guide*—a working document published in response to the need for written materials for those providing assistance after Hurricane Katrina in the U.S. Gulf region—can be downloaded from the NCP at http://www .ncptsd.va.gov/pfa/PFA.html. In contrast to debriefing techniques and defusing, PFA is not a specific therapeutic intervention. Instead, it outlines a modular framework for mental health professionals who provide individualized assistance to victims of natural disasters, terrorism, and other mass traumas.

PFA can be delivered in the field in diverse settings (such as shelters, hospitals, and mobile response units), and can be used with children, adolescents, and adults. Although modular, it is intended to be flexible, and the different components can be tailored to fit the specific needs of the individuals involved. The main goals of the intervention are to decrease the initial distress associated with exposure to trauma and to improve longer-term adaptive functioning.

The model emphasizes a nonintrusive, compassionate attitude on the part of clinicians. Notably, PFA discourages trauma debriefing in any form. Clinicians are encouraged to allow traumatized individuals to talk about their experiences as little or as much as they wish, but never to push for information or processing. The core components of PFA focus on practical assistance with immediate needs, providing safety and comfort, and establishing connections with primary support networks and social resources.

Cognitive-Behavioral Intervention

Generally in contrast to the approaches outlined previously, there is empirical evidence from several trials that a course of cognitive-behavioral therapy (CBT) in the weeks following a trauma can reduce the likelihood of subsequent PTSD—immediately posttreatment, at 6 months, and in one study, at 4 years posttrauma (for example, Bryant, Moulds, & Nixon, 2003; Bryant, Sackville, Dang, Moulds, & Guthrie, 1999; Echeburúa, De Corral, Sarasua, & Zubizarreta, 1996; Foa, Hearst-Ikeda, & Perry, 1995).

The first investigations of CBT for acute trauma survivors were conducted before the introduction of ASD as a diagnosis, and, as a result, included individuals who met symptomatic criteria for PTSD soon after trauma exposure. Initial results were not especially encouraging; interventions involving psychoeducation, anxiety management, cognitive techniques, and therapeutic exposure generally did not result in major, sustained symptom reduction relative to controls (Bryant & Harvey, 2000). However, many of these studies were limited by small sample sizes and widely varying degrees of impairment and symptomatology.

Later studies of CBT have shown more promise. In the first of two studies, Bryant, Harvey, Dang, & Sackville (1998) provided victims of motor vehicle or industrial accidents with five sessions of psychoeducation, anxiety management, prolonged exposure, *in vivo* exposure, and cognitive therapy. A control group received supportive counseling. Immediately posttreatment, as well as 6 months later, a significantly lower percentage of those who received CBT met PTSD diagnostic criteria as compared to controls. Bryant et al. (1999) next studied victims of more varied nonsexual traumas, who received cognitive and behavioral therapy, or supportive counseling. A similar pattern emerged, with a lower percentage of those who received prolonged exposure and cognitive interventions meeting PTSD criteria as compared to those receiving supportive treatment. Again, a significant difference remained between the two groups at a 6-month follow-up. However, 20 percent of the treatment group dropped out of the study, and the drop-outs were noted to have more severe ASD than therapy completers. Four years later, Bryant et al. (2003) reevaluated 41 of the participants from both of these studies and found that those who received supportive counseling were three times more likely to meet criteria for PTSD than the those receiving CBT; they also reported more intense and frequent posttraumatic symptoms overall. In a similar study, Ehlers et al. (2003) compared up to 12 sessions of CBT, use of a self-help booklet, and repeated clinician assessment in recent survivors of motor vehicle accidents (MVAs) who met criteria for PTSD. At 6 months follow-up, 11 percent of those who received CBT met criteria for PTSD, compared to 61 percent of the self-help group and 55 percent of those who received repeated assessments.

This literature suggests that CBT approaches can be effective in reducing symptoms and the risk of later PTSD in at least some of those suffering from ASD. Whether this effect is due to classic CBT or would occur with any treatment that involved therapeutic exposure to trauma memories is unclear. It should also be noted that the strongest studies with the largest samples have focused on survivors of motor vehicle accidents, disasters, and other noninterpersonal traumas. This makes it harder to generalize the results of such studies to the general clinical environment, since sexual and physical interpersonal traumas are often more common in clinical caseloads than are noninterpersonal events, can cause particularly severe symptoms, and generally lead to higher rates of PTSD. Although initial data are encouraging, more research is needed in this area to assess whether interventions that are helpful with acute survivors of MVAs and other noninterpersonal traumas are also helpful in victims of rape and domestic violence.

Intervention in Acute Posttraumatic Stress

The literature reviewed above, although generally limited to the treatment of screened samples of noninterpersonal trauma survivors in specialty clinics or, in some cases, battleground environments, provides important guidance for clinicians working with the acutely traumatized—in terms of both what one should and should not do. At the same time, however, these studies are similar to the cognitive-behavioral literature on treating more chronic posttraumatic disturbance in that they shed less light on the actual conduct of acute trauma therapy as it occurs in (and is constrained by) general clinical practice. The originators of the most effective interventions described in this chapter and elsewhere in this book are highly trained and specialized clinicians who devote much of their time to the study and treatment of acute trauma, often with relatively "pure" cases of ASD, in the context of relatively academic environments.

In contrast, most clinicians in the "real world" do not have such specialized training, and often deal with clients who (1) present with multiple old and new traumas and (2) frequently suffer from a broad range of comorbid, psychiatric conditions. In other words, the acute trauma survivor presenting to the average community mental health clinic is often someone who has a variety of needs—psychosocial, psychological, and sometimes physical or medical—for whom intervention ideally involves considerable assessment and carefully monitored treatment.

Given this complexity, and issues related to generalizability, the rest of this chapter is based on our clinical experience with acute trauma survivors in community mental health and trauma clinic settings, as informed by the existing psychological literature. The suggestions we offer, therefore, represent an attempt to balance empiricism with practicality, as is true for other chapters in this book.

Fortunately, once certain preconditions are met, much of the treatment of acute trauma parallels the intervention approach described in earlier chapters for more chronic posttraumatic reactions. For example, therapy continues to involve the steps of trauma processing outlined previously, that is, exposure, activation, disparity, counterconditioning, and extinction/resolution, as well as other cognitive-behavioral components, such as psychoeducation. However, when the client is an acute trauma survivor, assessment of readiness for treatment is a considerably larger issue, and the process of therapy requires even more attention to the appropriate focus, intensity, and pace of treatment.

Immediate Assessment

The evaluation of acutely traumatized individuals follows the general principles of assessment as presented in Chapter 3. It is especially important to remember that individual responses to acute trauma can differ dramatically and that there is no single, typical response—some survivors appear to be relatively unaffected, whereas others may have extreme and dramatic responses characterized by anger, tearfulness, erratic behavior, and tension reduction activities. Even seemingly asymptomatic responses can be deceiving, however, because an expressionless exterior may reflect dissociation, numbing, and significant internal distress. As a result, a common mistake made by evaluators is to assume that all of those who appear to be "in control" or otherwise euthymic soon after a trauma are necessarily coping well.

At the same time, however, the avoidant trauma survivor should not be forced or coerced into treatment, regardless of his or her inferred needs. High levels of dissociation or cognitive avoidance soon after a trauma may signal overwhelming distress and/or reduced affect regulation capacities. As noted in other chapters, too much (or sometimes any) exposure to traumatic memory in such cases may "overshoot the window" and retraumatize.

In general, we recommend that clinicians let acutely traumatized individuals talk as little or as much as they wish to during the assessment process. Pushing for details about the trauma, or encouraging victims to talk when they are reluctant to do so, should be avoided when possible. Obviously, however, certain issues are a critical part of assessment in the acute phase and may require some potentially intrusive questioning. The goal is to find a balance between providing gentle support while eliciting necessary information in a nonthreatening manner.

Critical issues to be assessed initially are among those described in Chapter 3. They include:

- *Physical safety.* Is there injury requiring medical attention? Does the individual have adequate access to shelter, clothing, and food? Does the victim of rape or domestic violence have a safe place to go, where he or she cannot be found by the perpetrator?
- *Suicidality.* Has the acute experience of personal loss, overwhelming shame, betrayal by an attachment figure, massively reduced function, or physical disfiguration resulted in suicidal thoughts and impulses? Is there a suicide plan? Are there methods (for example, pills, knives, guns) easily available?
- *Homicidality/potential for violence.* Has the trauma increased the likelihood of aggressive behavior, that is, in the service of revenge or punishment? Does the victim have access to a gun or other weapon? Is he or she making a credible threat? Does he or she have a history of violent behavior?
- *Psychosis.* Has the trauma resulted in psychotic symptoms? If so, do these symptoms interfere with his or her access to resources by impairing cognitive capacities and goal directedness? Do the symptoms place the individual at immediate risk for additional harm by impairing his or her judgment or understanding?
- *Other psychological debilitation.* Is the victim experiencing severe anxiety, depression, or dissociation such that his or her ability to behave in an appropriate, goal-directed manner is impaired? Is he or she overwhelmed or dramatically destabilized, either by extreme emotional distress or highly intrusive or debilitating posttraumatic stress symptoms?
- *Family or other sources of social support.* Are there relational or social resources available to the survivor that he or she can access in the acute aftermath of the trauma?
- *Trauma status.* Is the trauma over? The clinician may assume that a given trauma is now in the past, and thus is not a continuing threat. Unfortunately, many forms of interpersonal violence are repetitive and ongoing, resulting in both continuing danger to the victim and survival responses that may make psychotherapy difficult. Immediate assessment questions should include:
  - Does the perpetrator still have physical access to the victim?
  - Is the victim emotionally connected to the assailant in a way that will allow the assailant continuing access to him or her?

— If the perpetrator was arrested, was he or she incarcerated? If incarcerated, how long will he or she be imprisoned? Does the perpetrator have access to outside contacts who could still harm the victim?

Referral

Based on answers to these questions, immediate intervention may or may not be appropriate. When it is indicated, in many cases the clinician's first function is that of referral agent. If there are signs of significant psychological, medical, or psychosocial difficulties, the clinician will typically act on assessment by triaging to appropriate resources. For example:

- Injured or otherwise medically ill trauma victims should be referred for immediate medical attention or transported to the nearest emergency room.
- Those needing shelter, clothing, or food should be given information about social service agencies and/or shelters, and/or relevant caseworkers should be alerted to the clients' needs.
- Victims of rape and domestic violence should be referred to a local emergency room, crisis center, shelter, or appropriate service agency. If necessary, reports should be made to law enforcement, adult protection services, and/or child abuse agencies.
- Individuals who are psychotic or otherwise impaired by psychiatric symptoms to the extent that they cannot care for themselves, are at risk of harming themselves or others, or have become suicidal should be referred for psychiatric hospitalization.
- To the extent possible, and within the constraints of any confidentiality issues, attempts should be made to contact family and friends who may be able to assist the traumatized individual.

Treatment

Although some form of referral is often indicated for symptomatic individuals who have been exposed to acute trauma, the need for formal psychological treatment (as well as the client's perception of this need) varies from person to person. The reasons for this include the following:

- The time frame may not support psychological interventions. The first days and weeks after a traumatic event often involve emotional responses and symptoms that spontaneously resolve after a period of cognitive adjustment and consolidation—a process that can be interrupted or diverted by ill-timed psychological treatment (Bisson, 2003).
- As noted earlier, a significant number of people who undergo a potentially traumatic event are not, in fact, traumatized by the event; they may experience few if any lasting posttraumatic symptoms.

- For victims of more severe traumas, when physical injury is involved, medical attention takes priority over mental health evaluation and intervention.
- Beyond medical treatment, adequate shelter, clothing, and food are usually the first priority for survivors of floods, earthquakes, fires, and other disasters (National Institute for Mental Health, 2002). For many victims of rape or domestic violence, a major concern may be finding a place to stay that is safe from the perpetrator. In such situations, that is, when physical needs and safety are paramount—and as yet unmet—psychological treatment is often not an immediate focus (Briere & Jordan, 2005). To the extent that it is provided before (or instead of) these more immediate interventions, in fact, early psychotherapy may even be detrimental.

In the context of acute trauma, very early treatment may seem out of place, intrusive, and even anti-survival to the extent that it distracts from more immediate concerns. After the terrorist attacks of September 11, 2001, for example, anecdotal reports suggested that the services most immediately appreciated by victims and their families were assistance in locating other family members or victims, concrete advice, referral to social services, emotional encouragement, and, in some cases, the human contact and warmth associated with donuts, coffee, and support at the disaster site. In contrast, however, there were a few complaints that clinicians insisted that survivors discuss and process traumatic material, despite protestations of not needing or wanting clinical intervention. This latter group tended to characterize the effects of such treatment more negatively.

As interveners, it is important that we not be too rigidly attached to providing "clinical" services to acutely traumatized individuals—there are times when the most important thing we can offer is basic human contact, emotional support, and assisting in the survivor's connection with others.

In some cases, requests for mental health treatment do not come from the victim, but, instead, from family members, clergy, or relief workers. Such referral for clinical intervention can be critically important when the victim is unable or unwilling to seek out needed medical or psychological attention on his or her own. For example, intervention is clearly indicated when the victim is psychotic, suicidal, or otherwise at risk for immediate harm. In less extreme instances, however, trauma-exposed individuals may experience uninvited referrals and interventions as intrusive and irrelevant to their immediate concerns.

Despite these cautions, there is little question that some people are profoundly and immediately affected by traumatic events, and that early psychological intervention can be very helpful. In general, we suggest that formal psychological treatment for acute stress be considered if the following criteria are met:

- Assessment has indicated significant psychological impairment.
- Significant food, shelter, and medical issues are not present or are under control.
- The client indicates a desire to enter treatment.
- Major, clinically significant symptoms have persisted for at least one or two weeks *or* symptoms reflect potential danger to self or others—in which case intervention should be immediate.

Unfortunately, this list runs the risk of making things appear more cut-and-dried than they often are. Perhaps most significantly, in some cases where early intervention could be helpful, given the victim's level of impairment, the victim either denies significant symptoms or actively avoids treatment. As noted at various points in this book, a frequent aspect of acute posttraumatic response is some form of emotional or behavioral avoidance. The shock and numbing often associated with an overwhelming event may reduce the victim's access to (and therefore description of) his or her internal state. In some cases, the survivor may feel so overwhelmed by negative feelings that he or she understandably avoids conversations (for example, symptom disclosure) and activities (for example, treatment) that might activate posttraumatic distress, as per the symptoms of ASD and PTSD described in Chapter 2. Survivors may feel embarrassed or frightened by their symptoms, or by the trauma itself, and thus may be reluctant to disclose their experiences; others may consider emotional expression or help-seeking a sign of weakness. Still others may accept social messages that they should "put their past behind them" or "just get over it," in the hopes that, if suppressed or unacknowledged, trauma symptoms will remit on their own.

Together, these various responses can result in a conundrum for the clinician: the individual appears traumatized, but denies symptoms and rejects offers of treatment. Ultimately, the decision to disclose or to participate in therapy is largely the victim's alone. It is rarely wise to insist that even obviously symptomatic individuals enter psychological treatment if they do not want to be treated. On the other hand, when faced with such situations (for example, with a highly symptomatic rape victim who demands to be left alone, or an emotionally distressed police officer who fears stigmatization if he or she discloses PTSD symptoms or enters therapy), it is entirely appropriate for the clinician to gently discuss with the victim his or her current symptomatic state, the possible benefits of current or future therapy, and possible solutions to any barriers preventing him or her from seeking treatment. If it is clear that the victim is unwilling to engage in treatment, it is usually best not to push further. Instead, the clinician may consider one of the following:

- Offer information—either verbally or (preferably) in written form—that describes possible longer-term effects of trauma exposure and outlines ways to receive help in the future.
- Make a follow-up appointment for the victim a month after the current contact, noted on a written appointment slip.
- With the victim's permission, arrange for at least one follow-up phone call from the clinician "just to see how things are going."
- With the victim's permission and signed release form, meet with one or more significant others (for example, partner, family members) to discuss the victim's situation and the future availability of clinical services. Ideally, this is done with the victim present—in which case release forms may or may not be necessary.
- Refer the victim to a psychiatrist or other medical practitioner for evaluation for possible medication treatment. Some individuals, while concerned about possible stigma associated with psychotherapy, may be willing to consider medication to help with distressing symptoms, and may see such intervention as less pathologizing. Medication management, while not affording clients the opportunity to fully process trauma, may provide empathic support as well as a safe environment in which to express concerns. It may also "open the door" to the possibility of future psychological treatment.

In some cases, victims respond to these additional prompts or supports by eventually requesting psychological assistance, albeit well after the fact. For example, the individual may keep a flyer or appointment slip—"just in case"—and then refer to it when symptoms increase or fail to remit. In other instances, unfortunately, it may be years before the trauma survivor seeks mental health services, if at all. Even in these cases, however, the clinician's demeanor, helpfulness, and initial information at the time of the trauma may be remembered, and may influence later decisions to seek help.

Once it has been determined that treatment is both indicated and desired by the client, therapy generally proceeds as described in previous chapters. However, because acutely traumatized individuals are sometimes easily overwhelmed, and may rely to a greater extent on avoidance defenses, treatment must be provided with considerable attention to the principles of the self-trauma model, especially vis-à-vis the therapeutic window. Following are a series of special considerations to take into account when working with acute trauma.

Balanced Emotional Support and Compassion

As noted earlier, individuals acutely overwhelmed by traumatic events often have significant, immediate needs for human contact, support, and compassion. This need is often so strong that the less responsive clinician may be seen as uncaring or unapproachable, thereby potentially reducing his or her effectiveness. We suggest that the first moments of interaction with an acute trauma survivor be directed toward making empathic contact and communicating caring. This does not mean that the therapist should be excessively sympathetic, to the extent that his or her attentions suggest pity, nor should expressions of concern be intrusive. The goal should be to respond in a manner that communicates appreciation of the client's traumatic situation, provides emotional acceptance and warmth, yet remains professional and noninvasive. Survivors often remember such caring, professional helper responses, whether in the emergency room or at a disaster site, well into the future.

Active Relatedness

In classic psychotherapy, the clinician often works to communicate therapeutic neutrality, and may respond to client disclosures in a relatively reflective, nondirective manner. In contrast, therapy for trauma victims, perhaps especially those acutely exposed to traumatic events, is often more active and directly interactive with the client. To paraphrase Judith Herman (1992a), there is rarely a place for therapeutic neutrality in work with victims of violence and other trauma. Further, the potentially overwhelming quality of some acute posttraumatic presentations often requires that the therapist provide concrete advice, make direct referrals, and act as a strong relational figure—someone the client can temporarily rely upon. Importantly, this directive stance is rarely indicated for longer-term therapy, where the client's self-determination and self-directedness are more directly called upon and bolstered (see Chapter 9). Instead, active relatedness is typically a shorter-term response to the disorganizing and destabilizing effects of acute trauma exposure. As the client's immediate needs for structure, access to resources, and therapeutic guidance wanes, so too should the therapist's directiveness.

Greater Than Usual Accessibility

In more traditional, less emergent mental health contexts, contact boundaries are often negotiated between the client and therapist, typically limiting when the client may call or otherwise access the therapist. Such understandings discourage excessive dependency and allow the therapist to have uninterrupted periods of time when he or she is not "on duty." In acute trauma situations, however, the client may experience crises and/or intermittent episodes of overwhelming distress or grief that require more frequent contact. For this reason, professional assistance should be available to the acute trauma victim whenever necessary in the days, weeks, and early months following the trauma. In addition to providing the client with phone numbers for emergency rooms, crisis centers, or on-call or back-up clinicians, the emergency/trauma clinician should consider allowing more phone calls or impromptu sessions (ideally during normal work hours) than would be the case for regular psychotherapy. Because the client may have formed an especially strong attachment to the therapist early in the trauma recovery process, ongoing access to the clinician is often more appreciated (and often more helpful) than interventions provided by more impersonal settings, such as a crisis phone line or back-up clinician. Of course, it is almost never appropriate for even acute trauma clinicians to be available on a 24-hour basis. If the acute trauma survivor appears to require many mental health contacts within a short period of time, more intensive intervention (for example, psychiatric hospitalization) should be considered.

Case Work

Most psychotherapists and other mental health clinicians understandably prefer to focus their attention on evaluating and treating psychological disturbance rather than on other, more extratherapeutic tasks. However, as described earlier in this chapter, many acute trauma survivors require medical, social, legal, and other nonpsychological services above and beyond psychological treatment. The logistics inherent in accessing these additional services and resources are often daunting for the recently traumatized person. For example, in the context of loss, posttraumatic stress, and acute dysphoria, the client may have difficulty arranging for clinic appointments, locating appropriate social services (for example, disaster relief or crime victim support), housing or economic assistance, insurance personnel, or help with legal issues when law enforcement is (or should be) involved. Although assisting the client in such areas may seem to be beyond the therapist's job description, it is often difficult to separate casework issues from psychotherapeutic ones when the client's immediate world has been disrupted (for example, Young et al., 1998). In such situations, the clinician may need to call or write to governmental, legal, or other agencies to advocate for the client, resolve issues, or cut through red tape that the client could not resolve on his or her own.

Social Connection

The psychological effects of trauma include isolation and social disconnection—the survivor may feel that he or she has undergone experiences that cannot be fully understood or appreciated by others (Herman, 1992a). In disasters or other mass trauma phenomena, there also may be *actual* disconnection—during the chaos and confusion of acute traumatic events, victims may be separated from other victims, families, and friends, and helpers may not be able to reach all victims quickly or may themselves be affected by the event (Hobfoll, Dunahoo, & Monnier, 1995; Orner, Kent, Pfefferbaum, Raphael, & Watson, in press). For these reasons, intervention in acute trauma often includes reconnecting survivors with relational resources (for example, helping victims locate and establish contact with family members) and broad sources of social support (for example, involving clergy, when appropriate, or facilitating access to community resources and groups). In many cases, in fact, increasing social support and mobilizing community resources may be more immediately beneficial to the acute trauma survivor than classic psychological interventions (Orner et al., in press).

Psychoeducation

Most clinicians and researchers view psychoeducation as a critical component of treatment for acute trauma survivors. The acutely traumatized client should be provided with information regarding self-care, perhaps especially in the weeks and months following a major trauma. When appropriate, this includes counseling against excessive behavioral avoidance of trauma cues, such as entirely secluding oneself to avoid triggered memories of recent interpersonal violence, or attempting to avoid all conversations, thoughts, or reminders of a traumatic event. Similarly, the excessive use of alcohol or recreational drugs should be discouraged in the first weeks or months after a major trauma, since substance abuse may interfere with trauma processing and reduce inhibitions that otherwise would prevent self-destructive behaviors, suicidality, or danger to others. The general message, in this regard, is that excessive avoidance of trauma triggers and memories, although entirely understandable, potentially interferes with psychological recovery by undercutting the normal process of exposure, activation, and processing.

In some cases, such advice supports a form of *in vivo* desensitization. For example, a recent victim of a motor vehicle accident who drives only when absolutely necessary might be encouraged to drive more often, or to try driving progressively closer to the area where the accident occurred. Similarly, a self-secluding rape survivor might be asked to consider walking to the local store with a woman friend, or, if possible, attending a party (with a friend) where men are present but interaction with them is limited. In such instances, the clinician ideally does more than advise—he or she explains the underlying reasons for such advice. In our experience, clients who are advised that they should, in a sense, avoid avoidance are considerably more likely to try to do so if they understand the underlying rationale for such advice.

As described in Chapter 5, the client is typically informed of the range of symptoms and problems that are known potentially to follow acute exposure to traumatic events. This often includes the major symptoms of ASD and PTSD, as well as other cognitive or behavioral responses that seem relevant to the client's specific situation. Although, by definition, individuals appropriate for trauma therapy are to some extent symptomatic, few will experience the entire range of posttraumatic disturbance. Nevertheless, gentle, nonalarming education about possible posttraumatic outcomes can serve to validate and normalize what the client is already experiencing, so that he or she is less likely to feel stigmatized or mentally disordered.

Finally, the acutely traumatized client may benefit from information on how to identify potentially triggering situations and stimuli so that he or she can avoid excessive activation when it is problematic. As noted in Chapter 6, the benefit of this information is that the easily overwhelmed client will feel a greater sense of control to the extent that he or she is able to predict and, to some extent, reduce intrusive flashbacks and trauma-related emotional flooding.

Careful Attention to the Therapeutic Window

Although the relative balance between the effects of trauma memory activation and the client's level of self-capacity must be attended to in all trauma work, this issue is especially relevant to treating acute trauma survivors. Because such individuals are often in the midst of major, intrusive posttraumatic symptoms and equally powerful dysphoric emotions, it may be relatively easy to overshoot the therapeutic window by intervening too quickly or too evocatively. This is probably the most common error made by clinicians working with the acutely traumatized—beginning treatment too early and/or providing too much memory exposure and activation with a client who is acutely dysregulated and who has not yet had a chance to consolidate his or her psychological resources. Because the therapeutic window may initially be quite "small" in such cases, the clinician must approach trauma processing very carefully, and only attempt significant exposure activities when it is clear that the client has sufficient internal stability. In many cases, in fact, the various interventions outlined earlier in this chapter and elsewhere (for example, emotional support, case work, psychoeducation, and, in some instances, strengthening self-capacities) may be required before memory processing is considered. This is not to say that therapeutic exposure is contraindicated in work with acute trauma victims—recent research clearly indicates that it can be quite helpful. Instead the relevant issues are *how soon, how fast,* and *how intense.* Although (1) rapid treatment, (2) soon after a trauma, using

(3) prolonged therapeutic exposure might be most efficient for those acute survivors who can tolerate it, more often the best approach is to assess for emotional stability, and then to provide titrated exposure, only when indicated, only when the client is ready, and with careful attention to the therapeutic window.

Duration of Treatment

A final issue that may discriminate treatment of acute traumatic stress from treatment of more chronic posttraumatic states is that of therapy duration. In some cases, survivors of multiple traumatic events that have occurred over a number of years may require extended therapy before they show major and sustained clinical improvement. In contrast, some acute stress survivors respond to a considerably shorter treatment period. For example, Bryant and Harvey (2000) and Ehlers et al. (2003) describe empirically validated cognitive-behavioral treatments for ASD that range from 5 to 12 sessions. Although such brief therapy may not always be appropriate, for example when treating acute survivors who have undergone especially invasive or horrific experiences (for example, torture, gang rape, war atrocities), have substantial comorbidity, or have a history of unresolved prior traumas, the success of Bryant and colleagues makes an important point: many acutely traumatized individuals do not require extended treatment. The reasons for this are several. First, many acute traumas will resolve, to some extent, on their own—the role of therapy in such cases may be to provide more rapid and/or complete recovery. In contrast, PTSD and other, similar posttraumatic conditions are, by definition, more chronic, and thus typically represent more severe and treatment-resistant phenomena. Second, although chronic posttraumatic stress is associated with multiple risk factors (for example, inadequate affect regulation, excessive avoidance), this may not be the case for many acute trauma survivors. Finally, it is possible, although not yet proven, that early, successful intervention "catches" posttraumatic symptoms before they have a chance to generalize and elaborate over time, and thus require less comprehensive intervention.

It should be reemphasized that not all acute traumatic survivors respond to shorter-term treatment. A minority are likely to require considerably more extensive clinical attention. Nevertheless, as is true for all trauma therapy, the extent of treatment required to resolve a given instance of acute stress should not be determined by the clinician's preexisting assumptions or by what kind of therapy he or she habitually provides. In many cases, a positive outcome may result from less treatment than otherwise might be anticipated.

Suggested Reading

Bisson, J. I., McFarlane, A. C., & Rose, S. (2000). Psychological debriefing. In E. B. Foa, T. M. Keane, & M. J. Friedman (Eds.), *Effective treatments for PTSD* (pp. 39–59). New York: Guilford.

Blanchard, E. B., & Hickling, E. J. (1997). *After the crash: Assessment and treatment of motor vehicle accident survivors.* Washington, DC: American Psychological Association.

Bryant, R. A., & Harvey, A. G. (2000). *Acute stress disorder: A handbook of theory, assessment, and treatment.* Washington, DC: American Psychological Association.

National Child Traumatic Stress Network and National Center for PTSD. (2005). *Psychological First Aid: Field operations guide.* Retrieved October 25, 2005, from http://www.ncptsd.va.gov/pfa/PFA.html

Ritchie, E. C., Watson, P. J., & Friedman, M. J. (Eds.). (in press). *Interventions following mass violence and disasters: Strategies for mental health practice.* New York: Guilford.

Shalev, A. Y. (2002). Acute stress reactions in adults. *Biological Psychiatry, 51,* 532–544.

Solomon, S., Laor, N., & Mc Farlane A. C. (1996). Acute posttraumatic reactions in soldiers and civilians. In B. A. van der Kolk, A. C. Mc Farlane, & L. Weisaeth (Eds.), *Traumatic stress: The effects of overwhelming experience on mind, body and society* (pp. 102–114). New York: Guilford.

11

Biology and Psychopharmacology of Trauma

Catherine Scott and John Briere

This chapter is intended to be useful for psychiatrists and other medical practitioners as well as for nonphysician clinicians. Of necessity, some of the material presented here is relatively technical in nature. Because this information is more medically specialized, it may seem less relevant to the needs of some nonprescribing clinicians. It should be noted, however, that many trauma survivors who are in regular psychotherapy take psychiatric medications of one type or another. In this context, the nonprescribing therapist is often the professional most aware of the client's week-to-week psychological state and general physical functioning; in contrast, medical practitioners may only have a fraction of an hour—perhaps once a month—to evaluate medication effects. This ready access to the client's state may allow the pharmacologically informed therapist to detect drug side effects or emergent need for medication changes, which can then be communicated to the prescribing clinician. In other cases, severely traumatized or comorbid survivors are not receiving medication, but probably should be. Knowledge of trauma psychopharmacology can assist the nonmedical clinician in making appropriate psychiatric referrals and recommendations for such clients. Issues addressed in this chapter for the nonmedical psychotherapist include (1) the rationale for specific trauma-focused medications, (2) their primary actions on the human nervous system, (3) their major side effects, and (4) their limitations.

For medical practitioners who are interested in increasing their understanding of the practical psychopharmacology of posttraumatic stress and related psychiatric conditions, we include a detailed overview of the major trauma-relevant medications, their appropriate dosages, and their general indications and contraindications for posttraumatic symptom patterns. In this regard, the major clinical trials involving medications for posttraumatic distress are reviewed. This chapter also discusses strategies for medication management in the context of Axis I comorbidity and as an adjunct to trauma-focused psychotherapy. An in-depth discussion of the research in this area is beyond the scope of this book, however; the clinician is referred to the Suggested Reading at the end of the chapter for a more detailed review of the literature on trauma pharmacotherapy. We have also limited this chapter to the treatment of adult survivors. Trauma psychopharmacology for children and adolescents is a highly specialized area; although adolescents often respond to psychoactive medication in ways similar to adults, there are significant differences between adolescent and adult biology. The reader is referred to Donnelly, Amaya-Jackson, and March (1999) and Seedat and Stein (2001) for more information on the use of medication for traumatized children and adolescents.

Before discussing psychopharmacology, we briefly review the psychobiology of posttraumatic stress, since nervous system dysregulation is the specific target of psychiatric medication. However, because research in this area is still in its infancy, we present an overview of currently proposed biological models, rather than attempting to make a definitive statement about the exact physiological substrates of posttraumatic disturbance.

The Psychobiology of Trauma

There has been a surge of interest in recent years regarding the biology of posttraumatic stress. This research indicates that multiple systems and neurotransmitters are involved in posttraumatic disturbance, although some of the evidence is contradictory and not always easy to interpret. There are several immediate implications of this complexity:

1. There are probably multiple pathways to posttraumatic stress, and no one model will suffice to describe the entire pathophysiology involved.

2. Posttraumatic stress disorder (PTSD), as it is currently described, may not represent a single disorder, but rather a collection of outcomes that vary

widely depending on individual differences in genetics, underlying neurophysiology, stress response, and exposure to traumatic events.

3. There is unlikely to be one ideal medication for PTSD or other posttraumatic outcomes, but rather a range of pharmacological agents that may be of assistance in treating different symptom clusters.

The Hypothalamic–Pituitary Adrenal (HPA) Axis and the Adrenergic System

When stressed, the normal response of the body is to activate both the adrenergic and the glucocorticoid systems, releasing (among other compounds) norepinephrine and cortisol. Under healthy conditions these two systems regulate one another—cortisol appears to act as a "brake" on the adrenergic system, preventing sustained sympathetic activity. In PTSD, this balance is not maintained, and the responses of both systems become dysregulated (Raison & Miller, 2003).

The adrenergic system, also known as the sympathetic nervous system (SNS), is responsible for what is classically known as the *fight-or-flight* response. It is associated with maintaining arousal and attention and with the consolidation of memories. Typically, under conditions of stress or threat, the brain increases the synthesis and release of norepinephrine—primarily in the locus ceruleus and reticular activating system—to allow an appropriate response to the situation (for example, running away or fighting). When the stress is removed, the adrenergic system returns to its usual baseline state. This return to normal levels of arousal appears to be disrupted in PTSD. Adrenergic hyperactivity—involving the release of multiple neurotransmitters and neurohormones such as acetylcholine, epinephrine, and norepinephrine, as well as increased levels of their metabolites—has been demonstrated in individuals with PTSD. Such excess and sustained activation has been associated with multiple posttraumatic symptoms, including hyperarousal, reexperiencing, dissociation, aggression, and both generalized anxiety and panic attacks. In addition, increased adrenergic activity appears to assist in the encoding of emotionally laden memories (Southwick et al., 1999).

The adrenal glands—the end organs of the HPA axis—release both cortisol and adrenergic compounds. The cascade that results in cortisol production begins at the hypothalamus, which secretes corticotropin releasing factor (CRF). CRF stimulates the pituitary to secrete adrenocorticotropin hormone (ACTH), which, in turn, controls the release of cortisol by the adrenals. Cortisol is a hormone with multiple functions, including regulation of immune and stress responses. It has been proposed that cortisol, along with other compounds such as neuropeptide Y (NPY), may serve to modulate the activity of the adrenergic system (Southwick et al., 1999). NPY is an endogenous anxiolytic that appears to act in concert with cortisol (Kask et al., 2002). At moderate, or "tolerable" levels of stress, this means that blood levels of cortisol and NPY are typically high. However, when an individual is overwhelmed by trauma, this system may be overwhelmed as well, leading to a drop in levels of cortisol and NPY. The result is a limitation on the brain's capacity to down-regulate adrenergic arousal.

Decreased cortisol and NPY levels have been demonstrated in individuals living under chronically stressful conditions. Several lines of research have also demonstrated lower cortisol and NPY in individuals with PTSD (Yehuda, 2002). In addition, low levels of these neurochemicals after a trauma appear to be predictive of later PTSD (Morgan et al., 2001). In women with a history of sexual abuse who were raped, low cortisol predicted PTSD (Resnick, Yehuda, Pitman, & Foy, 1995). However, several studies in this area disagree. For example, DeBellis, et al. (1999) found elevated (as opposed to lower) cortisol in PTSD, and a few studies suggest that the relationship between cortisol and posttraumatic stress may be more complex than otherwise assumed (see Yehuda, 2002, for a discussion). Research in this area is ongoing, and current findings—although strongly suggestive—should not be considered definitive.

The HPA axis self-regulates by means of a negative feedback loop. Under "normal" circumstances, a low cortisol level would provide feedback to the hypothalamus and pituitary that would result in higher levels of CRF and ACTH—resulting ultimately in the stimulation of the adrenals to secrete more cortisol and balance the system. However, in PTSD, there appears to be enhanced negative feedback of the HPA axis—resulting in higher CRF without a concomitant increase in cortisol (Raison & Miller, 2003). In addition, individuals with PTSD appear to hypersuppress cortisol upon dexamethasone challenge (Yehuda, Halligan, Golier, Grossman, & Bierer, 2004). These data suggest that glucocorticoid receptors may become hypersensitive in some traumatized individuals, leading to lower baseline levels of cortisol and, therefore, increased sympathetic nervous system activity. It has therefore been proposed that the deficit is one of impaired glucocorticoid *signaling* rather than simply a problem of too little cortisol (Raison & Miller, 2003).

Taken together, these findings suggest the likelihood that there is a neurobiological window for optimal stress response, within which various brain compounds (such as NPY and cortisol) operate to "inhibit the continued release of [norepinephrine] so that the SNS does not overshoot" (Southwick, Morgan, Vythilingan, Krystal, & Charney, 2003, p. 1). In posttraumatic stress, there appears to be a co-occurrence of *increased* adrenergic activity with *decreased* glucocorticoid (cortisol) and NPY modulation. This imbalance may lead to the rapid and powerful consolidation of emotionally laden traumatic memories, which, under conditions of ongoing adrenergic stimulation, become intrusive and overwhelming, and lead to symptoms of hyperarousal, agitation, anxiety, and dissociation. HPA-related disruption of the normal immune response, especially under conditions of chronic stress (for example, prolonged torture, childhood physical or sexual abuse), may also contribute to chronic physical complaints and susceptibility to physical illness, as reported by some trauma survivors (Ehlert, Gaab, & Heinrichs, 2001).

Other Biological Correlates of PTSD

In addition to the role of the adrenergic and glucocorticoid systems, there is a significant body of literature investigating less well-established biological mechanisms in the development of PTSD. Serotonin has been implicated in the biology of posttraumatic stress, primarily due to the efficacy of selective serotonin reuptake inhibitors (SSRIs) in the treatment of PTSD (Friedman, 2000b). However, because serotonergic agents have effects on the locus ceruleus, where the adrenergic cell bodies reside, their effects may be more complex than simply increasing available serotonin. PTSD has also been associated with changes in serotonin transporters, opioid dysregulation, and high-normal thyroid hormone levels (Friedman, 2000b). Kindling, in which repeated stress is thought to sensitize limbic neurons so that reactions are set off by stimuli that were once sub-threshold, has also been proposed as a model for the development of PTSD, especially in conditions of chronic stress such as child abuse (Weiss & Post, 1998).

Findings From Neuroimaging Studies

Recent advances in neuroimaging technology allow us to view the brain as it functions *in vivo*, opening a window into how trauma affects both neuroanatomy and neurophysiology. While much of the data is limited by small sample sizes, there do appear to be some consistent findings. In general, PTSD has been associated with smaller brain white and gray matter, smaller hippocampal volumes, and smaller anterior cingulates (Villarreal & King, 2004). Small hippocampal volume has also been found in survivors of child abuse (irrespective of PTSD diagnostic status), and the volume loss correlates both with the severity of that abuse and with the severity of PTSD symptoms (Fennema-Notestine, Stein, Kennedy, Archibald, & Jernigan, 2002). A question that remains to be answered is whether smaller hippocampal volume might predate the trauma and therefore predispose an individual to develop PTSD, or whether the volume decrease occurs as a result of the neurobiological response to a traumatic event. To further complicate the picture, it is possible that *both* of these processes might occur, in an overlapping fashion, in some individuals.

In addition, imaging has demonstrated decreased activation of the hippocampus during verbal memory tasks in individuals with PTSD (Bremner et al., 2003), a finding that makes sense given that the hippocampus plays an important role in the consolidation of memory. Interestingly, treatment with the selective serotonin reuptake inhibitors (such as Prozac) has been shown to improve verbal memory as well as increase hippocampal volume (Villarreal & King, 2004). Similarly, researchers have found decreased recruitment of the anterior cingulate during trauma recall, an area of the brain thought to be associated with emotional responsiveness and affect regulation (Shin et al., 2001).

Integrating Biological Models With the Self-Trauma Model

The psychobiological models presented here are focused on nervous system pathology, as opposed to the more adaptation-oriented psychological conceptualizations described in earlier chapters. Biological theories tend to suggest that the symptoms of posttraumatic stress arise from excessive activation of the sympathetic nervous system, probably in combination with dysregulation of the HPA axis and related neurohormones, such that traumatic memories become overconsolidated, easily activated, and overwhelming in their capacity to produce negative emotions. Further, the continuous activation of the sympathetic system is thought to result in sustained autonomic arousal, and, in the presence of repeated stressors, hyperreactivity to subsequent stimuli.

In contrast, the psychological model described in earlier chapters suggests that posttraumatic reexperiencing (for example, flashbacks and intrusive trauma-related thoughts) represents a normal psychobiological process—the mind's attempts to desensitize traumatic memory by repeatedly evoking it in the context of safety (that is, the concepts of exposure, disparity, and extinction discussed in Chapter 8).

Although the integration of these two perspectives must remain speculative, we suggest that it is possible. We hypothesize that, as described in Chapter 8, the normal exposure/disparity/extinction process "works" only to the extent that reexperiencing phenomena (for example, intrusive thoughts and memories) do not exceed the individual's capacities to regulate and tolerate the associated painful affect. These affect regulation capacities, in turn, are likely to be partially a function of psychobiological phenomena such as the ability of the HPA axis to modulate sympathetic arousal.

Thus, it is possible that chronic PTSD and other posttraumatic responses arise when the natural exposure/extinction system is derailed—that is, when the emotional impacts of a stressor exceed the individual's existing affect regulation "window." This is perhaps especially true in those who already have a sensitive or dysregulated nervous system. In cases where reexperiencing appears to be effective—that is, when traumatic memories are successfully exposed and extinguished—we might expect to find less overwhelming stressors, a less "excitable" nervous system (and, therefore, more effective modulation via cortisol), higher levels of NPY, and less overall limbic sensitization.

It is interesting that both biological and psychological researchers have independently hypothesized the notion of a "window" within which optimal stress response occurs. Southwick, Morgan, Vythilingam, and Charney (2003) have suggested that "psychologically resilient individuals maintain SNS activation within a window of adaptive elevation, high enough to respond to danger but not so high as to produce incapacity, anxiety, and fear" (p. 1). As has been described in detail in Chapter 8, the self-trauma model (Briere, 2002a) posits a psychological window within which individuals can experience and tolerate emotion and distress without becoming overwhelmed.

Given the preceding discussion, successful treatments for PTSD and other stress disorders would probably involve some combination or subset of the following:

- Carefully titrated exposure to traumatic memory, so that even compromised biological and psychological systems are not overwhelmed
- Attempts to increase emotional/stress regulation through the psychological interventions described in Chapter 6, but also, in some instances, through medications thought to stabilize the limbic system and HPA axis
- A reduction in the overall anxiety/arousal "load" (that is, overactivity and hypersensitivity of the sympathetic nervous system) through relaxation training and memory desensitization, as well as dampening of sympathetic activation, when indicated, through medications that treat anxiety
- Use of medications to reduce comorbid anxiety, depression, or psychosis that otherwise add to overall distress or interfere with affect regulation

Although, as noted in this chapter, currently available medications are rarely sufficient to permanently resolve posttraumatic stress, some trauma survivors suffer from such high levels of anxiety, hyperarousal, and comorbid symptoms that psychotherapy alone is unlikely to be fully effective. As a result, successful treatment of posttraumatic states—especially in the case of severe or chronic symptoms—may sometimes involve both psychological and pharmacological interventions.

Trauma Psychopharmacology

As discussed throughout this volume, posttraumatic outcomes can be extremely complex. Similarly, tailoring treatment—whether it be psychotherapy, psychopharmacology, or a combination of the two—to a given individual's particular circumstances may be far from simple. Although the medications indicated for the treatment of PTSD and related disorders are relatively few in number, the practice of using them and encouraging compliance requires considerable knowledge and attention. It is rarely sufficient to write a prescription and tell the client to return in a month for follow-up. Specific concerns associated with using medications with trauma survivors include the following:

- *Compliance.* Trauma survivors often have a difficult time remembering to take their medications—the result of distractibility, high levels of emotional activation, and, sometimes, dissociation. This may be even more of a concern if a medication regimen requires pills at multiple time points during the day.
- *Anxiety.* Many of the antidepressant medications used to treat PTSD can increase the levels of anxiety that some individuals experience in the initial days of treatment, and in some instances can precipitate panic attacks. Trauma survivors who are highly dissociated, somatically preoccupied, and anxious, or who present with panic attacks, are likely to respond to these medications with more anxious symptoms than are other, less traumatized individuals.
- *Sedation.* Certain psychotropic medications can cause feelings of "dullness," sedation, or of "not being myself" in some individuals. Trauma survivors, in particular, may feel that these side effects impair their ability to sense and respond to danger. Paradoxically, although hypervigilance can be an extremely debilitating component of posttraumatic stress, many individuals do not want to lose the sense of control and safety that "being on edge" provides them.
- *Sleep.* Similarly, although trauma survivors frequently report disturbed and erratic sleep, they may resist taking sleep medications for fear that they will sleep through potential danger.
- *Memory processing.* Some medications, particularly the benzodiazepines (and some "street" and recreational drugs as well) may interfere with the psychological processing of traumatic memories, as described in more detail following. As a result, the costs and benefits of using such drugs should be carefully considered when the client is undergoing psychotherapy or otherwise addressing traumatic material.
- *Substance abuse.* The use of illicit and other addictive substances is highly comorbid with posttraumatic stress and may be problematic in combination with certain medications.
- *Distrust of authority.* Many trauma survivors, especially victims of interpersonal violence or political torture, may be distrustful of authority figures, including—in

some cases—therapists or physicians, and may therefore be reluctant to take prescribed medications. For example, they may fear that the clinician is trying to control them through drugs, or even, in rare instances, poison them.

- *Overmedication.* The chronic and extreme distress that some trauma survivors experience may induce helplessness and frustration in the clinician, leading him or her to medicate clients more aggressively than is appropriate, or to overprescribe addictive anti-anxiety medications.

Given these concerns, we make the following initial recommendations:

- Close follow-up of traumatized clients, preferably within a week of starting a new medication
- Patience regarding the client's occasional unwillingness to take medications—it may take more than one visit for him or her to develop the trust necessary to start a psychotropic regimen
- Slow dose increases to avoid side effects that may decrease compliance
- Adequate education about potential side effects, so that, if they occur, they do not surprise or alarm the client, or cause him or her to prematurely discontinue medication that ultimately would be tolerable
- Gentle encouragement and support around fears of being overmedicated and therefore less responsive to danger
- Careful consideration of any potential for abuse or overdose when prescribing medications for relief of anxiety

Psychotherapy and Psychopharmacology

Throughout this volume, we focus on the importance of processing traumatic material in the context of a supportive therapeutic relationship. In some instances, however, posttraumatic symptoms may be so overwhelming that the individual is unable to participate in therapy altogether, or becomes so anxious and distressed with even low levels of activation that therapy proceeds at a very slow pace. In other situations, comorbid psychological conditions (most commonly depression) interfere with the client's ability to participate fully in psychotherapy. In the worst case, the client may drop out of treatment after a very few sessions, often without explanation, and without returning therapist phone calls.

Psychotropic medications can be a useful adjunct to trauma-focused psychotherapy under such conditions, especially in the early phase of treatment. Appropriate pharmacological intervention can provide some initial relief of intense distress—partly via medication effects on posttraumatic symptomatology, and partly via the placebo effect. Medication that improves sleep may be particularly helpful, since sleep disturbance is often one of the most debilitating symptoms of posttraumatic stress.

When some initial symptom reduction can be gained through the use of medication, clients may be more able and willing to engage in the often difficult work of trauma-focused psychotherapy. For clients who are suspicious of treatment, the experience of an initial benefit may help to improve the therapeutic alliance; for those whose negative experiences have caused them to believe there is no possibility of recovery, the demonstration of early symptom relief may provide a glimmer hope for the future. Seen in this light, pharmacotherapy can be a "stepping stone" in the process of helping clients to recover—a way to help them both enter into and stay engaged with psychotherapy.

Surprisingly, there have been no head-to-head comparisons of psychotherapy with psychopharmacological treatment for posttraumatic stress. Overall, however, medications are rarely curative by themselves, and, although helpful, may have less of an impact than psychological therapy. In the practice guidelines of the International Society for Traumatic Stress Studies (Foa, Keane, & Friedman, 2000), where the "gold standard" outcome studies for both psychotherapy (Rothbaum, Meadows, Resick, & Foy, 2000) and pharmacotherapy (Friedman, Davidson, Mellman, & Southwick, 2000) are reviewed, the amount of symptom reduction associated with psychotherapeutic interventions was considerably larger than that found for pharmacological interventions. While there are methodological problems associated with such direct comparisons (including possible differences in symptom severity between the participants in drug and psychotherapy studies), certainly there is no evidence to support the idea that pharmacotherapy for posttraumatic stress is intrinsically more effective than therapy. Nevertheless, in our experience, some individuals may "miss out" on the potential benefits of psychotherapy because their level of symptomatology means that they cannot tolerate—and therefore must avoid—even low levels of activation and distress. For these individuals, medication can be a powerful method of engaging them in psychotherapy, and thus may increase the possibility of recovery.

Treatment Outcome Studies and the Limitations of Medications in Posttraumatic Stress

This chapter reviews the medications used to treat posttraumatic states, their indications and side effects, and the major clinical trials (if any) investigating their use in traumatized individuals. There are, however, several limitations of this research that warrant discussion. Many studies of treatment outcome in PTSD, whether involving medication or psychotherapy, have looked at relatively "pure" PTSD, often associated with adult traumas of little complexity.

Individuals with comorbid diagnoses of major depression, personality disorders, obsessive-compulsive disorder, and other anxiety disorders are often excluded from such trials (Spinazzola, Blaustein, & van der Kolk, 2005). In addition, many studies exclude those who abuse substances, are suicidal, or who have significant dissociative symptoms. Remarkably, even despite these exclusions, drop-out rates approach 30 percent in many studies (Spinazzola et al., 2005).

Unfortunately, in the general population (that is, in nonscreened settings), PTSD is highly comorbid with other Axis I diagnoses. In fact, estimates place the comorbidity of PTSD with other Axis I disorders, summing across sex, at up to 80 percent (Kessler, Sonnega, Bromet, Hughes, & Nelson, 1995). As most clinicians working with trauma survivors in clinic and in private offices will attest, "pure" PTSD is relatively rare. Thus, it is not always easy to generalize the results of treatment outcome studies to the actual environment in which most clinicians practice—a world in which clients often present with a complex array of symptoms, and may respond less robustly to treatment or take longer to respond than the studies suggest.

Overall, there is considerable evidence that psychoactive medication is sometimes necessary, but rarely is sufficient in the treatment of PTSD and other trauma-related states. However, these limitations should not preclude the appropriate use of such medications in clinical practice. For example, a majority of the clients in our Psychological Trauma Program are taking at least one psychoactive medication—although, admittedly, these individuals may fall on the more severe end of the trauma severity-complexity continuum (Ehrlich & Briere, 2002).

Pregnancy and Lactation

As noted in Chapter 1, women are overrepresented among trauma survivors, and women who are in violent relationships are at particularly high risk for victimization when they are pregnant (Campbell & Lewandowski, 1997). For these reasons, it is important to consider the potential effects of medications used for posttraumatic stress on the developing fetus. Unfortunately, most psychiatric medications have not been studied enough in pregnant women to provide clear guidance on their safety. Instead, most are classified by the Food and Drug Administration (FDA) as pregnancy Category C, indicating possible adverse effects on the unborn child. Certain medications, such as the benzodiazepines, the antidepressant Paxil (paroxetine), and some of the mood stabilizers, are clearly contraindicated in pregnancy. Therefore, the decision to treat a pregnant woman with psychotropic medication involves a careful risk-benefit analysis. For example, are the symptoms severe enough that a woman is at risk for harming herself or her baby? Is the risk for harm due to intentional injury or self-neglect greater than the risk posed by use of a medication?

The antidepressants, especially the selective serotonin reuptake inhibitors (SSRIs), have been prescribed quite widely during pregnancy. However, in December 2005, the FDA changed the SSRI paroxetine (Paxil) from pregnancy category C to D, indicating positive evidence of risk. This change occurred as a result of preliminary data suggesting that exposure to this drug during the first trimester may increase the chance of congential malformations, espcially cardiac anomalies (Federal Drug Administration, 2005). It is unclear whether this might be a more general SSRI-related effect as opposed to one simply connected with paroxetine. Nonetheless, this change, which was announced rather suddenly, illustrates that there is much we stilll do not know about this class of medications.

To the extent possible, it is recommended that the use of psychotropics be avoided during the first trimester, since this is when the most crucial neurological development occurs in the fetus. If medication must be used, it should follow an honest discussion with the patient about the potential risks and side effects of whatever pharmacologic agent is being considered.

Most psychotropic medications are secreted in breast milk. The data on the effects of medications taken in by newborns through breast milk is minimal. Therefore, in circumstances where new mothers have symptoms severe enough to require pharmacological intervention, breast-feeding generally should be avoided.

In the tables throughout this chapter, we have listed the FDA pregnancy ratings, when known, for each drug. In addition, we have listed whether or not each medication is secreted in breast milk. For reference, the FDA pregnancy ratings are as follows (Physicians' Desk Reference, 2004):

- Category A: Controlled studies in humans show no risk
- Category B: No evidence of risk in humans despite adverse effects in animals, or in absence of human studies, no adverse effects seen in animals, but chance of harm remains a possibility
- Category C: Risk cannot be ruled out; adequate controlled studies in humans are lacking
- Category D: Positive evidence of risk in humans
- Category X: Contraindicated in pregnancy

Alternative Therapy and Psychotropic Medications

Alternative therapy (sometimes referred to as *complementary medicine*) is comprised of a rather loosely defined group of therapeutic modalities that are not often taught in medical schools or available in hospitals. Alternative therapy is generally distinguished from "conventional medicine" and includes such disparate therapies as herbal remedies, homeopathy, massage, chiropractic, acupuncture, vitamins, and energy healing, among others. We explore the use of herbal therapies in this chapter because there is considerable anecdotal evidence that some trauma survivors avail themselves of nontraditional remedies instead of (or in addition to) prescribed psychiatric medication.

Over the past two decades, the use of alternative therapies has become increasingly widespread in the United States; in 1997, 45 percent of respondents to a national phone survey had used at least one form of alternative therapy (Knaudt, Connor, Weisler, Churchill, & Davidson, 1999). While some forms of alternative therapies are provided by licensed practitioners, others are entirely unregulated. For example, herbal supplements, nutritionals, and vitamins, some of which can have significant side effects, are sold over the counter and are not regulated by the FDA.

There have been few systematic studies of alternative pharmacologic (that is, herbal or other "natural" remedies) for PTSD specifically. However, there is a growing literature on the use of alternative remedies more generally for symptoms of depression and anxiety. These include St. John's Wort (or Hypericin), Kava Kava, and SAMe. In addition, there is an abundance of scientifically unsubstantiated information available on the World Wide Web regarding the use of vitamins, tryptophan, and other supplements to treat psychiatric symptoms.

Demographic data have repeatedly indicated that individuals who seek out alternative forms of health care have higher rates of anxiety and depression (Davidson, Rampes, Eisen, Fisher, Smith, & Malik, 1998; Knaut et al., 1999). Possible reasons for this include diffuse, ill-defined physical complaints not well addressed by conventional medicine, attempts to find "natural" remedies for both physical and psychiatric complaints, and frustration and skepticism with the health care system, among others. Whatever the reason, it is important for mental health providers to be aware that their clients may be using alternative remedies and that they are often reluctant to share this information with their doctors and/or therapists. It is a common misconception that herbal or other supplements, because they are "natural," do not have any adverse effects; unfortunately, this is not the case.

An exhaustive review of potential problems with herbs and other supplements is beyond the scope of this chapter. A few critical points are worth mentioning, however.

St. John's Wort (Hypericin) is an herbal supplement available over the counter for treatment of depression and often recommended by alternative providers. It has some selective serotonin receptor inhibitor (SSRI) activity, which is presumed to be its mechanism of action. Therefore, it is critical that clients not take St. John's Wort concurrently with an SSRI, since this would increase the risk of serotonin syndrome (see the section on SSRIs, following, for a description of the SSRIs and serotonin syndrome). There are similar potential risks with the use of supplements containing tryptophan, a serotonin precursor. Tryptophan is widely recommended on Web sites as a "mood enhancer" and is available online and over the counter in various forms.

Some natural remedies act as stimulants and activate the sympathetic nervous system (for example, ephedra/ephedrine used for weight control, or yohimbine used for energy and male impotence). As described previously, trauma survivors frequently experience increased sympathetic nervous system activity and therefore are at risk of increased posttraumatic symptoms if they use stimulants. In one series of case reports (Southwick, Morgan, Charney, & High, 1999), dramatic symptom increases were noted in individuals with PTSD who took over-the-counter yohimbine. We therefore recommend that traumatized individuals avoid herbal or nonprescribed stimulants of all kinds.

Some clients may take supplements that do not come in labeled packaging, or that come from other countries. For example, at LAC+USC Medical Center, we see a number of individuals who have consulted with traditional Mexican spiritual healers, known as *Curanderos*. Sometimes, Curanderos will give herbs or other unlabeled pills to take as part of a healing ritual. In these cases, it is impossible to know exactly what the client is taking. If psychotropic medications are indicated, it is imperative to have a frank discussion with the client about the need to stop taking whatever remedy they are on because of concerns about potential interactions.

We have focused on the possible risks of herbal and other supplements in trauma survivors, whether alone or in combination with psychotropic medications. These risks are real and must be conveyed to the client as well as documented in the medical record. However, maintaining a supportive, nonjudgmental attitude is essential during any such discussion. Often, clients believe that they will be penalized for seeing alternative providers and are afraid to report what they are taking. In such situations, open communication among the nonprescribing therapist, the psychiatrist or other medical practitioner, and the client can be critical.

A Note on the Uses and Limitations of This Chapter

Much of what we present in the following sections is well-known, easily available information regarding the mechanism of action, side effects, contraindications, and dosing of various psychotropic medications. However, in the interest of brevity—and ease for the reader—we have not presented exhaustive general information about each medication. We have, however, focused on the application of such medication in posttraumatic stress, so that interested readers can further their knowledge in this ever-expanding area. Prescribing clinicians should view this book primarily as a guide to the literature on the use of psychopharmacology in trauma; they are referred to more complete and authoritative texts, as well as their own clinical knowledge, for specifics regarding the use of psychiatric medications in actual practice. In all cases, the prescribing clinician should consult the *Physicians' Desk Reference* (PDR, 2005) or other drug reference for the exact and proper dosage and regimen appropriate for any given client.

Medications for PTSD

Antidepressants

Selective Serotonin Reuptake Inhibitors

Most of the research on medications for PTSD has focused on the use of selective serotonin reuptake inhibitors (SSRIs). This is logical—SSRIs have demonstrated efficacy for the treatment of depression, generalized anxiety, and panic. Therefore, their use for PTSD, which includes symptoms that overlap with these disorders, is a natural extension. The results of research on SSRIs and PTSD have generally been encouraging, leading to the widespread use of these medications to treat posttraumatic stress. For example, SSRIs are listed as the first-line medication for PTSD in the "Treatment Recommendations for PTSD" made by the International Society for Traumatic Stress Studies (Friedman, Davidson, Mellman & Southwick, 2000).

There have been several randomized, double-blind, placebo-controlled studies of SSRIs in PTSD, using paroxetine (Paxil) (for example, Stein, Davidson, Seedat, & Beebe, 2003); sertraline (Zoloft) (for example, Brady et al., 2000; Davidson, Rothbaum, van der Kolk, Sikes, & Farfel, 2001); and fluoxetine (Prozac) (for example, Connor, Sutherland, Tupler, Malik, & Davidson, 1999). Results of this research indicate that SSRIs reduce symptoms in all three of the core symptom clusters of PTSD (that is, reexperiencing, hyperarousal, and avoidance).

Most studies have followed patients over a relatively short 12-week treatment period. Only one study of sertraline followed patients for 28 weeks following the acute phase of the study, to assess efficacy in preventing relapse (Davidson, Pearlstein, et al., 2001). The results suggested that sertraline is effective in preventing relapse of PTSD. However, they also indicated that those who received a placebo following discontinuation of this drug had a significant risk of relapsing back into PTSD. This implies that, in order for SSRI treatment to be effective in the long term, it must be maintained for a longer period of time than the usual 12-week duration of most clinical trials. In fact, for PTSD that lasts more than 3 months, studies indicate that treatment with an SSRI for 9 months to a year after symptom remission may be more appropriate (Davidson, 2004).

It is important to note that SSRIs, while helpful in PTSD, are not necessarily curative. In most studies, while 50–60 percent of participants responded, only 20–30 percent of those responders no longer met criteria for PTSD by the end of the study (Spinazzola, Blaustein, & van der Kolk, 2005). Put another way, this means that 70–80 percent of individuals in the study still had PTSD after treatment, albeit perhaps in an attenuated form.

In some of the early studies of SSRIs in PTSD, treatment appeared to be less successful in war veterans and in men than in civilians and women (for example, Hertzberg, Feldman, Beckham, Kudler, & Davidson, 2000). There was much discussion about why this might be the case. The original studies were done with participants who were male Vietnam-era veterans with PTSD that had persisted for many years—a cohort with, almost by definition, a particularly treatment-resistant form of the disorder. However, more recent studies in civilians have demonstrated no sex difference in response to these medications.

There are some interesting data that suggest that SSRIs may actually have direct effects on the anatomy and neurophysiology that underlie posttraumatic stress. In a small group of patients with borderline personality disorder, fluvoxamine (Luvox) was found to decrease the hyperresponsiveness of the HPA axis (as measured by dexamethasone challenge) in individuals with a history of childhood abuse (Rinne et al., 2003). Another recent study showed a 5 percent increase in hippocampal volume in individuals with PTSD who were treated for a year with paroxetine (Bremner & Vermetten, 2004). This information, while still preliminary, supports the notion that treatment with SSRIs may be most effective when used over a more extended period of time.

At the time of publication of this book, there are six SSRIs available on the market, listed in Table 11.1. They have been found to be equally effective in reducing symptoms and improving quality of life across most clinical trials for various DSM-IV-TR (Diagnostic and Statistical Manual of Mental Disorders; American Psychiatric Association, 2000) diagnoses (for example, Mace & Taylor, 2000). As discussed later in this chapter, they differ primarily in terms of side effects. This is an important consideration in choosing a medication for trauma survivors, because noncompliance is especially high in this population. At this time, only sertraline and paroxetine have received FDA

Table 11.1   SSRIs

Generic Name	Trade Name	Recommended Dosage	Half-Life	Pregnancy Category*	Present in Breast Milk
Citalopram	Celexa	10–60mg	35 hrs	C	Yes
Escitalopram	Lexapro	10–20mg	27–32 hrs	C	Yes
Fluoxetine	Prozac	10–80mg	4–6 wks	C	Yes
Fluvoxamine	Luvox	100–300mg	15 hrs	C	Yes
Paroxetine	Paxil	10–60mg	10–21 hrs	D	Yes
Sertraline	Zoloft	50–200mg	26 hrs	C	Yes

*See page 196 for a description of FDA pregnancy ratings.

approval for the treatment of PTSD. However, as the SSRIs are generally equally effective across disorders, decisions regarding choice of one medication over another are primarily based upon the judgment of the clinician.

SSRIs are generally considered to be safer than the older antidepressants (the tricyclics and monoamine oxidase inhibitors, described later in this chapter), and less lethal in overdose. However, they have been associated with a potentially life-threatening condition known as "serotonin syndrome" that results from excess central nervous system serotonin. Symptoms can range from tremor and diarrhea to delirium, neuromuscular rigidity, and hyperthermia. Serotonin syndrome can occur in cases of overdose, drug-drug interactions, or in rare instances, during therapeutic drug use.

Fluoxetine is the oldest SSRI, and it and fluvoxamine are the only SSRIs at this time that are available in a less expensive generic form. Fluvoxamine has a high incidence of side effects, however, and is used less frequently in routine practice than the other SSRIs. Generally, SSRIs are well tolerated, and have the benefit of being relatively nonlethal in overdose (as compared to, for example, the tricyclic antidepressants, which can be fatal when taken in quantities equaling a 15-day supply). However, they all share some potential side effects. These include anxiety, nervousness, sweating, headache, gastrointestinal upset (nausea, diarrhea, dyspepsia), dry mouth, somnolence, insomnia, and disruption of all phases of sexuality (erections in men, and libido and orgasms in both men and women). Although SSRIs treat symptoms of anxiety and are indicated for the treatment of Axis I anxiety disorders, they frequently increase anxiety in the initial days of treatment, and can sometimes precipitate panic attacks.

There are certain side effects that are associated more with some SSRIs than others. Fluoxetine tends to be activating, and is generally prescribed to be taken in the morning. Paroxetine (as well as fluvoxamine) tends to be more sedating and is typically taken in the evening. Paroxetine can also cause weight gain. Sertraline, escitalopram (Lexapro), and citalopram (Celexa) are more side effect–neutral, with fewer effects on sleep and weight. Some clinicians make decisions about which SSRI to give an individual client based upon the most advantageous use of these side effects, a strategy that we have found anecdotally to increase compliance; for example:

- Paroxetine in a nonpregnant client who is highly anxious and unable to sleep and is not bothered by potential weight gain
- Fluoxetine in a client who is tired and apathetic and has a hard time "getting going" in the morning
- Sertraline, citalopram, or escitalopram in a client who is particularly concerned about side effects

Given the potential side effects discussed, client education is essential. It is important to warn very anxious and hyperaroused clients that their anxiety may increase initially, and that this is a normal response to the medication. It is also crucial to inform clients about possible sexual side effects, and to assure men that erectile difficulties will resolve if the medication is stopped. In addition, it is essential to inform clients that antidepressants do not take effect immediately. Often, it takes up to 2 weeks for an initial response to occur; a full response may not take place until an individual has been taking a therapeutic dose for 4–6 weeks.

SSRIs also have the potential to cause significant symptoms if they are stopped abruptly, known as "discontinuation syndrome." Vomiting, diarrhea, nausea, anorexia, dizziness, headache, insomnia, irritability, disturbances of vision, fatigue, and tremor, as well as "electric shock" sensations in the back and arms have all been reported (for example, Coupland, Bell, & Potokar, 1996). Paroxetine, with its short half-life, has been noted to cause discontinuation symptoms more frequently than the other SSRIs (Barr, Goodman, & Price, 1994). Fluoxetine, with a long half-life, rarely causes such difficulties, and in fact is sometimes used short term to assist in tapering clients off of other SSRIs. Again, educating clients about the potential symptoms associated with stopping SSRIs is important—they should be encouraged to discontinue such medications only when tapered under the supervision of a prescribing clinician. The half-lives of the SSRIs are noted in Table 11.1 for reference purposes regarding this issue.

Other Serotonergic Agents

There has been a dramatic increase in the number of antidepressant medications available to clinicians over the past 15 years. In addition to the SSRIs,

Table 11.2   Other Serotonergic Agents

Generic Name	Trade Name	Recommended Dosage	Pregnancy Category*	Present in Breast Milk
Venlafaxine XR	Effexor XR	75–225mg daily	C	Yes
Bupropion	Wellbutrin	150–300mg daily (divided twice daily for the regular and SR forms, once daily for the XL)	B	Yes
Mirtazapine	Remeron	15–45mg at bedtime	C	Yes
Trazodone	Desyrel	150–600mg divided twice daily	C	Yes
Nefazodone	Serzone	200–600mg divided twice daily	C	Yes

*See page 196 for a description of FDA pregnancy ratings.

several newer medications have come onto the market that have effects on other neurotransmitters as well as serotonin. These have been demonstrated to be effective antidepressant medications in their own right; however, we know less about their efficacy in treating posttraumatic stress. In the coming years, our knowledge about these medications and their use in trauma will undoubtedly increase considerably. These agents are listed in Table 11.2.

Venlafaxine (Effexor). Venlafaxine is a potent serotonin-norepinephrine reuptake inhibitor that has been found to be effective in the treatment of depression. Its side effect profile is similar to that of the SSRIs. It tends to be activating rather than sedating, and has a relatively high likelihood of causing sexual side effects and a discontinuation syndrome (both of these are due to its serotonergic activity, and are similar to the side effects described above for the SSRIs). The regular form of venlafaxine was associated with elevations in blood pressure in some individuals; this is seen less with the extended-release form of the medication, venlafaxine XR. It is nevertheless appropriate to monitor blood pressure in individuals taking venlafaxine. There is almost no literature on the use of venlafaxine in PTSD, although given its similarity to the SSRIs, one would expect that it would be a useful treatment for this disorder. One open trial in refugees showed efficacy in five subjects (Smajkic et al., 2001); other than this trial, there have only been case reports of good response to venlafaxine in PTSD (for example, Hamner & Frueh, 1998).

Bupropion (Wellbutrin). Bupropion is unrelated to any other antidepressants. Its precise mechanism of action is unknown—it weakly inhibits the reuptake of serotonin and epinephrine, and more potently inhibits the reuptake of dopamine. It appears to have stimulant-like effects, and therefore it is usually recommended that bupropion be taken before five o'clock in the evening to prevent insomnia. In line with this activation, a substantial portion of individuals treated with bupropion experience agitation or restlessness, a side effect that must always be kept in mind when treating trauma survivors who may already complain of autonomic arousal. The most concerning side effect with bupropion is a 0.4 percent risk of causing seizures, which is four times that of other antidepressants. This risk is increased in patients with bulimia, and the medication is therefore contraindicated in those with a prior history of seizure disorder or a history of bulimia. Because some survivors of childhood abuse may engage in tension reduction behaviors, including bingeing/purging (as described in Chapter 2) it is important to ask about a history of eating disorders. Despite these concerns, bupropion is an effective antidepressant, and has the significant (and unique) added benefit of causing no sexual side effects.

There is only one report in the literature on the use of bupropion in PTSD. This may be due to concerns that bupropion could be too activating in those with significant posttraumatic distress and anxiety. Interestingly, in an open trial of 17 combat veterans with PTSD, bupropion was found to decrease hyperarousal but have no effect on intrusions or avoidance, or, in fact, on measures of overall PTSD severity (Canive, Clark, Calais, Qualls, & Tuason, 1998). Clearly, more research is needed before any recommendations can be made regarding the use of this medication in PTSD. Bupropion is available in three formulations—regular, sustained release (SR), and most recently, an extended release (XL) that is dosed only once a day. It may be that this XL formulation will have fewer acute side effects, such as anxiety and agitation, but this remains to be seen as the medication is used in clinical practice.

Mirtazapine (Remeron). Mirtazapine is another unique medication that has activity on both serotonin and norepinephrine, as well as some presynaptic alpha-adrenergic blockade. It has antagonism at some serotonin receptor sites, which is hypothesized to be the reason that it has less serotonergic side effects than do the SSRIs, including less sexual side effects. It is sedating and is usually given at night to help with sleep. Unfortunately, it also can cause significant weight gain. There have been several open trials and one small randomized controlled trial that have indicated good response to mirtazapine in PTSD (Davidson, Weisler, et al., 2003). One randomized open trial in Korean War veterans found mirtazapine to be superior to Zoloft in reducing symptoms of PTSD (Chung et al., 2004). There have also been case reports of the efficacy of Mirtazapine for PTSD-related nightmares and sleep disturbance (Lewis, 2002). It has been suggested that this may be due to alpha blockade, a topic that is discussed later in this chapter.

Trazodone (Desyrel). Trazodone is another serotonergic antidepressant that has alpha-adrenergic blocking activity. It is highly sedating, and is used most frequently in psychiatry as a sleep agent. There have been a few case reports and one open trial with six subjects investigating the use of trazodone in PTSD. These reports suggest mild to moderate efficacy across the PTSD symptom clusters (Hertzberg, Feldman, Beckham, & Davidson, 1996). Significant side effects, aside from sedation, include dry mouth, blurred vision, gastrointestinal upset, and in males, risk of priapism (painful sustained erection that may require emergent medical intervention).

Nefazodone (Serzone). Nefazodone is a potent blocker of postsynaptic serotonin, as well as a weak inhibitor of both serotonin and norepinephrine reuptake. It has been shown to have similar efficacy to the SSRIs in treating depression, and has the benefit of causing minimal sexual side effects. Nefazodone was widely used in those individuals for whom SSRI-related sexual dysfunction was problematic. Unfortunately, it has been associated with several cases of fatal liver failure, and has been taken off the market in the United States, Europe, and Canada. There have been no randomized controlled trials with Nefazodone; however, several open trials have shown efficacy not only for the three symptom clusters of PTSD, but for improved sleep as well (for example, Davis, Nugent, Murray, Kramer, & Petty, 2000).

Monoamine Oxidase Inhibitors

Monoamine oxidase inhibitors (MAOIs; listed in Table 11.3) are effective antidepressants that have largely been replaced by SSRIs because of their considerable side effects, and because of the dietary restrictions that must be followed when taking them. They are generally used for treatment of depression (especially the melancholic type) when other medications have failed. MAOIs inhibit the action of the enzyme monoamine oxidase, which breaks down epinephrine, norepinephrine, serotonin, and dopamine, thereby increasing the available levels of these neurotransmitters. MAOIs have significant side effects, including dizziness, headache, somnolence, weight gain, constipation, dry mouth, and sexual disturbances. MAOIs can also cause hypertensive crisis, especially in those individuals taking other sympathomimetic agents (such as cold preparations, decongestants, and weight reduction medications), or who eat tyramine-containing foods. The dietary

Table 11.3   Monoamine Oxidase Inhibitors

Generic Name	Trade Name	Recommended Dosage (daily)	Pregnancy Category*	Present in Breast Milk
Phenelzine	Nardil	15–19mg	Not known	Not known
Tranylcypromine	Parnate	30–60mg	Not known	Not known

*See page 196 for a description of FDA pregnancy ratings.

restrictions are critical, as monoamine oxidase also breaks down tyramine. When tyramine is not metabolized, it displaces epinephrine and norepinephrine in the nervous system and adrenal glands, which can lead to severe headache, sweating, neck rigidity, palpitations, and dramatic blood pressure elevations. On rare occasions, MAOI-induced hypertensive crisis can lead to cardiac arrhythmias and cerebral hemorrhage. Therefore, individuals taking MAOIs must avoid foods containing tyramine (including, but not limited to aged cheese, yeast extract, red wine, beer, pickled fish, preserved meats, fava beans, overripe bananas and avocados, caffeine, and chocolate). Clearly, MAOIs are not simple to take, and compliance can be very difficult.

There have been two randomized controlled trials of phenelzine in PTSD. One showed efficacy in reducing reexperiencing symptoms and in global improvement, but not the other symptom clusters; the other was not superior to placebo at all (Friedman et al., 2000). Open trials of phenelzine have had similarly equivocal results.

Tricyclic Antidepressants

The tricyclic antidepressants (TCAs; listed in Table 11.4) were introduced in the 1950s as a treatment for depression, and were the mainstay of pharmacotherapy for depression until the introduction of the SSRIs in the 1980s. TCAs have been used less frequently over the past two decades due to their side effects, which can be quite debilitating, and because of their potential lethality when taken in overdose. Common side effects of TCAs include sedation, dry mouth, gastrointestinal discomfort, constipation, blurry vision, sexual dysfunction, and weight gain. TCAs can also cause prolongation of the QTc interval on the electrocardiogram (EKG) and can, in some instances, lead to cardiac arrhythmias.

There have been four randomized clinical trials of TCAs in PTSD, and multiple open trials. Both imipramine and amitriptyline have shown effectiveness in reducing the reexperiencing and avoidant symptoms of PTSD, but not hyperarousal (Kosten, Frank, Dan, McDougle, & Giller, 1991; Davidson,

Table 11.4   Tricyclic Antidepressants

Generic Name	Trade Name	Recommended Dosage (daily)	Pregnancy Category*	Present in Breast Milk
Amitriptyline	Elavil	50–300mg	C	Yes
Clomipramine	Anafranil	100–250mg	C	Yes
Desipramine	Norpramin	100–300mg	C	Yes
Imipramine	Tofranil	75–300mg	C	Yes
Nortriptyline	Pamelor	74–150mg	C	Yes

*See page 196 for a description of FDA pregnancy ratings.

Kudler, et al., 1990). One study with desipramine showed no efficacy (Reist et al., 1989). Overall, TCAs appear to be less effective for PTSD than are SSRIs or the MAOIs (Friedman, Davidson, Mellman, & Southwick, 2000). However, all of the randomized controlled studies have involved veterans, not civilians, which may have affected the results.

Some clinicians take advantage of the sedating properties of the tricyclics and use them in low doses as adjunctive sleep medications in PTSD. There is, however, no research data to support this practice.

Like the SSRIs, TCAs can cause a discontinuation syndrome. These are thought to be due to cholinergic excess after the blockade of acetylcholine is removed. Discontinuation symptoms can include abdominal pain, nausea, vomiting, anorexia, chills, diaphoresis, diarrhea, fatigue, headache, malaise, myalgia, and weakness (Lejoyeux, Adès, Mourad, Solomon, & Dilsaver, 1996).

Benzodiazepines

Benzodiazepines are highly addictive medications that are used in psychiatry and general medicine for the treatment of anxiety. The most commonly used benzodiazepines are listed in Table 11.5. They act on gammaaminobutyric acid (GABA) and have many similarities to alcohol—in fact, they are used as the primary treatment in alcohol detoxification to prevent withdrawal. Their use is fraught with controversy due to the potential for abuse and dependence. Benzodiazepines are often used in combination with illegal recreational substances, as well as with alcohol, and can be purchased "on the street" as drugs of abuse. Concerns about abuse are especially relevant in the treatment of trauma survivors, who often present complaining of intense, overwhelming anxiety that appears to require immediate relief. For such individuals, benzodiazepines may initially seem a godsend—the only thing that seems to dramatically reduce their level of arousal and/or address their panic.

Table 11.5   Benzodiazepines

Generic Name	Trade Name	Recommended Dosage (used as needed two to three times daily, or taken at bedtime)	Pregnancy Category*	Present in Breast Milk
Alprazolam	Xanax	0.25–2mg	D	Yes
Clonazepam	Klonopin	0.5–2mg	D	Yes
Diazepam	Valium	2.5–10mg	D	Yes
Lorazepam	Ativan	1–2mg	D	Yes
Temazepam	Restoril	7.5–30mg at bedtime	D	Yes
Triazolam	Halcion	0.125–0.25mg at bedtime	D	Yes
Oxazepam	Serax	10–30mg at bedtime	D	Yes

*See page 196 for a description of FDA pregnancy ratings.

However, in the longer term, many people develop tolerance to the drugs' effects, requiring higher and higher doses to achieve the same result. Some individuals develop physiological and psychological dependence and find that these medications are extremely difficult to discontinue. As mentioned earlier, benzodiazepines have similar actions to alcohol—including a withdrawal syndrome that can be potentially fatal if not managed properly. Although benzodiazepines are excellent anti-anxiety medications, they are only a short-term solution—they treat anxiety when it happens, and for as long as the drug remains active in the bloodstream. Unlike SSRIs and other antidepressants that treat anxiety only after a therapeutic blood level has built up over several weeks, benzodiazepines only work "in the moment."

Another problem with the use of benzodiazepines in trauma survivors, aside from the problems related to abuse and dependence, is the alteration in consciousness that they produce. Benzodiazepines not only treat anxiety and panic, they may cause euphoria, disinhibition, sedation, diminished response to threat, impaired coordination, and feelings of being "zoned out" or "disconnected." It might appear, at first glance, that this reduction in arousal would be useful in the context of trauma-related psychotherapy. One might imagine, for example, that decreased arousal could reduce the likelihood that the client would be overwhelmed when discussing emotionally laden, traumatic material. However, this is not borne out in clinical practice. Instead, regular use of benzodiazepines may interfere with the processing of traumatic material in therapy, or may produce state-dependent treatment effects that do not persist once medication has been discontinued (Briere, 2002a).

Although this clinical observation has yet to be empirically validated in the specific context of psychotherapeutic interventions, research has clearly demonstrated that benzodiazepines affect both learning and memory performance. Triazolam has been shown to affect memory for emotional content, in a manner consistent with difficulties seen in those who have damage to the amygdala (Buchanan, Karafin, & Adolphs, 2003). Other studies have shown that lorazepam can cause impairment in the ability to learn behavioral strategies, a finding that may be due to impaired consolidation of long-term memory while under the influence of the medication (Matthews, Kirkby, & Martin, 2002). Similar impairments in learning and memory have been found with oxazepam and alcohol (Barbee, 1993; Mattila, Vanakoski, Kalska, & Seppala, 1998). These findings are not surprising, given that benzodiazepines are known amnestics and are used as such in anesthesia.

There are similar data regarding the effects of alcohol on memory and performance that may be generalizable to benzodiazepines, given its similar effects on GABA. Studies with alcohol have shown that information learned while under the effects of alcohol is best retrieved under the same conditions. Some research suggests that alcohol disrupts hippocampal-dependent information processing (that is, explicit or declarative memory) preferentially. This finding might explain why it is difficult to remember specific experiences that occurred while under the influence of alcohol (Melia, Ryabinin, Corodimas, Wilson, & LeDoux, 1996).

It is important to educate clients early on about these concerns if they are taking benzodiazepines. When clients are informed about the potential for addiction and possible longer-term impacts on trauma processing, those not yet addicted are often more careful in how they use these medications. In addition, those trauma survivors who are concerned about having less ability to sense danger often appreciate being informed about the potential for benzodiazepines to sedate and impair responsiveness. It may also be helpful to explain to patients that benzodiazepines work only in the short term—much as drinking a glass of wine will help to alleviate acute anxiety but will not treat it longer term.

Unfortunately, when trauma survivors present to medical emergency rooms with complaints of intense anxiety and panic, they are often prescribed benzodiazepines as sole agents, without being provided adequate information about potential problems. All too frequently, the medication prescribed is alprazolam (Xanax), which is the most highly addictive of this class of medication. Alprazolam also produces a type of euphoria that heightens the potential for psychological addiction. Alprazolam can produce a particularly bad withdrawal syndrome with rebound panic, and sometimes the need for medications to manage seizures. The frequent use of alprazolam in emergency room settings means that trauma therapists and mental health professionals often find that they need to intervene and educate clients who have already developed a problem with this medication. In one survey of primary care patients, trauma exposure was associated with increased lifetime use of benzodiazepines (Sansone, Hruschka, Vasudevan, & Miller, 2003).

There are very few studies examining the use of benzodiazepines in trauma victims. In the only randomized controlled investigation of benzodiazepines in trauma, alprazolam was noted to help with symptoms of anxiety during the course of the trial, but there was no decrease in posttraumatic symptoms or in risk of later development of PTSD (Braun, Greenberg, Dasberg, & Lerer, 1990). In an open study of clonazepam and alprazolam, administered within the first week posttrauma, benzodiazepine-treated patients showed a decrease in heart rate over time, but no other benefit was found at 6 months. In fact, more of the patients who received medication met diagnostic criteria for PTSD at 6 months than those who did not receive a benzodiazepine (Gelpin, Bonne, Peri, Brandes, & Shalev, 1996). Temazepam, given at bedtime for a week in victims of acute trauma, improved sleep and appeared to decrease symptoms of PTSD 1 week after discontinuation; however, there was no long-term follow-up (Mellman, Augenstein, & Byers, 1998). Clonazepam, given at bedtime in a small single-blind placebo-controlled study, was not superior to placebo across multiple sleep measures in combat-related PTSD (Cates, Bishop, Davis, Lowe, & Wooley, 2004).

Clearly, more research is needed to elucidate the utility of benzodiazepines in trauma survivors. At the present time, we advise that benzodiazepines be used with such individuals only for the management of intense anxiety and panic attacks. If used, these medications should be prescribed short term, and the initial treatment plan should include a discussion of risks and side effects as well as a plan for discontinuation. In addition, the clinician should have a discussion with the client regarding treatment with a less addictive, more long-term medication for intense, ongoing symptoms, such as an SSRI. Ideally, treatment with an SSRI would begin concomitantly with the benzodiazepine, with the benzodiazepine being tapered over the first 10–14 days of treatment. Close follow-up by the prescribing clinician is essential. In emergency settings, dispensing only enough medications to last 4 or 5 days is recommended as well—this ensures that the patient will not develop dependence before follow-up can occur.

Mood Stabilizers

As mentioned earlier, kindling has been hypothesized as one of the mechanisms by which PTSD develops under conditions of chronic stress. Because kindling theory was developed as a way to explain seizure disorders, this sparked interest in the use of mood stabilizing and anti-epileptic medications

Table 11.6   Mood Stabilizers

Generic Name	Trade Name	Recommended Dosage	Pregnancy Category*	Present in Breast Milk
Lithium	Lithobid	300–1800mg (divided two times daily, dosed to reach a blood level of 0.6–1.2 mEq/L)	D	Yes
Lamotrigine	Lamictal	50–200mg daily, dosed once	C	Yes
Valproate	Depakote	500–1500mg (divided two or three times daily, dosed to reach a blood level of 50–100micrograms/mL)	D	Yes
Carbamazepine	Tegretol	200–1200mg (divided twice daily, dosed to reach a blood level of 8–12micrograms/mL)	D	Yes
Topiramate	Topamax	100–400mg, divided twice daily	C	Yes
Gabapentin	Neurontin	300–2700mg divided three or four times daily	C	Yes

*See page 196 for a description of FDA pregnancy ratings.

in PTSD. These medications have also been used to treat aggression and irritability in PTSD and other psychiatric conditions. Only two medications have been FDA approved as mood stabilizers: lithium and valproic acid. Despite the fact that lithium is generally considered to be the "gold standard" for the treatment of classical bipolar disorder, there have been no clinical trials investigating its use in PTSD. Recently, there has been increased interest in using the atypical antipsychotic medications as mood stabilizers, and in fact there are now indications for their use in certain phases of bipolar disorder. These medications and their indications are discussed in the section on antipsychotics. The mood stabilizers are listed in Table 11.6.

Lithium. There are some studies suggesting that lithium may be helpful for the treatment of PTSD-related aggression (for example, Kitchner & Greenstein, 1985); however, there are no data investigating the use of this medication for PTSD. Lithium can cause weight gain, tremor, rash, kidney failure, and thyroid problems; it is also potentially fatal in overdose.

Lamotrigine (Lamictal). The only randomized clinical trial of a mood stabilizer in PTSD was a very small study of lamotrigine, a newer medication that affects N-methyl-D-aspartate (NDMA) (Hertzberg et al., 1999). Lamotrigine was associated with improvements over placebo in the reexperiencing and avoidance/numbing symptoms of PTSD. Given the small sample size of this study, little can be extrapolated from these findings until more research has been done. Lamotrigine is well documented as an effective mood stabilizer, as well as having antidepressant effects. Its most concerning potential side effect is *Stevens Johnson Syndrome*, a rare but life-threatening form of erythema multiforme that presents as a rash over the body, particularly the palms, soles, and backs of hands and feet. It can also involve lesions of the mucous membranes, and in severe cases, the kidneys, lungs, and digestive tract. For this reason, it must be slowly titrated with close observation.

Valproate (Depakote). Of all the mood stabilizers, valproate is probably most commonly used for the control of aggression and irritability. However, there have only been three small open trials, in addition to multiple case reports, investigating its use in PTSD. Results have been positive, but somewhat equivocal—one of the open trials reported benefit in all three symptom clusters of PTSD, the others in reexperiencing/hyperarousal and hyperarousal/avoidance, respectively (for example, Clark, Canive, Calais, Qualls, & Tuason, 1999; Petty et al., 2002). Valproate can cause weight gain, mental dullness, and liver damage. It can also be fatal in overdose.

Carbamazepine (Tegretol). Carbamazepine is another anticonvulsant frequently used as a mood stabilizer, although it is not FDA approved as such. In several small open trials, carbamazepine was effective in reducing all three symptom clusters of PTSD (for example, Keck, McElroy, & Friedman, 1992; Looff, Grimley, Kuller, Martin, & Shonfield, 1995). Carbamazepine is generally well tolerated, although it can cause bone marrow suppression that may have serious consequences. Blood counts, as well as liver and kidney functions, therefore need to be monitored periodically. Common side effects include gastrointestinal upset, weight gain, and sedation. Carbamazepine can be lethal in overdose.

Topiramate (Topamax). Topiramate is a newer anticonvulsant that is used as an add-on mood stabilizer. It has the added benefit of assisting with weight loss, a notable effect as most of the more commonly used mood stabilizers can cause significant weight gain. In case reports and in two small open trials (Berlant, 2004; Berlant & van Kammen, 2002), topiramate appeared to be effective across the three symptom clusters of PTSD. Topiramate has also been reported to be particularly effective in reducing PTSD-related nightmares and flashbacks. Its most notable side effect is cognitive dulling, which some individuals find intolerable.

Gabapentin (Neurontin). Gabapentin is another newer anticonvulsant that is used frequently in psychiatry as an add-on mood stabilizer, as well as an adjunct in the management of anxiety and aggression. It has the benefit of having relatively few side effects and being less risky in overdose. To date there have been only case reports and retrospective chart reviews of its use as an adjunct to other medications for PTSD. Initial reports suggest that gabapentin may be useful for sleep disturbance and nightmares in PTSD (Hamner, Brodrick, & Labbate, 2001).

Given this discussion, and the lack of adequate data regarding the use of mood stabilizers, they cannot be recommended as a first-line treatment for PTSD. They are probably most appropriate for use in those who do not respond adequately to treatment with SSRIs or other antidepressants, and in those who have significant behavioral disturbances due to aggression or agitated hyperarousal.

Adrenergic Agents

As described earlier in this chapter, dysregulation of the adrenergic system is clearly part of the biological underpinning of PTSD and other posttraumatic outcomes. Despite research that has demonstrated adrenergic hyperactivity in these states, there has been surprisingly little investigation of the use of anti-adrenergic compounds in the treatment of posttraumatic stress. The most commonly used adrenergic agents are listed in Table 11.7.

Beta-Adrenergic Blockade

Propranolol (Inderal). Propranolol is a nonselective beta-adrenergic blocking agent that has effects on both the central and peripheral nervous systems. While primarily used in general medicine as an antihypertensive and antiarrhythmic medication, propranolol is also used in psychiatry to treat aggression, social phobia, and performance anxiety.

The only randomized controlled trial of a beta-blocker in trauma is a pilot study investigating the use of a course of propranolol in acute trauma survivors with heart rates of at least 90 beats per minute (Pitman et al., 2002). At 1-month follow-up, fewer victims treated with the beta-blocker met PTSD criteria. However, this difference disappeared by 3 months. Surprisingly, those in the treatment group did not have a significantly greater heart rate decrease after receiving propranolol (at a dose of 40 milligrams) than did those who received a placebo. The authors suggest that this may indicate a need for higher doses in order to effectively counteract trauma-related

Table 11.7   Adrenergic Agents

Generic Name	Trade Name	Recommended Dosage	Pregnancy Category*	Present in Breast Milk
Propranolol	Inderal	Initial dose 40mg twice daily. Titration as tolerated to a maximum of 320mg. Usual doses in psychiatry total 120–160mg daily. (Inderal exists in a long-acting form, but there are no studies of its use in psychiatry.)	C	Yes
Clonidine	Catapres	Initial dose 0.1mg twice daily. The dose may be increased by 0.1mg per day as indicated clinically—usual doses range from 0.2 to 0.6mg daily.	C	Yes
Prazosin	Minipress	Initial dose 1mg daily. Slowly increase as tolerated. The doses used in PTSD have ranged from 1 to 4 mg daily, although the dose limit for prazosin in medical settings is up to 15 mg.	C	Yes

*See page 196 for a description of FDA pregnancy ratings.

adrenergic conditioning. Smaller open studies, one in acute trauma survivors (Vaiva et al., 2003), one in children with PTSD (Famularo, Kinscherff, & Fenton, 1988), and a two-client case report (Dias & Jones, 2004) suggest that propranolol may be useful in reducing both current symptoms of posttraumatic stress and later risk for PTSD. It is worth noting that these studies, with the exception of Dias and Jones (2004), involved short courses of treatment, followed by a slow taper before discontinuation, with doses of 40 milligrams three or four times daily.

Frequent side effects of beta-blockers include gastrointestinal upsets (nausea, vomiting, diarrhea, abdominal pain), cold extremities and exacerbation of Raynaud's phenomenon, sleep disturbance, dizziness, and fatigue. Beta-blockers can also cause congestive heart failure and bronchospasm; they are therefore contraindicated in individuals who have preexisting congestive heart failure, bronchospasm, and bronchial asthma, as well as those who have sinus bradycardia or first-degree heart block. In overdose, propranolol can lead to significant cardiac damage.

Alpha-Adrenergic Blockade

Clonidine (Catapres). Clonidine, a presynaptic alpha 2-adrenergic agonist, suppresses the release of norepinephrine both centrally and peripherally. It is used as an antihypertensive agent, and as an adjunct in the treatment for the autonomic symptoms associated with opiate withdrawal. In open trials, clonidine has been reported as helpful for symptoms of hyperarousal, hypervigilance, sleep disruption, exaggerated startle response, nightmares, behavioral irritability, and aggression in studies of combat veterans (Kolb, Burris, & Griffiths, 1984), Cambodian refugees (Kinzie & Leung, 1989), and children with PTSD (Harmon & Riggs, 1996).

The most common side effects of clonidine include dry mouth, drowsiness, sedation, dizziness, and constipation. Clonidine acts relatively rapidly and can cause severe hypotension acutely, within 30–60 minutes after administration. It must therefore be carefully dosed and monitored. Clonidine should not be given to those with severe cardiovascular disease, and care should be taken on discontinuation to avoid rebound hypertension.

A significant problem with the use of clonidine is the development of physiological tolerance, leading to a gradual return of symptoms that sometimes do not respond to higher doses. There have been a few case reports describing the use of guanfacine instead of clonidine, but these are too small in number to recommend its use (for example, Horrigan & Barnhill, 1996).

Prazosin (Minipress). The use of prazosin as an alternative to clonidine in the treatment of PTSD has recently been investigated. Prazosin is an antihypertensive agent that blocks alpha1-adrenergic receptors centrally and peripherally. Initial case reports of the use of prazosin in PTSD described particular efficacy for sleep disturbance and trauma-related nightmares. Open trials of prazosin in both combat- and noncombat-related PTSD, as well as one small placebo controlled trial in combat veterans, have reported "moderate" improvement in overall PTSD symptoms, again with particular emphasis on improvement in sleep and nightmares (Raskind et al., 2003; Taylor & Raskind, 2002).

The most common side effects of prazosin are nausea, dizziness, headache, drowsiness, weakness, lack of energy, and palpitations. Prazosin has been noted to cause syncope (sudden loss of consciousness), which is believed in most cases to be due to hypotension. There are no absolute contraindications; however, care must be taken in patients who have preexisting heart disease, and blood pressure must be closely monitored. In overdose, alpha-blockers can cause significant cardiac problems, as well as fatality in very high doses.

A Final Note on Adrenergic Agents

Although there are clear research data that alpha- and beta-adrenergic blockers can be useful adjuncts in the treatment of posttraumatic stress, the investigations to date have been limited to case reports, open trials, and a handful of controlled trials with very few subjects. The data suggest that beta-blockers may be helpful in treating those individuals who suffer from intense symptoms of hyperarousal, while alpha-blockers may be most helpful in those with intractable sleep disturbance and nightmares. Practical precautions to take with patients when prescribing these medications include (1) explaining the nature of and rationale for treatment with these agents, including the fact that their use in psychiatry is "off label," (2) communicating with and obtaining clearance from patients' internists regarding using blood pressure-lowering agents, and (3) close monitoring of vital signs, especially in the first few weeks of treatment.

Antipsychotics

The antipsychotics are medications that block dopamine in the central nervous system. They differ from each other primarily in the extent of dopamine blockade, the specific receptors that they affect, and their side effects. The "typical" antipsychotics, (for example, haloperidol [Haldol], fluphenazine [Prolixin], chlorpromazine [Thorazine]) were seen as a miracle cure for schizophrenia when they were first introduced in the 1950s. However, because they affect dopamine, they have potentially serious and debilitating motor side effects. The "extrapyramidal symptoms" (EPS—so called because they are thought to originate from the basal ganglia, rather than from the motor "pyramids" of the brainstem) occur often in the first few days or weeks of treatment, and manifest in three ways: (1) Parkinsonism—tremor, rigidity, shuffling gait; (2) akathisia—the subjective experience of feeling restless and unable to sit still; and (3) dystonia—stiffening of the limbs, jaw, or neck, often occurring quite acutely and requiring immediate medical intervention. Tardive dyskinesia (TD) usually occurs after long-term treatment with antipsychotics, although it has also been reported early in treatment and after treatment is terminated. TD is characterized by rhythmic involuntary movements of the mouth, jaw, tongue, and lips (such as chewing, smacking, and pursing) as well as the extremities. TD is generally irreversible, and can be quite disfiguring and debilitating.

Table 11.8   Atypical Antipsychotics

Generic Name	Trade Name	Recommended Dosage	Major Side Effects	Pregnancy Category*	Present in Breast Milk
Risperidone	Risperdal	0.5–6mg daily	Akathisia, EPS in higher doses, hyperprolactinemia	C	Yes
Olanzapine	Zyprexa	5–30mg daily	Sedation, weight gain, increased risk for diabetes	C	Yes
Quetiapine	Seroquel	50–600mg daily, in divided doses	Sedation, weight gain, rare risk of cataracts	C	Yes
Ziprasidone	Geodon	40–160mg daily, in divided doses	Rare risk of prolonged QTc on EKG—screening EKG recommended before starting therapy	C	Yes
Aripiprazole	Abilify	10–30mg daily	Agitation	C	Yes
Clozapine	Clozaril	100–800mg daily, in divided doses	Sedation, drooling, weight gain, increased risk for diabetes, agranulocytosis	B	Yes

*See page 196 for a description of FDA pregnancy ratings.

The typical antipsychotics have also been associated with a condition known as *neuroleptic malignant syndrome* (NMS), a potentially life-threatening reaction that is characterized by altered mental status, autonomic dysfunction, fever, and muscle rigidity. In overdose, they can cause arrythmias, and can be fatal.

In the 1980s, a new class of antipsychotics was developed, referred to as "atypical" to distinguish them from the older medications. These newer medications, as a class, have significantly less risk of motor side effects. They also are relatively benign in overdose. Because of this lower risk, they are being used for an increasingly wide spectrum of nonpsychotic psychiatric disturbances, including mania, depression, severe anxiety, personality disorders, aggression, insomnia, and trauma. In fact, the FDA has recently approved the use of several atypical antipsychotics for the treatment of various phases of bipolar disorder. The atypical antipsychotics are listed in Table 11.8.

The use of these medications in nonpsychotic individuals, nonetheless, remains controversial. While the incidence of movement disorders and NMS is greatly reduced with atypical antipsychotics, the risk is not eliminated. The annual incidence of TD with typical antipsychotics has been estimated to be 5 percent in adults; for the atypicals, the annual incidence is around 0.8 percent (Correll, Leucht, & Kane, 2004). However, several lines of research have suggested that individuals with mood disorders have a higher likelihood of developing TD from antipsychotics than do those who have primary psychotic disorders. In one study, depressed individuals treated with typical antipsychotics developed TD at an annual rate of 13.5 percent (Kane, 1999). Such data have yet to be replicated using the newer generation of medications. However, given the high comorbidity of PTSD and depression, it might be reasonable to extrapolate from these data that traumatized individuals could also be at higher risk for these debilitating side effects. Given this potential risk, caution is warranted when using antipsychotics for this broader array of symptoms.

Another emerging concern with the use of the atypicals is *metabolic syndrome*—a clustering of obesity, impaired glucose tolerance, hypertension, and increased lipids. Metabolic syndrome has been noted to be higher in those with severe mental illnesses than in the general population (for a variety of reasons, including lifestyle and poor self-care among others) but has also been associated with psychotropic medications, particularly olanzapine, clozapine, and quetiapine. Recent studies have shown high discontinuation rates with all antipsychotics, and researchers and clinicians are beginning to reevaluate the risk-benefit profiles associated with their use (for example, Lieberman et al., 2005).

Antipsychotics for PTSD

Only three of the atypical antipsychotics have been evaluated for efficacy in trauma. These are risperidone (Risperdal), olanzapine (Zyprexa), and quetiapine (Seroquel). Ziprasidone (Geodon) and aripiprazole (Abilify) are newer to the market, and it is likely that, in the coming years, their use in trauma will be investigated as well. There is one case report in the literature discussing the efficacy of clozapine (Clozaril) in PTSD with psychosis (Hamner, 1996). Given the dearth of literature, and the significant side effects associated with the use of this medication, however, it would be prudent to continue to restrict its use to those individuals who are psychotic and highly treatment resistant, as is the usual practice.

Risperidone (Risperdal). There have been four randomized controlled trials of risperidone in PTSD. All were limited by small sample size, the presence of significant comorbidity, and the use of other psychotropic medications. Two of these found that low-dose risperidone was helpful in the treatment of irritability and intrusive reexperiencing (Monnelly, Ciraulo, Knapp, & Keane, 2003; Reich, Winternitz, Hennen, Watts, & Stanculescu, 2004); another found efficacy on the hyperarousal subscale of the CAPS (Bartzokis, Lu, Turner, Mintz, & Saunders, 2005). The last investigated the use of risperidone in veterans with PTSD who also had psychotic symptoms. These individuals had a modest improvement in their psychotic symptoms, but no statistically significant reduction in PTSD symptoms (Hamner, Deitsch, Brodrick, Ulmer, & Lorberbaum, 2003). In addition, there have been multiple case reports indicating that risperidone may be helpful for nightmares, intrusive reexperiencing, hyperarousal, and aggression in PTSD (for example, Krashin & Oates, 1999; Monnelly & Ciraulo, 1999). Of the atypicals, risperidone has the highest risk of extrapyramidal symptoms; it also carries some risk of weight gain and is mildly sedating.

Olanzapine (Zyprexa). There have been two small randomized controlled trials using olanzapine as an adjunctive treatment in nonpsychotic combat veterans with PTSD. The first indicated moderate response in symptoms of PTSD compared to placebo, but no significant difference in clinical global improvement (Stein, Kline, & Matloff, 2002). The second found a high placebo-response rate and no statistical benefit to olanzapine over placebo (Butterfield et al., 2001). There have been several open trials and case reports suggesting the effectiveness of olanzapine in treating PTSD-associated insomnia, nightmares, intrusive reexperiencing, and depressive symptoms (for example, Jakovljevic, Sagud, & Mihaljevic-Peles, 2003; Pivac, Kozaric-Kovacic, & Muck-Seler, 2004). Olanzapine has a significant risk of weight gain (which patients often find intolerable) and has been associated with the development of diabetes and metabolic syndrome.

Quetiapine (Seroquel). There have been no randomized controlled trials of quetiapine in PTSD. An open trial of quetiapine in 20 veterans as adjunctive therapy indicated effectiveness across all PTSD symptom clusters, particularly the reexperiencing symptoms, and in positive symptoms of psychosis (Hamner, Deitsch, Brodrick, Ulmer, & Lorberbaum, 2003). However, the participants in this study had severe PTSD, and their posttreatment symptom scores, while showing improvement, remained high. Retrospective chart review of quetiapine as adjunctive therapy in treatment-resistant veterans shows promise for reduction of symptoms in all symptom clusters, whereas case reports suggest effectiveness for reducing flashbacks (for example, Sokolski, Denson, Lee, & Reist, 2003).

Taken together, these data suggest that, for treatment-refractory PTSD, particularly when there are psychotic symptoms present, atypical antipsychotics may be a useful addition to pharmacotherapy. However, given the high risk of side effects, and the limited amount of data regarding their use for nonpsychotic posttraumatic stress, caution is recommended. It may be particularly difficult to convince highly anxious, distrustful individuals, especially those who do not want to be sedated, that antipsychotics are a reasonable alternative. At the present time, there is no indication that the antipsychotics are as effective as the SSRIs for PTSD, nor is there any evidence to suggest that antipsychotics represent a first-line choice for PTSD (Friedman, Davidson, Mellman, & Southwick, 2000).

Medications for Trauma-Related Psychosis

As noted earlier in this volume, posttraumatic stress is occasionally accompanied by psychosis. Severe trauma can lead to brief psychotic disorder with marked stressors (BPDMS), and can exacerbate symptoms in those with an underlying psychotic disorder such as schizophrenia. PTSD has been found to occur four times more frequently in people with psychotic depression than in those with nonpsychotic depression (Zimmerman & Mattia, 1999). Some individuals may have intense reexperiencing symptoms that can be very difficult to distinguish from psychotic symptoms; others may have trauma-associated fear and avoidance responses that generalize to a wide range of stimuli and are hard to discriminate from paranoid delusions. Although there is no *DSM-IV* category for "PTSD with psychotic features," there do appear to be some individuals with PTSD who have psychotic symptoms, who do not appear to have another underlying psychotic disorder, and who do not meet criteria for psychotic depression. (See Chapter 2 for a more complete discussion of this issue and the diagnostic dilemma involved.)

In instances when trauma leads acutely to psychosis, the recommended treatment is antipsychotic medication. Often, as in BPDMS, the psychotic symptoms resolve over a relatively brief time period. In such situations, the antipsychotic may be tapered off over a course of several weeks, with close monitoring for recurrence as well as for the development of other posttraumatic symptomatology. The literature on BPDMS (and on its predecessor in *DSM-III* [APA, 1987], "Acute Reactive Psychosis") is extremely sparse, and there are no clinical trials investigating the use of medications specifically for this condition.

Major depression with psychotic features, a not uncommon disorder in trauma survivors (see Chapter 2), is a particularly difficult condition both to diagnose and treat. When PTSD occurs comorbidly with psychotic depression, treatment with both an antidepressant (generally an SSRI) and an antipsychotic is indicated (see Schatzberg, 2003, for a review). Tricyclic anti-depressants as monotherapy have generally been found to be ineffective for psychotic depression, as have SSRIs and antipsychotic medications when used alone (for example, Schatzberg, 2003; Simpson, El Shesahai, Rady, Kingsbury, & Fayek, 2003). Overall, response rates with the combination of an SSRI and an atypical antipsychotic have ranged in the area of 50–60 percent. Over the course of treatment the symptoms of PTSD, depression, and psychosis should be followed closely. The decision to continue antipsychotic medication once psychotic symptoms have resolved must be made on an individual basis. This involves an assessment of risk of recurrence, prior history of psychosis, severity of depression, current levels of stress, and presence or absence of debilitating medication side effects. Recent research indicates that treatment with an antipsychotic for at least 4 months is associated with a decreased risk of relapse (Rothschild & Duval, 2003).

There is an emerging literature on the use of medications that inhibit the HPA axis, such as mifepristone, for psychotic depression. This practice is based in the finding that psychotic depression appears to be associated with abnormal HPA axis activity and elevated cortisol levels (Schatzberg, 2003). Note that the reconciliation of this finding with the generally *low* HPA axis activity and *low* cortisol associated with PTSD, as described earlier, is as yet unclear. Some recent research has suggested that nonpsychotic depression in trauma survivors is biologically (in terms of HPA axis activity) more similar to PTSD than it is to "regular" depression that is not associated with trauma (Yehuda, Halligan, Golier, Grossman, & Bierer, 2004). Perhaps, as research continues, we will find a similar biological difference between psychotic depression that is associated with trauma and PTSD, and psychotic depression that occurs in the absence of trauma. This conundrum, again, illustrates the complexity associated with studying and treating trauma. As of yet, there is no data looking at the use of HPA inhibition in psychotic depression that is comorbid with PTSD.

For those situations where PTSD is accompanied by psychotic symptoms in the absence of depression or another Axis I disorder, the literature provides little in the way of direction. Clinical and anecdotal experience suggest that, as for PTSD with comorbid psychotic depression, treatment with an antidepressant and an antipsychotic is indicated, with similar close follow-up and assessment of the need for ongoing medication. In our experience, antipsychotics are rarely helpful when the reexperiencing symptoms of PTSD mimic psychosis. (See Table 11.8.)

Medications for Acute Traumatic Stress

As described in Chapter 6, there is a dearth of literature on acute stress disorder (ASD). This is especially apparent in the area of pharmacological treatment. There have been very few randomized controlled trials of medications for acute stress; in fact, when treating acute trauma victims, clinicians must often extrapolate from the literature on PTSD in order to provide treatment that is validated and up to date. Most of the literature on treating victims in the emergency setting, or in a less emergent but nonetheless acute setting, focuses on psychosocial rather than pharmacological interventions (see Chapter 10).

Benzodiazepines

Acute survivors of trauma are often in a great amount of distress, with significant anxiety, panic attacks, agitation, and sleep disturbance. Victims (and often their families and loved ones) may request that medical practitioners provide sedating medications to relieve the intense distress associated with the trauma. In addition, clinicians may have their own emotional reactions to traumatic material and to the distress of their clients, which may prompt them to provide powerful medications for immediate symptomatic relief. Unfortunately, the literature is equivocal on the benefits to be derived from acutely treating the anxiety that acute trauma victims experience.

As described earlier, the benzodiazepines, although technically effective for the amelioration of acute anxiety, are not useful treatments for acute trauma, and, in fact, even may be associated with an increased risk for PTSD when used acutely (Gelpin et al., 1996). Some have suggested that the benzodiazepines be used acutely in order to prevent the memory consolidation that might lead to PTSD; again, this hypothesis has not been borne out in clinical practice. Nevertheless, there are situations in which acute distress (for example, following a gang rape or witnessing the murder of a family member), especially in the emergency room setting, can only be adequately addressed by using a benzodiazepine. Under these circumstances, cautious use is acceptable, preferably in conjunction with beginning an SSRI or other antidepressant. However, because of the especially high risk for abuse and dependence associated with alprazolam, its use is not recommended. (See Table 11.5.)

Antidepressants

There have been very little data collected on the use of antidepressants in the acutely traumatized. In a single, small open trial of imipramine in pediatric burn victims who met ASD criteria, moderate improvement across all three symptom clusters was seen after 7 days (Robert, Blakeney, Villarreal, Rosenberg, & Meyer, 1999). Surprisingly, there has been no research on the use of SSRIs in acute traumatic stress, despite the fact that SSRIs are the first-line medication treatment for PTSD and appear to have efficacy for all three of its symptom clusters.

Despite the absence of empirical data, in actual clinical practice, clinicians often prescribe SSRIs for those individuals who have been diagnosed with ASD or who are otherwise experiencing acute posttraumatic symptoms, particularly panic attacks. In addition, SSRIs are often prescribed in the hope that they will prevent the development of lasting posttraumatic disturbance. The use of SSRIs in ASD seems reasonable, given (1) the fact that the *DSM-IV* criteria for ASD are similar to those for PTSD, and (2) the data mentioned earlier suggesting that SSRIs may "reregulate" the HPA dysfunction thought to be involved in posttraumatic stress.

For these reasons, the SSRIs are a reasonable choice for those individuals suffering from ASD who require intervention with medications. In light of the problems associated with the use of benzodiazepines, an SSRI is probably the best candidate for intervening in the acute anxiety of ASD, since these medications are clearly efficacious in the treatment of both generalized anxiety and panic attacks, in addition to PTSD. Clearly, however, research is needed to clarify this issue. (See Tables 11.1–11.4.)

Adrenergic Agents

As described earlier, the use of adrenergic medications in trauma is theoretically promising, but the few studies done to date have indicated equivocal results. Propranolol given to acute trauma survivors appears to reduce risk for PTSD initially, but this difference disappeared by 3 months (Pitman et al., 2002). However, script-driven imagery at 3 months revealed decreased physiological reactivity in those who had received the treatment as compared to controls. There has been some speculation that adrenergic blockade, if given within hours of a trauma, might work to prevent sensitization of the adrenergic system; this has yet to be adequately studied, however. At this time, no definitive recommendation regarding these agents in acute trauma can be made. (See Table 11.7.)

Other Agents

As with the SSRIs, there is very little literature on the use of other psychotropic agents in ASD. Research is necessary to evaluate the potential benefit of mood stabilizers to interfere at an early stage with the kindling that might lead to PTSD.

Medications for Sleep

Disturbances of sleep can be one of the most distressing and debilitating aspects of posttraumatic stress. Trauma survivors often complain of initial insomnia, frequent nighttime wakenings, nightmares, early morning wakenings, and subjective feelings of being not rested even when they have slept. Sleep studies have been inconclusive in terms of the underlying physiological mechanisms of disordered sleep in traumatized individuals. Although some research has indicated that trauma leads to disordered rapid eye movement (REM) sleep and that nightmare sufferers have more frequent nighttime wakenings (Harvey, Jones, & Schmidt 2003; Mellman, Bustamante, Fins, Pigeon, & Nolan, 2002), other studies have found no correlation between subjective complaints of sleep disturbance and abnormalities on polysomnographic sleep studies in the laboratory (for example, Hurwitz, Mahowald, Kuskowski, & Engdahl, 1998). Regardless, sleep problems remain a frequent complaint in trauma survivors. Finding medication that improves the quality and quantity of sleep without causing daytime drowsiness or oversedation can be challenging.

The literature on treating PTSD-related sleep disturbance is limited. However, many of the medications that improve posttraumatic symptomatology can help with sleep—including the mood stabilizers, the antipsychotics, the tricyclics, and some other antidepressants. Many of these medications are also sedating, and clinicians can take advantage of this side effect by prescribing them to be taken at night. Although the SSRIs as a class do improve symptoms across all three clusters of PTSD symptomatology, they can sometimes cause an increase in levels of anxiety and activation, especially in the first few weeks of treatment, and often require the addition of a sleep agent. The major non-benzodiazepine sleep agents are listed in Table 11.9.

Trazodone (Desyrel). Trazodone, as discussed earlier, is a highly sedating antidepressant. In fact, it is used more commonly as a sleep agent (in low doses) than as a treatment for depression. Trazodone is an effective hypnotic, and it does not cause dependence or withdrawal. However, it can cause a feeling of being "hung over," associated with daytime drowsiness, that some patients cannot tolerate. There are no reports of its use as sleep agent in PTSD survivors, but a few case reports suggest that trazodone improves sleep as well as other symptoms of PTSD (Hertzberg, Feldman, Beckham, &

Table 11.9   Non-benzodiazepine sleeping medications

Generic Name	Trade Name	Recommended Doses (for sleep)	Pregnancy Category*	Present in Breast Milk
Trazodone	Desyrel	50–200 mg	C	Yes
Diphenhydramine	Benadryl	25–50mg	Not known	Not known
Hydroxizine	Atarax, Vistaril	50–100 mg	Not known	Not known
Zolpidem	Ambien	5–10mg	B	Yes
Zaleplon	Sonata	5–10mg	C	Yes
Eszopiclone	Lunesta	1–3mg	C	Not known

*See page196 for a description of FDA pregnancy ratings.

Davidson, 1996). Trazodone is generally considered a safe adjunct to other psychotropics. See pages 204–205 for more information on this medication.

Antihistamines. There is no specific literature on the use of antihistamines in PTSD. However, diphenhydramine (Benadryl, which is available over the counter) and hydroxyzine (Atarax, Vistaril) are used commonly as sleep agents because of their sedating properties (Ringdahl, Pereira, & Delzell, 2004). They have relatively few side effects, little risk associated with overdose, and no potential for abuse or dependence. The major problem with their use as sleep agents is dry mouth and the potential for morning drowsiness.

Zolpidem (Ambien). Zolpidem is a commonly prescribed non-benzodiazepine sleep agent. It has a rapid onset of action and causes minimal daytime sedation, due to a short half-life of about 2.5 hours. Compared to benzodiazepines, it has significantly fewer effects on cognition and memory (Terzano, Rossi, Palomba, Smerieri, & Parrino, 2003), and appears to have less risk of abuse. In a series of case reports on the use of zolpidem in veterans with PTSD, it was found to be an effective sleep agent with no development of tolerance over treatment periods of up to 20 months (Dieperink & Drogemuller, 1999). However, caution is warranted as the manufacturer notes the potential for tolerance and rebound insomnia in some individuals, as well as psychological dependence, and recommends limiting the use of this medication to no more than three weeks. The main side effects associated with zolpidem are headache, drowsiness, fatigue, and dizziness. Zolpidem has also been noted to cause perceptual disturbances shortly after administration; this is thought to be due to the rapid induction of a hypnotic or dreamlike state associated with peak plasma levels. It is also available in a controlled release formulation (Zolpidem CR), which has a longer length of action.

Zaleplon (Sonata). Zaleplon is another non-benzodiazepine hypnotic. It is ultra-short acting, with a half-life of about 1 hour. There have been no studies investigating its use in PTSD. However, because of its short length of action, zaleplon may be a good choice for those traumatized individuals who are particularly concerned about sedation and decreased responsiveness to threats. Conversely, for individuals who suffer from early wakening, or who wake frequently throughout the night due to trauma-related nightmares, the effects of zaleplon may not be long lasting enough. The main side effects associated with zaleplon are headache, nausea, and dizziness. Zaleplon can also cause a hypnagogic state similar to that cause by zolpidem (Terzano et al., 2003).

Eszopiclone (Lunesta). Eszoplicone is the newest non-benzodiazepine sleep agent, and is related to zolpidem and zaleplon. It appears to be generally well tolerated. Its use in PTSD has not been investigated. The main side effects are a bad taste in the mouth on waking, which some report as intolerable, and headache, as well as the possibility of a hypnagogic state, as described earlier.

Benzodiazepines. As discussed earlier in this chapter, there are significant risks associated with the use of benzodiazepines. If at all possible, clinicians should try other agents before using benzodiazepines as sleep agents. The risk for physiological and psychological dependence is high, as is the potential for abuse. This being said, there are times when no other treatment for the severe insomnia associated with posttraumatic stress is adequate. In such cases, benzodiazepines should be prescribed for short periods of time only, and with careful monitoring of patterns of use and reported need for dose increases. (See Table 11.5.)

Strategy for Medicating Sleep Disturbances in Posttraumatic Stress

The recommendations for medicating posttraumatic sleep disturbance can be summarized as follows:

- Maximize use of current psychotropic regimen for sleep efficacy (for example, paroxetine, TCAs, trazodone, mirtazapine, antipsychotics, mood stabilizers). Often this can be accomplished by switching from twice daily to once daily at bedtime dosing.
- If necessary, add a nonaddictive sleep agent such as trazodone or an antihistamine.

- Switch to one of the non-benzodiazepine hypnotics such as zolpidem or zaleplon.
- If these are ineffective, judicious use of a benzodiazepine may be supportable.

Medications for Dissociation

The literature on pharmacological approaches to the treatment of dissociative symptomatology is extremely sparse, and many clinicians make the presumption that medications will not be helpful for dissociation. To some extent, this is correct; currently available medications do not do much for such symptoms as amnesia, cognitive disengagement, depersonalization, rapid switching from one state to another, or losing track of time. However, because dissociative symptoms do appear to intensify under stress, much of the literature encourages treatment of the conditions that may occur comorbidly with dissociative disorders, including depression, anxiety, and PTSD.

A few open trials (for example, Bohus et al., 1999) have suggested that naltrexone may help to reduce dissociative symptoms and posttraumatic flashbacks in borderline patients, while others have described its effectiveness in reducing self-injurious behavior in dissociative identity disorder (Loewenstein, in press).

The differentiation of posttraumatic reexeperiencing from psychotic hallucinations (as described in detail in Chapter 3) can be particularly difficult in highly dissociated individuals. Unfortunately, some clients are treated unnecessarily, sometimes for long periods of time, with antipsychotics that have little effect and have significant side effects, because they were incorrectly judged to be psychotic. Some clinicians find that low doses of antipsychotics are helpful in treating the anxiety and intrusive symptoms of PTSD that can accompany dissociation (Loewenstein, in press). However, in our anecdotal experience there are times when such medications can in fact increase dissociative responses by decreasing awareness of the environment, much in the way benzodiazepines do.

Morgan, Krystal, and Southwick (2003), in a review, suggest several approaches that might be beneficial for dissociation, given what we know about the biology of dissociative states: (1) treatment of hyperarousal with adrenergic blockers, as traumatized individuals often dissociate when stressed or overwhelmed, (2) treatment with medications that affect GABAergic neurons, such as SSRIs, and (3) use of medications that affect N-methyl-D-aspartate (NMDA), such as lamotrigine. However, these recommendations are based on presumptions about biology rather than clinical outcome data.

Our general approach to the treatment of dissociation involves psychotherapy as the primary intervention; in the best case scenario, as clients process trauma and learn skills that assist with affect regulation and interpersonal relatedness, dissociation recedes as part of the clinical picture. However, when dissociating clients have significant posttraumatic, depressive, or other anxiety symptoms, treatment with pharmacotherapy is appropriate.

Medications for Other Comorbid Disorders

As described in Chapter 2, PTSD is highly comorbid with other Axis I disorders, including depression, other anxiety disorders, and psychotic disorders. The trauma-focused clinician should not presume that psychotherapy for traumatic stress will necessarily address this broader range of symptoms. In cases where clients present with one or more comorbid disorders, appropriate pharmacological treatment for these conditions is recommended. Fortunately, when depression or other anxiety symptoms are involved, SSRIs are the treatment of choice, and symptoms of posttraumatic stress can be treated simultaneously. As described earlier, clear psychotic symptoms require the addition of an antipsychotic medication. The general principles of medication management in trauma survivors, described earlier in this chapter, especially regarding side effects and concerns about overmedication, are relevant when treating comorbidities as well as when treating posttraumatic stress.

This chapter has reviewed the wide range of medications that appear to be helpful in the treatment of posttraumatic stress. Two points should be reemphasized, however.

First, there is little reason to believe, based on the extant clinical literature, that psychiatric medication can, by itself, resolve most cases of PTSD or other forms of posttraumatic disturbance. Such medication is often helpful, but tends to be palliative rather than curative. In many cases medication will effect some level of symptom reduction but will not completely remove all symptomatology, and may only be effective for certain posttraumatic symptom clusters. In addition, among those clients who experience significant symptom remission, a significant proportion will relapse when medication is discontinued. Finally, some clients are unable or unwilling to tolerate the side effects of psychotropic medication, regardless of whether or not the drug might technically be effective.

Second, although psychiatric medication will rarely permanently resolve all posttraumatic symptoms in a given client, it is often helpful. In our experience, the effective use of medication can provide initial symptom relief (medically and via the placebo effect)—sometimes before initial psychotherapy effects. This initial medical result may increase compliance, discourage clinical drop-out, and reduce the sleep deprivation and/or autonomic hyper-arousal that contributes significantly to many clients' distress. In this way, psychiatric medication may provide benefits that allow the client to partici-pate in psychotherapy long enough for the more substantial and enduring effects of psychological intervention to emerge.

Suggested Reading

Davidson, J. R. T. (2004). Long-term treatment and prevention of posttraumatic stress disorder. *Journal of Clinical Psychiatry, 65,* 44–48.

Friedman, M. J. (2000). What might the psychobiology of posttraumatic stress dis-order teach us about future approaches to pharmacotherapy? *Journal of Clinical Psychiatry, 61* (Suppl. 7), 44–51.

Friedman, M. J., Davidson, J. R. T., Mellman, T. A., & Southwick, S. M. (2000). Pharmacotherapy. In E. B. Foa, T. M. Keane, & M. J. Friedman (Eds.), *Effective treatments for PTSD: Practice guidelines from the International Society for Traumatic Stress Studies* (pp. 84–105, 326–329). New York: Guilford.

Expert Consensus Guideline Series. (1999). Treatment for posttraumatic stress dis-order: The Expert Consensus Panels for PTSD. *Journal of Clinical Psychiatry, 60* (supl. 16), 3–76.

Morgan, C. A., Krystal, J. H., & Southwick, S. M. (2003). Toward early pharmaco-logical posttraumatic stress intervention. *Biological Psychiatry, 53,* 834–843.

12

Conclusions

This book has provided an overview of the assessment and treatment of various forms of posttraumatic distress and disorder. In it, we have offered a general philosophy of intervention that stresses a nonpathologizing, growth-oriented, and, ultimately, hopeful view of recovery from trauma. We have suggested that human relationships provide not only the context for a huge amount of violence in our world, but also the essential environment in which the effects of violence can be addressed. Healing relationships need not always involve psychotherapy; many people recover from trauma exposure without seeking professional assistance, instead processing and resolving their injuries in the context of family, friendship, and other relationships.

Unfortunately, some posttraumatic outcomes are of sufficient severity and chronicity that a more specialized relationship is often necessary: in Western culture, it is generally referred to as *psychotherapy*. Probably regardless of culture, some trauma effects appear to require a supportive other who is trained to listen and respond in an empathic and relatively objective manner and who is able to call on a variety of techniques and approaches that directly address psychological injury. We have outlined the range of interventions that are relevant to this process. At the same time, clinical techniques—although often providing great specificity and efficiency in treating posttraumatic stress—generally require an additional element: a caring, safe, and supportive therapeutic relationship in which the past can be explored and processed.

This focus on the therapeutic relationship is sometimes dismissed by proponents of shorter-term therapy, who may consider the relational effects of therapy to be nonspecific or "placebo" phenomena. We suggest, in contrast, that the therapeutic relationship activates important psychological and physiological processes that—far from being placebo effects—serve to evoke, countercondition, and otherwise process traumatic (especially relational) memories. Therapeutic intervention in these attachment-relational processes requires considerable training and skill, in part because relational dynamics also affect the therapist. At the same time, the largely cognitive-behavioral activities of exposure, activation, disparity, counterconditioning, and extinction/resolution can be found—in one form or another—in most effective trauma therapies. In fact, it is hard to imagine how successful psychological treatment for posttraumatic stress could fail to include at least some of these components.

The need for both relational and cognitive-behavioral interventions in the treatment of chronic and/or complex posttraumatic disturbance is not particularly surprising, especially when real-world clinical practice is examined. Probably all good trauma therapy is cognitive-behavioral, to the extent that it involves exploration of traumatic material (exposure) in a safe relationship (disparity) wherein the client is encouraged to feel and think about what happened to him or her (emotional and cognitive activation and processing). On the other hand, most effective therapy for complex trauma effects is also relational and "psychodynamic," involving the effects of activated attachment relationships and interpersonal processes.

Ultimately, the complex interrelationships between exposure to adverse events, biology, psychology, culture, social support, and symptomatology mean that no two trauma survivors are clinically similar. A corollary of this fact is that the therapy required to intervene in posttraumatic outcomes will necessarily differ from case to case, as a function of a wide variety of variables. As we hope has been apparent in this book, this means that trauma treatment must be flexible, inclusive of various perspectives, relevant to the client's specific issues and concerns, and responsive to his or her specific relational context. In some cases, it also may include carefully chosen and monitored psychiatric medication. In combination with the remarkable survival capacity of traumatized people, such therapy can be a powerful agent for psychological recovery and, in many cases, growth.

References

Abueg, F. R., & Fairbank, J. A. (1992). Behavioral treatment of posttraumatic stress disorder and co-occurring substance abuse. In P. A. Saigh (Ed.), *Posttraumatic stress disorder: A behavioral approach to assessment and treatment* (pp. 111–146). Needham Heights, MA: Allyn & Bacon.

Acierno, R., Resnick, H. S., Kilpatrick, D. G., Saunders, B. E., & Best, C. L. (1999). Risk factors for rape, physical assault, and posttraumatic stress disorder in women: examination of differential multivariate relationships. *Journal of Anxiety Disorders, 13,* 541–563.

Ahearn, E. P., Krohn, A., Connor, K. M., & Davidson, J. R. (2003). Pharmacologic treatment of posttraumatic stress disorder: A focus on antipsychotic use. *Annals of Clinical Psychiatry, 15,* 193–201.

Alexander, F., et al. (1946). *Psychoanalytic therapy: Principles and activations.* New York: Ronald Press.

Alexander, P. C. (1992). Effect of incest on self and social functioning: A developmental psychopathology perspective. *Journal of Consulting and Clinical Psychology, 60,* 185–195.

Alexander, Y., & Brenner, E. H. (Eds.). (2001). *Terrorism and the law.* Ardsley, NY: Transnational.

Allen, J. G. (2001). *Traumatic relationships and serious mental disorders.* Chichester, UK: Wiley.

Allen, J. G. (2005). *Coping with trauma: Hope through understanding* (2nd ed.). Washington, DC: American Psychiatric Press.

American Psychiatric Association. (1987). *Diagnostic and statistical manual of mental disorders* (3rd ed., Rev.). Washington, DC: Author.

American Psychiatric Association. (2000). *Diagnostic and statistical manual of mental disorders* (4th ed., Text Revision). Washington, DC: Author.

American Psychiatric Association. (2001). *Practice guideline for the treatment of patients with borderline personality disorder.* Washington, DC: Author.

Amir, N., Stafford, J., Freshman, M. S., & Foa, E. B. (1998). Relationship between trauma narratives and trauma pathology. *Journal of Traumatic Stress, 11,* 385–393.

Amnesty International. (2002). *Amnesty International, Report 2002.* Retrieved February 3, 2004, from http://web.amnesty.org/web/ar2002.nsf/home

Anderson, J. R., & Bower, G. H. (1972). Recognition and retrieval processes in free recall. *Psychological Review, 79*, 97–123.

Andrews, B., Brewin, C. R., Rose, S., & Kirk, M. (2000). Predicting PTSD symptoms in victims of violent crime: the role of shame, anger, and childhood abuse. *Journal of Abnormal Psychology, 109*, 69–73.

Armstrong, J. G., & Kaser-Boyd, N. (2003). Projective assessment of psychological trauma. In D. Segal & M. Hilsenroth (Eds.), *The comprehensive handbook of psychological assessment, Volume 2: Personality assessment* (pp. 500–512). New York: Wiley.

Atkeson, B., Calhoun, K., Resick, P., & Ellis, E. (1982). Victims of rape: Repeated assessment of depressive symptoms. *Journal of Consulting and Clinical Psychology, 50*, 96–102.

Baker, R. (1992). Psychosocial consequences for tortured refugees seeking asylum and refugee status in Europe. In M. Basoglu (Ed.), *Torture and its consequences: Current treatment approaches* (pp. 83–106). Cambridge: Cambridge University Press.

Baldwin, M. W., Fehr, B., Keedian, E., Seidel, M., & Thompson, D. W. (1993). An exploration of the relational schemata underlying attachment styles: Self-report and lexical decision approaches. *Personality and Social Psychology Bulletin, 19*, 746–754.

Barbee, J. G. (1993). Memory, benzodiazepines, and anxiety: Integration of theoretical and clinical perspectives. *Journal of Clinical Psychiatry, 54*(Suppl.), 86–97.

Barr, L. C., Goodman, W. K., & Price, L. H. (1994). Physical symptoms associated with paroxetine discontinuation. *American Journal of Psychiatry, 151*, 289.

Bartzokis, G., Lu, P. H., Turner, J., Mintz, J., & Saunders, C. S. (2005). Adjunctive risperidone in the treatment of chronic combat-related posttraumatic stress disorder. *Biological Psychiatry, 57*, 474–479.

Basoglu, M. (1992). *Torture and its consequences: Current treatment approaches.* Cambridge: Cambridge University Press.

Bassuk, E. L., Dawson, R., Perloff, J. N., & Weinreb, L. F. (2001). Post-traumatic stress disorder in extremely poor women: Implications for health care clinicians. *Journal of the American Medical Women's Association, 56*, 79–85.

Bassuk, E. L., Melnick, S., & Browne, A. (1998). Responding to the needs of low-income and homeless women who are survivors of family violence. *Journal of the American Medical Women's Association, 53*, 57–64.

Beck, J. S. (1995). *Cognitive therapy: Basics and beyond.* New York: Guilford.

Becker, E., Rankin, E., & Rickel, A. U. (1998). *High risk sexual behavior: Intervention with vulnerable populations.* New York: Plenum.

Beckham, J. C., Moore, S. D., Feldman, M. E., Hertzberg, M. A., Kirby, A. C., & Fairbank, J. A. (1998). Health status, somatization, and severity of posttraumatic stress disorder in Vietnam combat veterans with posttraumatic stress disorder. *American Journal of Psychiatry, 155*, 1565–1569.

Bem, S. L. (1976). Sex typing and the avoidance of cross-sex behavior. *Journal of Personality and Social Psychology, 33*, 48–54.

Berah, E. F., Jones, H. J., & Valent, P. (1984). The experience of a mental health team involved in the early phase of a disaster. *Australia and New Zealand Journal of Psychiatry, 18,* 354–358.

Berlant, J. L. (2004). Prospective open-label study of add-on and monotherapy topiramate in civilians with chronic nonhallucinatory posttraumatic stress disorder. *BMC Psychiatry, 4,* 24.

Berlant, J. L., & van Kammen, D. P. (2002). Open-label topiramate as primary, or adjunctive therapy in chronic civilian posttraumatic stress disorder: A preliminary report. *Journal of Clinical Psychiatry, 63,* 15–20.

Berliner, L., & Briere, J. (1998). Trauma, memory, and clinical practice. In L. Williams (Ed), *Trauma and memory* (pp. 3–18). Thousand Oaks, CA: Sage.

Bernstein, E. M., & Putnam, F. W. (1986). Development, reliability, and validity of a dissociation scale. *Journal of Nervous and Mental Diseases, 174,* 727–734.

Bernstein, I. H., Ellason, J. W., Ross, C. A., & Vanderlinden, J. (2001). On the dimensionalities of the Dissociative Experiences Scale (DES) and the Dissociation Questionnaire (DIS-Q). *Journal of Trauma and Dissociation, 2,* 103–123.

Berthold, S. M. (2000). War traumas and community violence: Psychological, behavioral, and academic outcomes among Khmer refugee adolescents. *Journal of Multicultural Social Work, 8,* 15–46.

Best, C. L., & Ribbe, D. P. (1995). Accidental injury: approaches to assessment and treatment . In J. R. Freedy & S. E. Hobfoll (Eds.), *Traumatic stress: From theory to practice* (pp. 315–337). New York: Plenum.

Bisson, J. I. (2003). Single-session early psychological interventions following traumatic events. *Clinical Psychology Review, 23,* 481–499.

Bisson, J. I., McFarlane, A. C., & Rose, S. (2000). Psychological debriefing. In E. B. Foa, T. M. Keane, & M. J. Friedman (Eds.), *Effective treatments for PTSD* (pp. 39–59). New York: Guilford.

Blake, D. D., Weathers, F. W., Nagy, L. M., Kaloupek, D. G., Gusman, F. D., Charney, D. S., & Keane, T. M. (1995). The development of a clinician-administered PTSD scale. *Journal of Traumatic Stress, 8,* 75–90.

Blanchard, E. B., & Hickling, E. J. (1997). *After the crash: Assessment and treatment of motor vehicle accident survivors.* Washington, DC: American Psychological Association.

Bohus, M. J., Landwehrmeyer, G. B., Stiglmayr, C. E., Limberger, M. F., Bohme, R., & Schmahl, C. G. (1999). Naltrexone in the treatment of dissociative symptoms in patients with borderline personality disorder: An open-label trial. *Journal of Clinical Psychiatry, 60,* 598–603.

Bowlby, J. (1982). *Attachment and loss. Vol. 1: Attachment* (2nd ed.). New York: Basic Books.

Bowlby, J. (1988). *A secure base: Parent-child attachment and healthy human development.* New York: Basic Books.

Bradley, R. G., Greene, J., Russ, E., Dutra, L., & Westen, D. (2005). A multidimensional meta-analysis of psychotherapy for PTSD. *American Journal of Psychiatry, 162,* 214–227.

Brady, K., Pearlstein, T., Asnis, G. M., Baker, D., Rothbaum, B., Sikes, C. R., & Farfel, G. M. (2000). Efficacy and safety of sertraline treatment of posttraumatic stress disorder: A randomized controlled trial. *Journal of the American Medical Association, 283,* 1837–1844.

Brady, K. T., Killeen, T., Brewerton, T. D., & Lucerini, S. (2000). Comorbidity of psychiatric disorders and posttraumatic stress disorder. *Journal of Clinical Psychiatry, 61*(Suppl. 7), 22–32.

Braun, P., Greenberg, D., Dasberg, H., & Lerer, B. (1990). Core symptoms of posttraumatic stress disorder unimproved by alprazolam treatment. *Journal of Clinical Psychiatry, 51,* 236–238.

Bremner, J. D., Southwick, S., Brett, E., Fontana, A., Rosenheck, R., & Charney, D. S. (1992). Dissociation and posttraumatic stress disorder in Vietnam combat veterans. *American Journal of Psychiatry, 149,* 328–332.

Bremner, J. D., & Vermetten, E. (2004). Neuroanatomical changes associated with pharmacotherapy in posttraumatic stress disorder. *Annals of the New York Academy of Sciences, 1032,* 154–157.

Bremner, J. D., Vythilingham, M., Vermetten, E., Southwick, S. M., McGlashan, T., Nazeer, A., Khan, S., Vaccarino, L. V., Soufer, R., Garg, P. K., Ng, C. K., Staib, L. H., Duncan, J. S., & Charney, D. S. (2003). MRI and PET study of deficits in hippocampal structure and function in women with childhood sexual abuse and posttraumatic stress disorder. *American Journal of Psychiatry, 160,* 924–932.

Brennan, K. A., & Shaver, P. R. (1995). Dimensions of adult attachment, affect regulation, and romantic relationship functioning. *Personality and Social Psychology Bulletin, 21,* 267–283.

Breslau, N., Chilcoat, H. D., Kessler, R. C., & Davis, G. C. (1999). Previous exposure to trauma and PTSD effects of subsequent trauma: results from the Detroit Area Survey of Trauma. *American Journal of Psychiatry, 156,* 902–907.

Breslau, N., Davis, G. C., Andreski, P., & Peterson, E. L. (1991). Traumatic events and posttraumatic stress disorder in an urban population of young adults. *Archives of General Psychiatry, 48,* 216–222.

Breslau, N., Kessler, R. C., Chilcoat, H. D., Schultz, L. R., Davis, G. C., & Andreski, P. (1998). Trauma and posttraumatic stress disorder in the community: The 1996 Detroit Area Survey of Trauma. *Archives of General Psychiatry, 55,* 626–632.

Breslau, N., Wilcox, H. C., Storr, C. L., Lucia, V., & Anthony, J. C. (2004). Trauma Exposure and PTSD: A non-concurrent prospective study of youth in urban America. *Journal of Urban Health, 81,* 530–544.

Brewin, C. R., Andrews, B., & Rose, S. (2000). Fear, helplessness, and horror in posttraumatic stress disorder: investigating DSM-IV criterion A2 in victims of violent crime. *Journal of Traumatic Stress, 13,* 499–509.

Brewin, C. R., Andrews, B., & Valentine, J. D. (2000). Meta-analysis of risk factors for posttraumatic stress disorder in trauma-exposed adults. *Journal of Consulting and Clinical Psychology, 68,* 748–766.

Briere, J. (1992a). *Child abuse trauma: Theory and treatment of the lasting effects.* Newbury Park, CA: Sage.

Briere, J. (1992b). Medical symptoms, health risk, and child sexual abuse (Editorial). *Mayo Clinic Proceedings, 67,* 603–604.

Briere, J. (1995). *Trauma Symptom Inventory professional manual.* Odessa, FL: Psychological Assessment Resources.

Briere, J. (1996). *Therapy for adults molested as children* (2nd ed.). New York: Springer.

Briere, J. (1998). *Brief Interview for Posttraumatic Disorders (BIPD).* Unpublished psychological test, University of Southern California.

Briere, J. (2000a). *Inventory of Altered Self Capacities (IASC).* Odessa, FL: Psychological Assessment Resources.

Briere, J. (2000b). *Cognitive Distortions Scale (CDS).* Odessa, FL: Psychological Assessment Resources.

Briere, J. (2001). *Detailed Assessment of Posttraumatic Stress (DAPS).* Odessa, FL: Psychological Assessment Resources.

Briere, J. (2002a). Treating adult survivors of severe childhood abuse and neglect: Further development of an integrative model. In J. E. B. Myers, L. Berliner, J. Briere, C. T. Hendrix, T. Reid, & C. Jenny (Eds.), *The APSAC handbook on child maltreatment* (2nd ed.; pp. 175–202). Newbury Park, CA: Sage.

Briere, J. (2002b). *Multiscale Dissociation Inventory.* Odessa, FL: Psychological Assessment Resources.

Briere, J. (2003). Integrating HIV/AIDS prevention activities into psychotherapy for child sexual abuse survivors. In L. Koenig, A. O'Leary, L. Doll, & W. Pequenat (Eds.), *From child sexual abuse to adult sexual risk: Trauma, revictimization, and intervention* (pp. 219–232). Washington DC: American Psychological Association.

Briere, J. (2004). *Psychological assessment of adult posttraumatic states: Phenomenology, diagnosis, and measurement* (2nd ed.). Washington, DC: American Psychological Association.

Briere, J. (2005, October). *Treating complex psychological trauma: PTSD, borderline personality, and beyond.* Workshop presented for the Institute for the Advancement of Human Behavior, Baltimore, MD.

Briere, J. (in press). Dissociative symptoms and trauma exposure: Specificity, affect dysregulation, and posttraumatic stress. *Journal of Nervous and Mental Disease.*

Briere, J., & Armstrong, J. (in press). Psychological assessment of posttraumatic dissociation. In E. Vermetten, M. Dorahy, & D. Spiegel (Eds.), *Traumatic dissociation: Neurobiology and treatment.* Washington, DC: American Psychiatric Press.

Briere, J., & Elliott, D. M. (2000). Prevalence, characteristics, and long-term sequelae of natural disaster exposure in the general population. *Journal of Traumatic Stress, 13,* 661–679.

Briere, J., & Elliott, D. M. (2003). Prevalence and symptomatic sequelae of self-reported childhood physical and sexual abuse in a general population sample of men and women. *Child Abuse and Neglect, 27,* 1205–1222.

Briere, J., & Gil, E. (1988). Self-mutilation in clinical and general population samples: Prevalence, correlates, and functions. *American Journal of Orthopsychiatry, 68,* 609–620.

Briere, J., & Jordan, C. (2004). Violence against women: Outcome complexity and implications for treatment. *Journal of Interpersonal Violence, 19,* 1252–1276.

Briere, J., & Runtz, M. R. (2002). The Inventory of Altered Self-Capacities (IASC): A standardized measure of identity, affect regulation, and relationship disturbance. *Assessment, 9,* 230–239.

Briere, J., Scott, C., & Weathers, F. (2005). Peritraumatic and persistent dissociation in the presumed etiology of PTSD. *American Journal of Psychiatry, 162,* 2295–2301.

Briere, J., & Spinazzola, J. (2005). Phenomenology and psychological assessment of complex posttraumatic states. *Journal of Traumatic Stress, 18,* 401–412.

Briere, J., Weathers, F. W., & Runtz, M. (2005). Is dissociation a multidimensional construct? Data from the Multiscale Dissociation Inventory. *Journal of Traumatic Stress, 18,* 221–231.

Briere, J., & Zaidi, L. Y. (1989). Sexual abuse histories and sequelae in female psychiatric emergency room patients. *American Journal of Psychiatry, 146,* 1602–1606.

Brown, P. J., Read, J. P., & Kahler, C. W. (2003). Comorbid posttraumatic stress disorder and substance use disorders: Treatment outcomes and the role of coping. In P. Ouimette & P. J. Brown (Eds.), *Trauma and substance abuse: Causes, consequences, and treatment of comorbid disorders* (pp. 171–188). Washington, DC: American Psychological Association.

Brown, P. J., & Wolfe, J. (1994). Substance abuse and post-traumatic stress disorder comorbidity. *Drug and Alcohol Dependence, 35,* 51–59.

Bryant, R. A., & Harvey, A. G. (1999). Postconcussive symptoms and posttraumatic stress disorder after mild traumatic brain injury. *Journal of Nervous and Mental Disease, 187,* 302–305.

Bryant, R. A., & Harvey, A. G. (2000). *Acute stress disorder: A handbook of theory, assessment, and treatment.* Washington, DC: American Psychological Association.

Bryant, R. A., & Harvey, A. G. (2002). Delayed-onset posttraumatic stress disorder: A prospective evaluation. *Australian and New Zealand Journal of Psychiatry, 36,* 205–209.

Bryant, R. A., Harvey, A. G., Dang, S. T., & Sackville, T. (1998). Assessing acute stress disorder: psychometric properties of a structured clinical interview. *Psychological Assessment, 10,* 215–220.

Bryant, R. A., Moulds, L. M., & Nixon, R. V. D. (2003). Cognitive behaviour therapy of acute stress disorder: A four-year follow-up. *Behaviour Research and Therapy, 41,* 489–494.

Bryant, R. A., Sackville, T., Dang, S., Moulds, M., & Guthrie, R. (1999). Treating acute stress disorder: An evaluation of cognitive behavior therapy and counseling techniques. *American Journal of Psychiatry, 156,* 1780–1786.

Buchanan, T. W., Karafin, M. S., & Adolphs, R. (2003). Selective effects of triazolam on memory for emotional, relative to neutral, stimuli: Differential effects on gist versus detail. *Behavioral Neuroscience, 117,* 517–525.

Burt, M. R. (1980). Cultural myths and support for rape. *Journal of Personality and Social Psychology, 38,* 217–230.

Butcher, J. N., Dahlstrom, W. G., Graham, J. R., Tellegen, A., & Kaemmer, B. (1989). *Minnesota Multiphasic Personality Inventory (MMPI-2). Manual for administration and scoring.* Minneapolis: University of Minnesota Press.

Butcher, J. N., Williams, C. L., Graham, J. R., Archer, R. P., Tellegen, A., Ben-Porath, Y. S., & Kaemmer, B. (1992). *MMPI-A (Minnesota Multiphasic Personality Inventory–Adolescent): Manual for administration, scoring, and interpretation.* Minneapolis: University of Minnesota Press.

Butterfield, M. I., Becker, M. E., Connor, K. M., Sutherland, S., Churchill, L. E., & Davidson, J. R. (2001). Olanzapine in the treatment of post-traumatic stress disorder: A pilot study. *International Clinical Psychopharmacology, 16,* 197–203.

Campbell, J. C. (2002). Health consequences of intimate partner violence. *Lancet, 359,* 1331–1336.

Campbell, J. C., & Lewandowski, L. A. (1997). Mental and physical health effects of intimate partner violence on women and children. *Psychiatric Clinics of North America, 20,* 353–374.

Campbell, J. C., & Soeken, K. L. (1999). Forced sex and intimate partner violence: Effects on women's risk and women's health. *Violence Against Women, 5,* 1017–1035.

Canive, J. M., Clark, R. D., Calais, L. A., Qualls, C., & Tuason, V. B. (1998). Bupropion treatment in veterans with posttraumatic stress disorder: An open study. *Journal of Clinical Psychopharmacology, 18,* 379–383.

Carlson, E. A. (1998). A prospective longitudinal study of attachment disorganization/disorientation. *Child Development, 69,* 1107–1128.

Carlson, E. B. (1997). *Trauma assessments: A clinician's guide.* New York: Guilford.

Carlson, E. B., & Dalenberg, C. J. (2000). A conceptual framework for the impact of traumatic experiences. *Trauma, Violence, and Abuse: A Review Journal, 1,* 4–28.

Carlson, E. B., Newman, E., Daniels, J., Armstrong, J., Roth, D., & Loewenstein, R. (2003). Distress in response to and perceived usefulness of trauma research interviews. *Journal of Trauma and Dissociation, 4,* 131–142.

Carlson, E. B., Putnam, F. W., Ross, C. A., Torem, M., Coons, P., Dill, D. L., Loewenstein, R. J., & Braun, B. G. (1993). Validity of the Dissociative Experiences Scale in screening for multiple personality disorder: A multicenter study. *American Journal of Psychiatry, 150,* 1030–1036.

Cassidy, J., & Mohr, J. J. (2001). Unsolvable fear, trauma, and psychopathology. *Clinical Psychology: Science and Practice, 8,* 275–298.

Cates, M. E., Bishop, M. H., Davis, L. L., Jowe, J. S., & Woolley, T. W. (2004). Clonazepam for treatment of sleep disturbances associated with combat-related posttraumatic stress disorder. *Annals of Pharmacotherapy, 38,* 1395–1399.

Chard, K. M., Weaver, T. L., & Resick, P. A. (1997). Adapting cognitive processing therapy for child sexual abuse survivors. *Cognitive and Behavioral Practice, 4,* 31–52.

Chilcoat, H. D., & Breslau, N. (1998). Investigations of causal pathways between PTSD and drug use disorders. *Addictive Behaviors, 23,* 827–840.

Chu, J. A. (1988). Ten traps for therapists in the treatment of trauma survivors. *Dissociation: Progress in the Dissociative Disorders, 1,* 24–32.

Chu, J. A. (1992). The therapeutic rollercoaster: Dilemmas in the treatment of childhood abuse survivors. *Journal of Psychotherapy: Practice and Research, 1,* 351–370.

Chu, J. A. (1998). *Rebuilding shattered lives: The responsible treatment of complex posttraumatic stress and dissociative disorders.* New York: Guilford.

Chu, J. A., Frey, L. M., Ganzel, B. L., & Matthews, J. A. (1999). Memories of childhood abuse: Dissociation, amnesia, and corroboration. *American Journal of Psychiatry, 156,* 749–755.

Chung, M. Y., Min, K. H., Jun, Y. J., Kin, S. S., Kin, W. C., & Jun, E. M. (2004). Efficacy and tolerability of mirtazapine and sertraline in Korean veterans with posttraumatic stress disorder: A randomized open label trial. *Human Psychopharmacology, 19*(7), 489–494.

Clark, R. D., Canive, J. M., Calais, L. A., Qualls, C. R., & Tuason, V. B. (1999). Divalproex in posttraumatic stress disorder: An open-label clinical trial. *Journal of Traumatic Stress, 12,* 395–401.

Classen, C. C., Nevo, R., Koopman, C., Nevill-Manning, K., Gore-Felton, C., Rose, D. S., & Spiegel, D. (2002). Recent stressful life events, sexual revictimization, and their relationship with traumatic stress symptoms among women sexually abused in childhood. *Journal of Interpersonal Violence, 17,* 1274–1290.

Classen, C. C., Palesh, O. G., & Aggarwal, R. (2005). Sexual revictimization: A review of the empirical literature. *Trauma, Violence, and Abuse: A Review Journal, 6,* 103–129.

Cloitre, M., Koenen, K. C., Cohen, L. R., & Han, H. (2002). Skills training in affective and interpersonal regulation followed by exposure: A phase-based treatment for PTSD related to childhood abuse. *Journal of Consulting and Clinical Psychology, 70,* 1067–1074.

Cochran, S. V. (2005). Evidence-based assessment with men. *Journal of Clinical Psychology, 61,* 649–660.

Coe, M. T., Dalenberg, C. J., Aransky, K. M., & Reto, C. S. (1995). Adult attachment style, reported childhood violence history and types of dissociative experiences. *Dissociation: Progress in the Dissociative Disorders, 8,* 142–154.

Coffey, S. F., Dansky, B. S., & Brady, K. T. (2003). Exposure-based, trauma-focused therapy for comorbid posttraumatic stress disorder-substance use disorder. In P. Ouimette & P. J. Brown (Eds.), *Trauma and substance abuse: Causes, consequences, and treatment of comorbid disorders* (pp. 127–146). Washington, DC: American Psychological Association.

Coker, A. L., Smith, P. H., Thompson, M. P., McKeown, R. E., Bethea, L., & Davis, K. E. (2002). Social support protects against the negative effects of partner violence on mental health. *Journal of Women's Health and Gender-Based Medicine, 11,* 465–476.

Cole, P. M., & Putnam, F. W. (1992). Effect of incest on self and social functioning: A developmental psychopathology perspective. *Journal of Consulting and Clinical Psychology, 60,* 174–184.

Collins, N. L., & Read, S. J. (1990). Adult attachment, working models, and relationship quality in dating couples. *Journal of Personality and Social Psychology, 58,* 644–663.

Connor, K. M., Sutherland, S. M., Tupler, L. A., Malik, M. L., & Davidson, J. R. (1999). Fluoxetine in post-traumatic stress disorder: Randomised, double-blind study. *British Journal of Psychiatry, 175,* 17–22.

Cook, A., Spinazzola, J., Ford, J., Lanktree, C., Blaustein, M., Cloitre, M., DeRosa, R., Hubbard, R., Kagan, R., Mallah, K., Olafson, E., & van der Kolk, B. (2005). Complex trauma in children and adolescents. *Psychiatric Annals, 35,* 390–398.

Cooper, B. S., Kennedy, M. A., & Yuille, J. C. (2001). Dissociation and sexual trauma in prostitutes: Variability of responses. *Journal of Trauma and Dissociation, 2,* 27–36.

Correll, C. U., Leucht, S., & Kane, J. M. (2004). Lower risk for tardive dyskinesia associated with second-generation antipsychotics: A systematic review of 1-year studies. *American Journal of Psychiatry, 161,* 414–425.

Cottler, L. B., Compton, W. M., Mager, D., Spitznagel, E. L, & Janka, A. (1992). Posttraumatic stress disorder among substance users from the general population. *American Journal of Psychiatry, 149,* 664–670.

Coupland, N. J., Bell, C. J., & Potokar, J. P. (1996). Serotonin reuptake inhibitor withdrawal. *Journal of Clinical Psychopharmacology, 16,* 356–362.

Courtois, C. A. (1988). *Healing the incest wound: Adult survivors in therapy.* New York: Norton.

Courtois, C. A. (1999). *Recollections of sexual abuse: Treatment principles and guidelines.* New York: Norton.

Currier, G., & Briere, J. (2000). Trauma orientation and detection of violence histories in the psychiatric emergency service. *Journal of Nervous and Mental Disease, 188,* 622–624.

Dalenberg, C. J. (2000). *Countertransference and the treatment of trauma.* Washington, DC: American Psychological Association.

David, D., Kutcher, G. S., Jackson, E. I., & Mellman, T. A. (1999). Psychotic symptoms in combat-related posttraumatic stress disorder. *Journal of Clinical Psychiatry, 60,* 29–32.

Davidson, J. R. T. (1994). Issues in the diagnosis of posttraumatic stress disorder. In R. S. Pynoos (Ed.), *Posttraumatic stress disorder: A clinical review* (pp. 1–15). Lutherville, MD: Sidran.

Davidson, J. R. T. (2004). Long-term treatment and prevention of posttraumatic stress disorder. *Journal of Clinical Psychiatry, 65,* 44–48.

Davidson, J. R. T, Book, S. W, Colket, J. T, Tupler, L. A, Roth, S. H., David, D., Hertzberg, M. A., Mellman, T. A., Beckham, J. C., Smith, R. D., Davison, R. M., Katz, R. J., & Feldman, M. E. (1997). Assessment of a new self-rating scale for posttraumatic stress disorder. *Psychological Medicine, 27,* 153–160.

Davidson, J. R. T., & Foa, E. B. (Eds.). (1993). *Posttraumatic stress disorder: DSM-IV and beyond.* Washington, DC: American Psychiatric Press.

Davidson, J. R. T., Kudler, H., Smith, R., Mahorney, S. L., Lipper, S., Hammett, E., Saunders, W. B., & Cavenar, J. O. (1990). Treatment of posttraumatic stress disorder with amitriptyline and placebo. *Archives of General Psychiatry, 47,* 259–266.

Davidson, J. R. T., Pearlstein, T., Londborg, P., Brady, K. T., Rothbaum, B., Bell, J., Maddock, R., Hegel, M. T., & Farfel, G. (2001). Efficacy of sertraline in preventing relapse of posttraumatic stress disorder: Results of a 28-week double-blind, placebo-controlled study. *American Journal of Psychiatry, 158,* 1974–1981.

Davidson, J. R. T., Rampes, H., Eisen, M., Fisher, P., Smith, R. D., & Malik, M. (1998). Psychiatric disorders in primary care patients receiving complementary medical treatments. *Comprehensive Psychiatry, 39,* 16–20.

Davidson, J. R. T., Rothbaum, B. O., van der Kolk, B. A., Sikes, C. R., & Farfel, G. M. (2001). Multi-center, double-blind comparison of sertraline and placebo in the treatment of posttraumatic stress disorder. *Archives of General Psychiatry, 58,* 485–492.

Davidson, J. R. T., Weisler, R. H., Butterfield, M. I., Casat, D. C., Connor, K. M., Barnett, S., & Van Meter, S. (2003). Mirtazapine vs. placebo in posttraumatic stress disorder: A pilot trial. *Biological Psychiatry, 53,* 188–191.

Davidson, P. R., & Parker, K. C. H. (2001). Eye movement desensitization and reprocessing (EMDR): a meta-analysis. *Journal of Consulting and Clinical Psychology, 69,* 305–316.

Davis, L. L., Nugent, A. L., Murray, J., Kramer, G. L., & Petty, F. (2000). Nefazodone treatment for chronic posttraumatic stress disorder: An open trial. *Journal of Clinical Psychopharmacology, 20,* 159–164.

De Bellis, M. D., Baum, A. S., Birmaher, B., Keshavan, M. S., Eccard, C. H., Boring, A. M., Jenkins, F., & Ryan, N. D. (1999). Developmental traumatology, Part I: Biological stress systems. *Biological Psychiatry, 45,* 1259–1270.

Derogatis, L. R. (1983). *SCL-90-R administration, scoring, and procedures manual II for the revised version* (2nd ed.). Towson, MD: Clinical Psychometrics Research.

Dias, C. P., & Jones, J. (2004, April). *Propranolol in the treatment of hyperarousal symptoms in posttraumatic stress disorder.* Paper presented at the West Coast Colleges of Biological Psychiatry, Pasadena, CA.

Dieperink, M. E., & Drogemuller, L. (1999). Zolpidem for insomnia related to PTSD. *Psychiatric Services, 50,* 421.

Dobie, D. J., Kivlahan, D. R., Maynard, C., Bush, K. R., Davis, T. M., Bradley, K. A. (2004). Posttraumatic stress disorder in female veterans: Association with self-reported health problems and functional impairment. *Archives of Internal Medicine, 164,* 394–400.

Donnelly, C. L., Amaya-Jackson, L., & March, J. S. (1999). Psychopharmacology of pediatric posttraumatic stress disorder. *Journal of Child and Adolescent Psychopharmacology, 9,* 203–220.

Duran, E., & Duran, B. (1995). *Native American postcolonial psychology.* Albany: State University of New York Press.

Echeburúa, E., De Corral, P., Sarasua, B., & Zubizarreta, I. (1996). Treatment of acute posttraumatic stress disorder in rape victims: An experimental study. *Journal of Anxiety Disorders, 10,* 185–199.

Ehlers, A., Clark, D. M., Hackman, A., McManus, F., Fennell, M., Herbert, C., & Mayou, R. A. (2003). A randomized controlled trial of cognitive therapy, self-help, and repeated assessment as early interventions for PTSD. *Archives of General Psychiatry, 60,* 1024-1032.

Ehlert, U., Gaab, J., & Heinrichs, M. (2001). Psychoneuroendocrinological contributions to the etiology of depression, posttraumatic stress disorder, and stress-related bodily disorders: The role of the hypothalamus-pituitary-adrenal axis. *Biological Psychology, 57,* 141–152.

Ehrlich, C., & Briere, J. (2002). The Psychological Trauma Clinic at Los Angeles County-USC Medical Center. *Los Angeles Psychologist, 16,* 12–13.

Elliott, D. M. (1992). *Traumatic Events Survey.* Unpublished psychological test. Los Angeles: Harbor-UCLA Medical Center.

Elliott, D. M. (1994). Impaired object relationships in professional women molested as children. *Psychotherapy, 31,* 79–86.

Elliott, D. M. (1997). Traumatic events: Prevalence and delayed recall in the general population. *Journal of Consulting and Clinical Psychology, 65,* 811–820.

Elliott, D. M., & Briere, J. (2003). *Prevalence and symptomatic sequelae of physical and sexual domestic violence in a general population sample of women.* Unpublished manuscript, University of Southern California, Los Angeles, CA.

Elliott, D. M., Mok, D., & Briere, J. (2004). Adult sexual assault: Prevalence, symptomatology, and sex differences. *Journal of Traumatic Stress, 17,* 203–211.

EMDR Institute. (2004). *A brief description of EMDR.* Retrieved June 10, 2005, from http://www.emdr.com/briefdes.htm

Epstein, R. S., Fullerton, C. S., & Ursano, R. J. (1998). Posttraumatic stress disorder following an air disaster: A prospective study. *American Journal of Psychiatry, 155,* 934–938.

Erickson, M. F., & Egeland, B. (2002). Child neglect. In J. E. B. Myers, L. Berliner, J. Briere, C. T. Hendrix, C. Jenny, & T. A. Reid (Eds.), *The APSAC handbook on child maltreatment* (2nd ed.; pp. 3–20). Thousand Oaks, CA: Sage.

Expert Consensus Guideline Series. (1999). Treatment for posttraumatic stress disorder: The Expert Consensus Panels for PTSD. *Journal of Clinical Psychiatry, 60*(Suppl. 16), 3–76.

Falsetti, S. A., & Resnick, H. S. (1997). Frequency and severity of panic attack symtoms in a treatment seeking sample of trauma victims. *Journal of Traumatic Stress, 10,* 683–689.

Famularo, R., Kinscherff, R., & Fenton, T. (1988). Propranolol treatment for childhood PTSD acute type. *American Disorders of Childhood, 142,* 1244–1247.

Farber, B. A., & Hall, D. (2002). Disclosure to therapists: What is and is not discussed in psychotherapy. *Journal of Clinical Psychology, 58,* 359–370.

Farley, M. (Ed.). (2003). *Prostitution, trafficking, and traumatic stress.* Binghamton, NY: Hayworth.

Fauerbach, J. A., Richter, L., & Lawrence, J. W. (2002). Regulating acute posttrauma distress. *Journal of Burn Care and Rehabilitation, 23,* 249–257.

Fennema-Notestine, C., Stein, M. B., Kennedy, C. M., Archibald, S. L., Jernigan, T. L. (2002). Brain morphometry in female victims of intimate partner violence with and without posttraumatic stress disorder. *Biological Psychiatry, 51,* 1089–1101.

Finkelhor, D., Hotaling, G., Lewis, I. A., & Smith, C. (1990). Sexual abuse in a national survey of adult men and women: Prevalence, characteristics, and risk factors. *Child Abuse and Neglect, 14,* 19–28.

Finkelhor, D., & Yllo, K. (1985). *License to rape: Sexual abuse of wives.* New York: Holt, Rinehart, & Winston.

Fitzgerald, S. G., & Gonzalez, E. (1994). Dissociative states induced by relaxation training in a PTSD combat veteran: Failure to identify trigger mechanisms. *Journal of Traumatic Stress, 7,* 111–115.

Flack, W. F., Litz, B. T., & Keane, T. M. (1998). Cognitive-behavioral treatment of warzone-related PTSD. In V. M. Follette, J. I. Ruzek, & F. R. Abueg (Eds.), *Cognitive-behavioral therapies for trauma* (pp. 77–99). New York: Guilford.

Foa, E. B. (1995). *Posttraumatic Stress Diagnostic Scale.* Minneapolis: National Computer Systems.

Foa, E. B., Hearst-Ikeda, D., & Perry, K. J. (1995). Evaluation of a brief cognitive-behavioral program for the prevention of chronic PTSD in recent assault victims. *Journal of Consulting and Clinical Psychology, 63,* 948–55.

Foa, E. B., Keane, T. M., & Friedman, M. J. (Eds.). (2000). *Effective treatments for PTSD: Practice guidelines from the International Society of Traumatic Stress Studies.* New York: Guilford.

Foa, E. B., & Kozak, M. J. (1986). Emotional processing of fear: Exposure to corrective information. *Psychological Bulletin, 99,* 20–35.

Foa, E. B., Molnar, C., & Cashman, L. (1995). Changes in rape narrative during exposure therapy for posttraumatic stress disorder. *Journal of Traumatic Stress, 8,* 675–690.

Foa, E. B., & Rothbaum, B. O. (1998). *Treating the trauma of rape: Cognitive-behavioral therapy for PTSD.* New York: Guilford.

Foa, E. B., Zinbarg, R., & Rothbaum, B. O. (1992). Uncontrollability and unpredictability in post-traumatic stress disorder: Experimental evidence. *Psychological Bulletin, 112,* 218–238.

Follette, V. M., Ruzek, J. I., & Abueg, F. R. (Eds.). (1998). *Cognitive-behavioral therapies for trauma.* New York: Guilford.

Ford, J. D., Courtois, C. A., Steele, K., van der Hart, O., & Nijenhuis, E. R. S. (2005). Treatment of complex postraumatic self-regulation. *Journal of Traumatic Stress, 18,* 437–447.

Foy, D. W., Resnick, H. S., Sipprelle, R. C., & Carroll, E. M. (1987). Premilitary, military, and postmilitary factors in the development of combat-related Posttraumatic Stress Disorder. *Behavior Therapist, 10,* 3–9.

Frank, A. F., & Gunderson, J. G. (1990). The role of the therapeutic alliance in the treatment of schizophrenia. *Archives of General Psychiatry, 47,* 228–236

Frayne, S. M., Seaver, M. R., Loveland, S., Christiansen, C. L., Spiro, A., Parker, V. A., & Skinner, K. M. (2004). Burden of medical illness in women with depression and posttraumatic stress disorder. *Archives of Internal Medicine, 164,* 1306–1312.

Freedman, S. A., Gluck, N., Tuval-Mashiach, R., Brandes, D., Peri, T., & Shalev, A. Y. (2002). Gender differences in responses to traumatic events: A prospective study. *Journal of Traumatic Stress, 15,* 407–413.

Freedman, S. A., & Shalev, A. Y. (2000). Prospective studies of the recently traumatized. In A. Y. Shalev, R. Yehuda, & A. C. McFarlane (Eds.), *International handbook of human response to trauma* (pp. 249–261). New York: Kluwer.

Friedman, M. J. (2000a). *Posttraumatic stress disorder.* Kansas City, MO: Compact Clinicals.

Friedman, M. J. (2000b). What might the psychobiology of posttraumatic stress disorder teach us about future approaches to pharmacotherapy? *Journal of Clinical Psychiatry, 61*(Suppl. 7), 44–51.

Friedman, M. J., Davidson, J. R. T., Mellman, T. A., & Southwick, S. M. (2000). Pharmacotherapy. In E. B. Foa, T. M. Keane, M. J. Friedman (Eds.), *Effective treatments for PTSD: Practice guidelines from the International Society for Traumatic Stress Studies* (pp. 84–105, 326–329). New York: Guilford.

Friedman, M. J., & Jaranson, J. M. (1994). The applicability of the PTSD concept to refugees. In A. J. Marsella, T. H. Borneman, S. Ekblad, & J. Orley (Eds.), *Amid peril and pain: The mental health and well-being of the world's refugees* (pp. 207–228). Washington, DC: American Psychological Association.

Fullerton, C. S., Ursano, R. J., & Wang, L. (2004). Acute stress disorder, posttraumatic stress disorder, and depression in disaster or rescue workers. *American Journal of Psychiatry, 161,* 1370–1376.

Galea, S., Ahern, J., Resnick, H. S., Kilpatrick, D. G., Bucuvalas, M. J., Gold, J., & Vlahov, D. (2002). Psychological sequelae of the September 11 terrorist attacks in New York City. *New England Journal of Medicine, 346,* 982–987.

Gelpin, E., Bonne, O., Peri, T., Brandes, D., & Shalev, A. Y. (1996). Treatment of recent trauma survivors with benzodiazepines: A prospective study. *Journal of Clinical Psychiatry, 57,* 390–394.

Gilboa, D., Friedman, M., Tsur, H., & Fauerbach, J. A. (1994). The burn as a continuous traumatic stress: Implications for emotional treatment during hospitalization. *Journal of Burn Care and Rehabilitation, 15,* 86–94.

Goin, M. K. (1997). A psychoanalyst's look at common and uncommon factors in psychodynamic and cognitive-behavioral psychotherapies. *Journal of Practical Psychiatry and Behavioral Health, 3,* 308–309.

Goin, M. K. (2002). When it really hurts to listen: Psychotherapy in the aftermath of September 11. *Psychiatric Services, 53,* 561–562.

Goldberg, J., True, W. R., Eisen, S. A., & Henderson, W. G. (1990). A twin study of the effects of the Vietnam war on posttraumatic stress disorder. *Journal of the American Medical Association, 263,* 1227–1232.

Goodman, L. A., Corcoran, C. B., Turner, K., Yuan, N., & Green, B. L. (1998). Assessing traumatic event exposure: General issues and preliminary findings for the Stressful Life Events Screening Questionnaire. *Journal of Traumatic Stress, 11,* 521–542.

Green, B. L., Grace, M. C., Lindy, J. D., & Gleser, G. C. (1990). War stressor and symptom persistence in posttraumatic stress disorder. *Journal of Anxiety Disorder, 4,* 31–39.

Green, B. L., & Solomon S. D. (1995). The mental health impact of natural and technological disasters. In J. R. Freedy & S. E. Hobfoll (Eds.), *Traumatic stress: From theory to practice* (pp. 163–180). New York: Plenum.

Grilo, C. M., Martino, S., Walker, M. L., Becker, D. F., Edell, W. S., & McGlashan, T. H. (1997). Controlled study of psychiatric comorbidity in psychiatrically hospitalized young adults with substance use disorders. *American Journal of Psychiatry, 154*, 1305–1307.

Hamner, M. B. (1996). Clozapine treatment for a veteran with comorbid psychosis and PTSD. *American Journal of Psychiatry, 153*, 841.

Hamner, M. B., Brodrick, P. S., & Labbate, L. A. (2001). Gabapentin in PTSD: A retrospective, clinical series of adjunctive therapy. *Annals of Clinical Psychiatry, 13*, 141–146.

Hamner, M. B., Deitsch, S. E., Brodrick, P. S., Ulmer, H. G., & Lorberbaum, J. P. (2003). Quetiapine treatment in patients with posttraumatic stress disorder: An open trial of adjunctive therapy. *Journal of Clinical Psychopharmacology, 23*, 15–20.

Hamner, M. B., Faldowski, R. A., Ulmer, H. G., Frueh, B. C., Huber, M. G., & Arana, G. W. (2003). Adjunctive risperidone treatment in post-traumatic stress disorder: A preliminary controlled trial of effects on comorbid psychotic symptoms. *International Clinical Psychopharmacology, 18*, 1–8.

Hamner, M. B., & Frueh, B. C. (1998). Response to venlafaxine in a previously antidepressant treatment-resistant combat veteran with post-traumatic stress disorder. *International Clinical Psychopharmacology, 13*, 233–234.

Harmon, R. J., & Riggs, P. D. (1996). Clonidine for posttraumatic stress disorder in preschool children. *Journal of the American Academy of Child and Adolescent Psychiatry, 35*, 1247–1249.

Hart, S. N., Brassard, M. R., Binggeli, N. J., & Davidson, H. A. (2002). Psychological maltreatment. In J. E. B. Myers, L. Berliner, J. Briere, C. T. Hendrix, C. Jenny, & T. A. Reid (Eds.), *The APSAC handbook on child maltreatment* (2nd ed.; pp. 79–104). Thousand Oaks, CA: Sage.

Haugaard, J. J. (2004). Recognizing and treating uncommon behavioral and emotional disorders in children and adolescents who have been severely maltreated: borderline personality disorder. *Child Maltreatment, 9*, 139–145.

Harvey, A. G., & Bryant, R. A. (2000). Two-year prospective evaluation of the relationship between acute stress disorder and posttraumatic stress disorder following mild traumatic brain injury. *American Journal of Psychiatry, 157*(4), 626–628.

Harvey, A. G., & Bryant, R. A. (2002). Acute stress disorder: A synthesis and critique. *Psychological Bulletin, 128*, 886–902.

Harvey, A. G., Jones, C., & Schmidt, D. A. (2003). Sleep and posttraumatic stress disorder: A review. *Clinical Psychology Review, 23*, 377–407.

Herman, J. L. (1992a). *Trauma and recovery: The aftermath of violence—from domestic abuse to political terror.* New York: Basic Books.

Herman, J. L. (1992b). Complex PTSD: A syndrome in survivors of prolonged and repeated trauma. *Journal of Traumatic Stress, 5*, 377–392.

Herman, J. L., Perry, C., & van der Kolk, B. A. (1989). Childhood trauma in borderline personality disorder. *American Journal of Psychiatry, 146*, 490–494.

Herpertz, S., Gretzer, A., Steinmeyer, E. M., Muehlbauer, V., et al. (1997). Affective instability and impulsivity in personality disorder: Results of an experimental study. *Journal of Affective Disorders, 44*, 31–37.

Hertzberg, M. A., Butterfield, M. I., Feldman, M. E., Beckham, J. C., Sutherland, S. M., Connor, K. M., & Davidson, J. R. T. (1999). A preliminary study of lamotrigine for the treatment of posttraumatic stress disorder. *Biological Psychiatry, 45,* 1226–1229.

Hertzberg, M. A., Feldman, M. E., Beckham, J. C., & Davidson, J. R. T. (1996). Trial of trazodone for posttraumatic stress disorder using a multiple baseline group design. *Journal of Clinical Psychopharmacology, 16,* 294–298.

Hertzberg, M. A., Feldman, M. E., Beckham, J. C., Kudler, H. S., & Davidson, J. R. T. (2000). Lack of efficacy for fluoxetine in PTSD: A placebo controlled trial in combat veterans. *Annals of Clinical Psychiatry, 12,* 101–105.

Hesse, E., Main, M., Abrams, K. Y., & Rifkin, A. (2003). Unresolved states regarding loss or abuse can have "second generation" effects: Disorganization, role inversion, and frightening ideation in the offspring of traumatized, non–maltreating parents. In M. F. Solomon & D. Siegel (Eds.), *Healing trauma: Attachment, mind, body, and brain* (pp. 57–106). New York: Norton.

Hickling, E. J., Gillen, R., Blanchard, E. B., Buckley, T. C., & Taylor, A. E. (1998). Traumatic brain injury and posttraumatic stress disorder: A preliminary investigation of neuropsychological test results in PTSD secondary to motor vehicle accidents. *Brain Injury, 12,* 265–274.

Hobfoll, S. E., Dunahoo, C. A., & Monnier, J. (1995). Conservation of resources and traumatic stress. In J. R. Freedy & S. E. Hobfoll (Eds.), *Traumatic stress: From theory to practice* (pp. 29–47). New York: Plenum.

Holbrook, T. L., Hoyt, D. B., Stein, M. B., & Sieber, W. J. (2001). Perceived threat to life predicts posttraumatic stress disorder after major trauma: risk factors and functional outcome. *Journal of Trauma: Injury, Infection, and Critical Care, 51,* 287–293.

Horowitz, M. J. (1978). *Stress response syndromes.* New York: Jason Aronson.

Horowitz, M. J., Siegel, B., Holen, A., Bonanno, G. A., Milbrath, C., & Stinson, C. H. (1997). Diagnostic criteria for complicated grief disorder. *American Journal of Psychiatry, 154,* 904–910.

Horrigan, J. P., & Barnhill, L.J. (1996). The suppression of nightmares with guanfacine. *Journal of Clinical Psychiatry, 57,* 371.

Horvath, A. O., & Luborsky, L. (1993). The role of the therapeutic alliance in psychotherapy. *Journal of Consulting and Clinical Psychology, 64,* 561–573.

Hurwitz, T. D., Mahowald, M. W., Kuskowski, M., & Engdahl, B. E. (1998). Polysomnographic sleep is not clinically impaired in Vietnam combat veterans with chronic posttraumatic stress disorder. *Biological Psychiatry, 44,* 1066–1073.

Jacobson, E. (1938). *Progressive relaxation.* Chicago: University of Chicago Press.

Jaycox, L. H., Foa, E. B., & Morral, A. R. (1998). Influence of emotional engagement and habituation on exposure therapy for PTSD. *Journal of Consulting and Clinical Psychology, 66,* 185–192.

Jakovljevic, M., Sagud, M., & Mihaljevic-Peles, A. (2003). Olanzapine in the treatment-resistant, combat-related PTSD—a series of case reports. *Acta Psychiatrica Scandinavica, 107,* 394–396.

Janoff-Bulman, B. (1992). *Shattered assumptions: Towards a new psychology of trauma.* New York: Free Press.

Jones, E., & Wessely, S. C. (2003). "Forward psychiatry" in the military: Its origins and effectiveness. *Journal of Traumatic Stress, 16,* 411–419.

Jordan, C. E., Nietzel, M. T., Walker, R., & Logan, T. K. (2004). *Intimate partner violence: Clinical and practice issues for mental health professionals.* New York: Springer.

Jordan, R. G., Nunley, T. V., & Cook, R. R. (1992). Symptom exaggeration in a PTSD inpatient population: Response set or claim for compensation. *Journal of Traumatic Stress, 5,* 633–642.

Kane, J. M. (1999). Tardive dyskinesia in affective disorders. *Journal of Clinical Psychiatry, 60*(Suppl. 5), 43–47.

Kask, A., Harro, J., von Horsten, S., Redrobe, J. P., Dumont, Y., & Quirion, R. (2002). The neurocircuitry and receptor subtypes mediating anxiolytic-like effects of neuropeptide Y. *Neuroscience and Behavioral Reviews, 26,* 259–283.

Keane, T. M. (1995). The role of exposure therapy in the psychological treatment of PTSD. *National Center for PTSD Clinical Quarterly, 5,* 1, 3–6.

Keck, P., McElroy, S., & Friedman, L. (1992). Valproate and carbamazepine in the treatment of panic and posttraumatic stress disorders, withdrawal states, and behavioral dyscontrol syndromes. *Journal of Clinical Psychopharmacology, 12,* 368–418.

Kendler, K. S., Bulik, C. M., Silberg, J., Hettema, J. M., Myers, J., & Prescott, C. A. (2000). Childhood sexual abuse and adult psychiatric and substance use disorders in women: An epidemiological and cotwin control analysis. *Archives of General Psychiatry, 57,* 953–959.

Kendler, K. S., Myers, J., & Prescott, C. A. (2002). The etiology of phobias: An evaluation of the stress-diathesis model. *Archives of General Psychiatry, 59,* 242–248.

Kernberg, O. F. (1976). *Borderline conditions and pathological narcissism.* New York: Aronson.

Kessler, R. C., Sonnega, A., Bromet, E., Hughes, M., & Nelson, C. B. (1995). Posttraumatic stress disorder in the national comorbidity survey. *Archives of General Psychiatry, 52,* 1048–1060.

Khantzian, E. J. (1997). The self-medication hypothesis of substance use disorders: A reconsideration and recent applications. *Harvard Review of Psychiatry, 4,* 231–244.

Kilpatrick, D. G, & Resnick, H. S. (1993). Posttraumatic stress disorder associated with exposure to criminal victimization in clinical and community populations. In J. R. T. Davidson & E. B. Foa (Eds.), *Posttraumatic stress disorder: DSM-IV and beyond* (pp. 113–143). Washington, DC: American Psychiatric Press.

Kinzie, J. D., & Leung, P. (1989). Clonidine in Cambodian patients with posttraumatic stress disorder. *Journal of Nervous and Mental Disease, 177,* 546–550.

Kirmayer, L. J. (1996). Confusion of the senses: Implications of ethnocultural variation in somatoform and dissociative disorders for PTSD. In A. J. Marsella, M. J. Friedman, E. T. Gerrity, & R. M. Scurfield (Eds.), *Ethnocultural aspects of posttraumatic stress disorder: Issues, research, and clinical applications* (pp. 131–163). Washington, DC: American Psychological Association.

Kitchner, I., & Greenstein, R. A. (1985). Low dose lithium carbonate in the treatment of post traumatic stress disorder: Brief communication. *Military Medicine, 150,* 378–381.

Knaudt, P. R., Connor, K. M., Weisler, R. H., Churchill, L. E., & Davidson, J. R. T. (1999). Alternative therapy use by psychiatric outpatients. *Journal of Nervous & Mental Disease, 187,* 692–695.

Koenen, K. C., Harley, R. M., Lyons, M. J., Wolfe, J., Simpson, J. C., Goldberg, J., Eisen, S. A., & Tsuang, M. T. (2002). A twin registry study of familial and individual risk factors for trauma exposure and posttraumatic stress disorder. *Journal of Nervous and Mental Disease, 190,* 209–218.

Kohlenberg, R. J., & Tsai, M. (1998). Healing interpersonal trauma with the intimacy of the therapeutic relationship. In V. M. Follette & J. I. Ruzek (Eds.), *Cognitive-behavioral therapies for trauma* (pp. 305–320). New York: Guilford.

Kosten, T. R., Frank, J. B., Dan, E., McDougle, C. J., & Giller, E. L. (1991). Pharmacotherapy for posttraumatic stress disorder using phenelzine or imipramine. *Journal of Nervous and Mental Disorders, 179,* 366–370.

Kolb, L. C., Burris, B. C., & Griffiths, S. (1984). Propranolol and clonidine in the treatment of the chronic post-traumatic stress disorders of war. In B. A. van der Kolk (Ed.), *Post traumatic stress disorder: Psychological and biological sequelae* (pp. 98–108). Washington, DC: American Psychiatric Press.

Koopman, C., Classen, C., & Speigel, D. (1996). Dissociative responses in the immediate aftermath of the Oakland/Berkeley firestorm. *Journal of Traumatic Stress, 9,* 521–540.

Koss, M. P. (1993). Detecting the scope of rape: A review of prevalence research methods. *Journal of Interpersonal Violence, 8,* 198–222.

Krashin, D., & Oates, E. W. (1999). Risperidone as an adjunct therapy for posttraumatic stress disorder. *Military Medicine, 164,* 605–606.

Kubany, E. S., & Watson, S. B. (2002). Cognitive trauma therapy for formerly battered women with PTSD: Conceptual bases and treatment outlines. *Cognitive and Behavioral Practice, 9,* 111–127.

Kudler, H., & Davidson, R. T. (1995). General principles of biological intervention following trauma. In J. R. Freedy & S. E. Hobfoll (Eds.), *Traumatic stress: From theory to practice* (pp. 73–98). New York: Plenum.

Kulka, R. A., Schlenger, W. E., Fairbank, J. A., Hough, R. L., Jordan, B. K., Marmar, C. R., & Weiss, D. S. (1988). *The National Vietnam Veterans Readjustment Study (NVVRS): Description, current status, and initial PTSD prevalence estimates.* Washington, DC: Veterans Administration.

Kulka, R. A., Schlenger, W. E., Fairbank, J. A., Hough, R. L., Jordan, B. K., Marmar, C. R., & Weiss, D. S. (1990). *Trauma and the Vietnam War generation.* New York: Brunner/Mazel.

Lambert, M. J., & Bergin, A. E. (1994). The effectiveness of psychotherapy. In A. E. Bergin & S. L. Garfield (Eds.), *Handbook of psychotherapy and behavior change* (4th ed.; pp. 143–189). New York: Wiley.

Lawrence, J. W., Fauerbach, J. A., & Munster, A. M. (1996). Early avoidance of traumatic stimuli predicts chronicity of intrusive thoughts following burn injury. *Behaviour Research and Therapy, 34,* 643–646.

LeDoux, J. (1998). *The emotional brain.* New York: Simon & Schuster.

Leff, J. P. (1988). *Psychiatry around the globe: A transcultural view* (2nd ed.). London: Gaskell.

Lee, A., Isaac, M. K., & Janca, A. (2002). Post-traumatic stress disorder and terrorism. *Current Opinion in Psychiatry, 15,* 633–637.

Lejoyeux, M., Adès, J., Mourad, I., Solomon, J., & Dilsaver, S. (1996). Antidepressant withdrawal syndrome: Recognition, prevention and management. *CNS Drugs, 5,* 278–292.

Leskela, J., Dieperink, M. E., & Thuras, P. (2002). Shame and posttraumatic stress disorder. *Journal of Traumatic Stress, 15,* 223–226.

Leskin, G. A., & Sheikh, J. I. (2002). Lifetime trauma history and panic disorder: findings from the National Comorbidity Survey. *Journal of Anxiety Disorders, 16,* 599–603.

Lewis, J. D. (2002). Mirtazapine for PTSD nightmares. *American Journal of Psychiatry, 159,* 1948–1949.

Lieberman, J. A., Stroup, T. S., McEvoy, J. P., Swartz, M. S., Rosenheck, R. A., Perkins, D. O., Keefe, R. S., Davis, S. M., Davis, C. E., Lebowitz, B. D., Severe, J., & Hsiao, J. K. (2005). Effectiveness of antipsychotic drugs in patients with chronic schizophrenia. *New England Journal of Medicine, 353,* 1209–1223.

Lindley, S. E., Carlson, E. B., & Benoit, M. (2004). Basal and dexamethasone suppressed salivary cortisol concentrations in a community sample of patients with posttraumatic stress disorder. *Biological Psychiatry, 55,* 940–945.

Linehan, M. M. (1993a). *Cognitive-behavioral treatment of borderline personality disorder.* New York: Guilford.

Linehan, M. M. (1993b). *Skills training manual for treating borderline personality disorder.* New York: Guilford.

Loewenstein, R. J. (in press) Psychopharmacologic treatments for dissociative identity disorder. *Psychiatric Annals.*

Loo, C. M., Fairbank, J. A., Scurfield, R. M., Ruch, L. O., King, D. W., Adams, L. J., & Chemtob, C. M. (2001). Measuring exposure to racism: Development and validation of a Race-Related Stressor Scale (RRSS) for Asian American Vietnam veterans. *Psychological Assessment, 13,* 503–520.

Looff, D., Grimley, P., Kuller, F., Martin, A., & Shonfield, L. (1995). Carbamazepine for PTSD. *Journal of the American Academy of Child and Adolescent Psychiatry, 34,* 703–704.

Luterek, J. A., Orsillo, S. M., & Marx, B. P. (2005). An experimental examination of emotional experience, expression, and disclosure in women reporting a history of child sexual abuse. *Journal of Traumatic Stress, 18,* 237–244.

Luxenberg, T., & Levin, P. (2004). The utility of the Rorschach in the assessment and treatment of trauma. In J. Wilson & T. Keane (Eds.), *Assessing psychological trauma and PTSD* (2nd ed.; pp. 190–225). New York: Guilford.

Mace, S., & Taylor, D. (2000). Selective serotonin reuptake inhibitors: A review of efficacy and tolerability in depression. *Expert Opinion in Pharmacotherapy, 1,* 917–933.

Maida, C. A., Gordon, N. S., Steinberg, A. M., & Gordon, G. (1989). Psychosocial impact of disasters: Victims of the Baldwin Hills fire. *Journal of Traumatic Stress*, 2, 37–48.

Main, M., & Morgan, H. J. (1996). Disorganization and disorientation in infant strange situation behavior: Phenotypic resemblance to dissociative states. In L. K. Michelson & W. J. Ray (Eds.), *Handbook of dissociation: Theoretical, empirical, and clinical perspectives* (pp. 107–138). New York: Plenum.

Manson, S. M., Beals, J., O'Nell, T. D., Piasecki, J., Bechtold, D. W., Keane, E. M., & Jones, M. C. (1996). Wounded spirits, ailing hearts: PTSD and related disorders among American Indians. In A. J. Marsella, M. J. Friedman, E. T. Gerrity, & R. M. Scurfield (Eds.), *Ethnocultural aspects of posttraumatic stress disorder: Issues, research, and clinical applications* (pp. 255–283). Washington, DC: American Psychological Association.

March, J. S. (1993). What constitutes a stressor? The "criterion A" issue. In J. R. T. Davidson & E. B. Foa (Eds.), *Posttraumatic stress disorder: DSM-IV and beyond* (pp. 37–54). Washington, DC: American Psychiatric Association Press.

Marsella, A. J., Bornemann, T., Ekblad, S., & Orley, J. (Eds.). (1994). *Amidst peril and pain: The mental health and wellbeing of world's refugees*. Washington, DC: American Psychological Association.

Marsella, A. J., Friedman, M. J., Gerrity, E. T., & Scurfield, R. M. (Eds.). (1996). *Ethnocultural aspects of posttraumatic stress disorder: Issues, research, and clinical applications*. Washington, DC: American Psychological Association.

Marshall, R. D., Spitzer, R. L., & Liebowitz, M. R. (1999). Review and critique of the new DSM-IV diagnosis of acute stress disorder. *American Journal of Psychiatry*, 156, 1677–1685.

Matthews, A., Kirkby, K. C., & Martin, F. (2002). The effects of single-dose lorazepam on memory and behavioural learning. *Journal of Psychopharmacology*, 16, 345–354.

Mattila, M. J., Vanakoski, J., Kalska, H., & Seppala, T. (1998). Effects of alcohol, zolpidem, and some other sedatives and hypnotics on human performance and memory. *Pharmacology, Biochemistry and Behavior, 59,* 917–923.

Mattis, J. S., Bell, C. C., Jagers, R. J., & Jenkins, E. J. (1999). A critical approach to stress-related disorders in African Americans. *Journal of the National Medical Association, 91,* 80–85.

Mayou, R. A., Bryant, B., & Ehlers, A. (2001). Prediction of psychological outcomes one year after a motor vehicle accident. *American Journal of Psychiatry, 158,* 1231–1238.

Mayou, R. A., Ehlers, A., & Hobbs, M. (2000). A three–year follow-up of psychological debriefing for road traffic accident victims. *British Journal of Psychiatry*, 176, 589–593.

McCann, I. L., & Pearlman, L. A. (1990). *Psychological trauma and the adult survivor: Theory, therapy, and transformation*. New York: Brunner/Mazel.

McFarlane, A. C. (1988). The phenomenology of post-traumatic stress disorders following a natural disaster. *Journal of Nervous and Mental Disorders, 176,* 22–29.

Meichenbaum, D. (1994). *A clinical handbook/practical therapist manual for assessing and treating adults with post-traumatic stress disorder (PTSD).* Waterloo, ONT: Institute Press.

Meichenbaum, D., & Fong, G. T. (1993). Toward a theoretical model of the role of reasons in nonadherence to health-related advice. In D. M. Wegner & J. W. Pennebaker (Eds.), *Handbook of mental control* (pp. 473–490). Englewood Cliffs, NJ: Prentice-Hall.

Melia, K. R., Ryabinin, A. E., Corodimas, K. P., Wilson, M. C., & LeDoux, J. E. (1996). Hippocampal-dependent learning and experience-dependent activation of the hippocampus are preferentially disrupted by ethanol. *Neuroscience, 74,* 313–322.

Mellman, T. A., Bustamante, V., Fins, A. I., Pigeon, W. R., & Nolan, B. (2002). REM sleep and the early development of posttraumatic stress disorder. *American Journal of Psychiatry, 159,* 1696–1701.

Mellman, T. A., Byers, P. M., & Augenstein, J. S. (1998). Pilot evaluation of hypnotic medication during acute traumatic stress response. *Journal of Traumatic Stress, 11,* 563–569.

Mendel, M. P. (1995). *The male survivor: The impact of sexual abuse.* Thousand Oaks, CA: Sage.

Mendelsohn, M., & Sewell, K. W. (2004). Social attitudes toward traumatized men and women: A vignette study. *Journal of Traumatic Stress, 17,* 103–111.

Miller, K. E., & Rasco, L. M. (2004). *The mental health of refugees: Ecological approaches to healing and adaptation.* Mahwah, NJ: Erlbaum.

Millon, T., Davis, R., & Millon, C. (1997). *MCMI-III manual* (2nd ed.). Minneapolis: National Computer Systems.

Mitchell, J. T. (1983). When disaster strikes . . . : The critical incident stress debriefing process. *Journal of Emergency Medical Services, 8,* 36–39.

Monnelly, E. P., & Ciraulo, D. A. (1999). Risperidone effects on irritable aggression in posttraumatic stress disorder. *Journal of Clinical Psychopharmacology, 19,* 377–378.

Monnelly, E. P., Ciraulo, D. A., Knapp, C., & Keane, T. (2003). Low-dose risperidone as adjunctive therapy for irritable aggression in posttraumatic stress disorder. *Journal of Clinical Psychopharmacology, 23,* 193–196.

Morey, L. C. (1991). *Personality Assessment Inventory: Professional manual.* Odessa, FL: Psychological Assessment Resources.

Morgan, C. A., Krystal, J. H., & Southwick, S. M. (2003). Toward early pharmacological posttraumatic stress intervention. *Biological Psychiatry, 53,* 834–843.

Morgan, C. A., Wang, S., Rasmusson, A., Hazlett, G., Anderson, G., & Charney, D. S. (2001). Relationship among plasma cortisol, catecholamines, neuropeptide Y, and human performance during exposure to uncontrollable stress. *Psychosomatic Medicine, 63,* 412–422.

Najavits, L. M. (2002). *Seeking safety: A treatment manual for PTSD and substance abuse.* New York: Guilford.

National Institute for Mental Health. (2002). *Mental health and mass violence—evidence-based early psychological intervention for victims/survivors of mass violence: A workshop to reach consensus.* NIMH Publication No. 02-5138. Washington, DC: U.S. Government Printing Office.

Neill, J. R. (1993). How psychiatric symptoms varied in World War I and II. *Military Medicine, 158,* 149–151.

Neuner, F., Schauer, M., Klaschik, C., Karunakara, U. K., & Elbert, T. (2004). A comparison of narrative exposure therapy, supportive counseling, and psychoeducation for treating posttraumatic stress disorder in an African refugee settlement. *Journal of Consulting and Clinical Psychology, 72,* 579–587.

Norris, F. (1992). Epidemiology of trauma: Frequency and impact of different potentially traumatic events on different demographic groups. *Journal of Consulting and Clinical Psychology, 60,* 409–418.

Norris, F., Friedman, M., Watson, P., Byrne, C., Diaz, E., & Kaniasty, K. (2002). 60,000 disaster victims speak, Part 1: An empirical review of the empirical literature, 1981–2001. *Psychiatry, 65,* 207–239.

North, C. S., Nixon, S. J., Shariat, S., Mallonee, S., McMillen, J. C., Spitznagel, E. L., & Smith, E. M. (1999). Psychiatric disorders among survivors of the Oklahoma City bombing. *Journal of the American Medical Association, 282,* 755–762.

North, C. S., Smith, E. M., & Spitznagel, E. L. (1994). Violence and the homeless: An epidemiologic study of victimization and aggression. *Journal of Traumatic Stress, 7,* 95–110.

Ogata, S. N., Silk, K. R., Goodrich, S., Lohr, N. E., et al. (1990). Childhood sexual and physical abuse in adult patients with borderline personality disorder. *American Journal of Psychiatry, 147,* 1008–1013.

Ogawa, J. R., Sroufe, L. A., Weinfield, N. S., Carlson, E. A., & Egeland, B. (1997). Development and the fragmented self: Longitudinal study of dissociative symptomatology in a nonclinical sample. *Development and Psychopathology, 9,* 855–879.

O'Leary, V. E. (1998). Strength in the face of adversity: Individual and social thriving. *Journal of Social Issues, 54,* 425–446.

Olsen, M. A., & Fazio, R. H. (2002). Implicit acquisition and manifestation of classically conditioned attitudes. *Social Cognition, 20,* 89–103.

Orlinski, D. E., Grawe, K., & Parks, B. K. (1994). Process and outcome in psychotherapy. In A. E. Bergin & S. L. Garfield (Eds.), *Handbook of psychotherapy and behavior change* (4th ed.; pp. 270–283). New York: Wiley

Orner, R., Kent, A. T., Pfefferbaum, B., Raphael, B., & Watson, P. (in press). Context for providing immediate intervention post-event. In E.C. Ritchi, P.J. Watson, & M. J. Friedman (Eds.), *Interventions following mass violence and disasters: Strategies for mental health practice.* New York: Guilford.

Ouimette, P., & Brown, P. J. (2003). *Trauma and substance abuse: Causes, consequences, and treatment of comorbid disorders.* Washington, DC: American Psychological Association.

Ouimette, P., Moos, R. H., & Brown, P. J. (2003). Substance use disorder-posttraumatic stress disorder comorbidity: A survey of treatments and proposed practice guidelines. In P. Ouimette & P. J. Brown (Eds.), *Trauma and substance abuse: Causes, consequences, and treatment of comorbid disorders* (pp. 91–110). Washington DC: American Psychological Association.

Ozer, E. J., Best, S. R., Lipsey, T. L., & Weiss, D. S. (2003). Predictors of posttraumatic stress disorder and symptoms in adults: A meta-analysis. *Psychological Bulletin, 129,* 52–73.

Pearlman, L. (2003). *Trauma and Attachment Belief Scale.* Los Angeles: Western Psychological Services.

Pearlman, L. A., & Courtois, C. A. (2005). Clinical applications of the attachment framework: Relational treatment of complex trauma. *Journal of Traumatic Stress, 18,* 449–459.

Pearlman, L. A., & Saakvitne, K. W. (1995). *Trauma and the therapist: Countertransference and vicarious traumatization in psychotherapy with incest survivors.* New York: Norton.

Pelcovitz, D., van der Kolk, B. A., Roth, S., Mandel, F., Kaplan, S., & Resick, P. (1997). Development of a criteria set and a structured interview for disorders of extreme stress (SIDES). *Journal of Traumatic Stress, 10,* 3–16.

Pennebaker, J. W. (1993). Putting stress into words: Health, linguistic, and therapeutic implications. *Behaviour Research and Therapy, 31,* 539–548.

Pennebaker, J. W., & Campbell, R. S. (2000). The effects of writing about traumatic experience. *National Center for PTSD Clinical Quarterly, 9,* 17–21.

Petty, F., Davis, L. L., Nugent, A. L., Kramer, G. L., Teten, A., Schmitt, A., & Stone, R. C. (2002). Valproate therapy for chronic, combat-induced posttraumatic stress disorder. *Journal of Clinical Psychopharmacology, 22,* 100–101.

Pfefferbaum, B. C., Call, J. A., Lensgraf, S. J., Miller, P. D., Flynn, B. W., Doughty, D. E., Tucker, P. M., & Dickson, W. L. (2001). Traumatic grief in a convenience sample of victims seeking support services after a terrorist incident. *Annals of Clinical Psychiatry, 13,* 19–24.

Physicians' Desk Reference. (2005). (59th ed.). Montvale, NJ: Thomson Healthcare.

Pinto, P. A., & Gregory, R. J. (1995). Posttraumatic stress disorder with psychotic features. *American Journal of Psychiatry, 152,* 471.

Pitman, R. K, Altman, B., Greenwald, E., Longpre, R. E., Macklin, M. L., Poiré, R. E., & Steketee, G. S. (1991). Psychiatric complications during flooding therapy for posttraumatic stress disorder. *Journal of Clinical Psychiatry, 52,* 17–20.

Pitman, R. K., Sanders, K. M., Zusman, R. M., Healy, F. C, Lasko, N. B., Cahill, L., & Orr, S. P. (2002). Pilot study of secondary prevention of posttraumatic stress disorder with propranolol. *Biological Psychiatry, 51,* 189–142.

Pivac, N., Kozaric-Kovacic, D., & Muck-Seler, D. (2004). Olanzapine versus fluphenazine in an open trial in patients with psychotic combat-related posttraumatic stress disorder. *Psychopharmacology, 175,* 451–456.

Plumb, J. C., Orsillo, S. M., & Luterek, J. A. (2004). A preliminary test of the role of experiential avoidance in post-event functioning. *Journal of Behavior Therapy and Experimental Psychiatry, 35,* 245–257.

Prigerson, H. G., Shear, M. K., Jacobs, S. C., Reynolds, C. F., Maciejewski, P. K., Davidson, J. R. T., Rosenheck, R. A., Pilkonis, P. A., Wortman, C. B., Williams,

J. B. W., Widiger, T. A., Frank, E., Kupfer, D. J., & Zisook, S. (1999). Consensus criteria for traumatic grief: a preliminary empirical test. *British Journal of Psychiatry, 174,* 67–73.

Pynoos, R. S., Steinberg, A. M., & Piacentini, J. C. (1999). A developmental psychopathology model of childhood traumatic stress and intersection with anxiety disorders. *Biological Psychiatry, 46,* 1542–1554.

Rachman, S. (1980). Emotional processing. *Behavior, Research, and Therapy, 18,* 51–60.

Raison, C. L., & Miller, A. H. (2003). When not enough is too much: The role of insufficient glucocorticoid signaling in the pathophysiology of stress-related disorders. *American Journal of Psychiatry, 169,* 1554–1565.

Rau, P. J., & Goldfried, M. R. (1994). The therapeutic alliance in cognitive-behaviour therapy. In A. O. Horvath & L. S. Greenberg (Eds.), *The working alliance: Theory, research and practice* (pp. 131–152). New York: Wiley.

Raskind, M. A., Peskind, E. R., Kanter, E. D., Petrie, E. C., Radant, A., Thompson, C. E., Dobie, D. J., Hoff, D., Rein, R. J., Straits-Troster, K., Thomas, R. G., & McFall, M. M. (2003). Reduction of nightmares and other PTSD symptoms in combat veterans by prazosin: A placebo-controlled study. *American Journal of Psychiatry, 160,* 371–373.

Read, J. (1997). Child abuse and psychosis: A literature review and implications for professional practice. *Professional Psychology: Research and Practice, 28,* 448–456.

Read, J., & Fraser, A. (1998). Abuse histories of psychiatric inpatients: To ask or not to ask? *Psychiatric Services, 49,* 355–359.

Reich, D. B., Winternitz, S., Hennen, J., Watts, T., & Stanculescu, C. (2004). A preliminary study of risperidone in the treatment of posttraumatic stress disorder related to childhood abuse in women. *Journal of Clinical Psychiatry, 65,* 1601–1606.

Reist, C., Kauffmann, C. D., Haier, R. J., Sangdahl, C., DeMet, E. M., Chicz-DeMet, A., & Nelson, J. N. (1989). A controlled trial of desipramine in 18 men with posttraumatic stress disorder. *American Journal of Psychiatry, 146,* 513–516.

Renzetti, C. M., & Curran, D. J. (2002). *Women, men, and society* (5th ed.). Boston: Allyn & Bacon.

Rimm, D. C., & Masters, J. (1979). *Behavior theory* (2nd ed.). New York. Academic Research.

Rinne, T., de Kloet, E. R., Wouters, L., Goekoop, J. G., de Rijk, R. H., & van den Brink, W. (2003). Fluvoxamine reduces responsiveness of HPA axis in adult female BPD patients with a history of sustained childhood abuse. *Neuro-psychopharmacology, 28,* 126–132.

Resick, P. A., & Schnicke, M. K. (1993). *Cognitive processing therapy for rape victims: A treatment manual.* Newbury Park: Sage.

Resnick, H. S., Yehuda, R., & Acierno, R. (1997). Acute post-rape cortisol, alcohol abuse, and PTSD symptom profile among recent rape victims. In R. Yehuda & A. C. McFarlane (Eds.), *Psychobiology of posttraumatic stress disorder* (vol. 821; pp. 433–436). New York: New York Academy of Sciences.

Resnick, H., Yehuda, R., Pitman, R., & Foy, D. (1995). Effect of previous trauma on acute plasma cortisol level following rape. *American Journal of Psychiatry, 152,* 1675–1677.

Ringdahl, E. N., Pereira, S. L., & Delzell, J. E., Jr. (2004). Treatment of primary insomnia. *Journal of the American Board of Family Practice, 17,* 212–219.

Ritchie, E. C., Watson, P. J., & Friedman, M. J. (Eds.). (in press). *Interventions following mass violence and disasters: Strategies for mental health practice.* New York: Guilford.

Rivard, J. M., Dietz, P., Martell, D., & Widawski, M. (2002). Acute dissociative responses in law enforcement officers involved in critical shooting incidents: The clinical and forensic implications. *Journal of Forensic Sciences, 47,* 1093–1100.

Robert, R., Blakeney, P. E., Villarreal, C., Rosenberg, L., & Meyer, W. J. (1999). Imipramine treatment in pediatric burn patients with symptoms of acute stress disorder: A pilot study. *Journal of the American Academy of Child and Adolescent Psychiatry, 38,* 873–882.

Roelofs, K., Keijsers, G. P. J., Hoogduin, K. A. L., Naring, G. W. B., & Moene, F. C. (2002). Childhood abuse in patients with conversion disorder. *American Journal of Psychiatry, 159,* 1908–1913.

Roemer, L., Orsillo, S. M., Borkovec, T. D., & Litz, B. T. (1998). Emotional response at the time of a potentially traumatizing event and PTSD symptomatology: A preliminary retrospective analysis of the DSM-IV criterion A-2. *Journal of Behavior Therapy and Experimental Psychiatry, 29,* 123–130.

Rogers, S., & Silver, S. M. (2002). Is EMDR an exposure therapy? A review of trauma protocols. *Journal of Clinical Psychology, 58,* 43–59.

Root, M. P. P. (1996). Women of color and traumatic stress in "domestic captivity": Gender and race as disempowering statuses. In A. J. Marsella, M. J. Friedman, E. T. Gerrity, & R. M. Scurfield (Eds.), *Ethnocultural aspects of posttraumatic stress disorder: Issues, research, and clinical applications* (pp. 363–387). Washington, DC: American Psychological Association.

Rose, S., Bisson, J., & Wessely, S. (2002). Psychological debriefing for presenting post traumatic stress disorder (PTSD) (Cochrane review). *Cochrane Library, 2.* Oxford, UK: Update software.

Rorschach, H. (1981). *Psychodiagnostics: A diagnostic test based upon perception* (P. Lemkau & B. Kronemberg, Eds. & Trans.; 9th ed.). New York: Grune & Stratton. (Original work published in 1921)

Ross, C. A., Anderson, G., & Clark, P. (1994). Childhood abuse and the positive symptoms of schizophrenia. *Hospital and Community Psychiatry, 45,* 489–491.

Ross, C. A., Joshi, S., & Currie, R. (1991). Dissociative experiences in the general population: A factor analysis. *Hospital and Community Psychiatry, 42,* 297–301.

Rosenman, S. (2002). Trauma and posttraumatic stress disorder in Australia: Findings in the population sample of the Australian National Survey of Mental Health and Wellbeing. *Australian and New Zealand Journal of Psychiatry, 36,* 515–520.

Rothbaum, B. O., Foa, E. G., Riggs, D. S., Murdock, T. B., & Walsh, W. (1992). A prospective examination of post-traumatic stress disorder in rape victims. *Journal of Traumatic Stress, 5,* 455–475.

Rothbaum, B. O., Meadows, E. A., Resick, P., & Foy, D. W. (2000). Cognitive-behavioral therapy. In E. B. Foa, T. M. Keane, M. J. Friedman (Eds), *Effective treatments for PTSD: Practice guidelines from the International Society for Traumatic Stress Studies* (pp. 60–83). New York: Guilford.

Rothschild, A. J., & Duval, S. E. (2003). How long should patients with psychotic depression stay on the antipsychotic medication? *Journal of Clinical Psychiatry, 64*, 390–396.

Ruch, L. O., & Chandler, S. M. (1983). Sexual assault trauma during the acute phase: An exploratory model and multivariate analysis. *Journal of Health and Social Behavior, 24*, 184–185.

Salter, A. C. (1995). *Transforming trauma: A guide to understanding and treating adult survivors of child sexual abuse.* Thousand Oaks, CA: Sage.

Samoilov, A., & Goldfried, M. R. (2000). Role of emotion in cognitive-behavior therapy. *Clinical Psychology: Science and Practice, 7*, 373–385.

Sansone, R. A., Hruschka, J., Vasudevan, A., & Miller, S. N. (2003). Benzodiazepine exposure and history of trauma. *Psychosomatics, 44*, 523–524.

Sar, V., Akyüz, G., Kundakci, T., Kiziltan, E., & Dogan, O. (2004). Childhood trauma, dissociation, and psychiatric comorbidity in patients with conversion disorder. *American Journal of Psychiatry, 161*, 2271–2276.

Schatzberg, A. F. (2003). New approaches to managing psychotic depression. *Journal of Clinical Psychiatry, 64*(Suppl. 1), 19–23.

Schnurr, P. P., & Green, B. L. (Eds.). (2004). *Trauma and health: Physical health consequences of exposure to extreme stress.* Washington DC: American Psychological Association.

Schore, A. N. (1994). *Affect regulation and the origin of the self: The neurobiology of emotional development.* Hillsdale, NJ: Erlbaum.

Schore, A. N. (1996). The experience-dependent maturation of a regulatory system in the orbital prefrontal cortex and the origin of developmental psychopathology. *Development and Psychopathology, 8*, 59–87.

Schore, A. N. (2003). *Affect dysregulation and disorders of the self.* New York: Norton.

Seedat, S., & Stein, D. J. (2001). Biological treatment of PTSD in children and adolescents. In S. Eth (Ed.), *PTSD in children and adolescents* (pp. 87–116). Washington, DC: American Psychiatric Press.

Segman, R. H., Cooper-Kazaz, R., Macciardi, F., Goltser, T., Halfon, Y., Dobroborski, T., & Shalev, A. Y. (2002). Association between the dopamine transporter gene and posttraumatic stress disorder. *Molecular Psychiatry, 7*, 903–907.

Selley, C., King, E., Peveler, R., Osola, K., Martin, N., & Thompson, C. (1997). Posttraumatic stress disorder symptoms and the Clapham rail accident. *British Journal of Psychiatry, 171*, 478–482.

Sells, D. J., Rowe, M., Fisk, D., & Davidson, L. (2003). Violent victimization of persons with co-occurring psychiatric and substance use disorders. *Psychiatric Services, 54*, 1253–1257.

Shalev, A. Y. (2002). Acute stress reactions in adults. *Biological Psychiatry, 51*, 532–544.

Shapiro, F. (1995). *Eye movement desensitization and reprocessing: Basic principles, protocols, and procedures.* New York: Guilford.

Shapiro, F. (2002). EMDR 12 years after its introduction: Past and future research. *Journal of Clinical Psychology, 58,* 1–22.

Shear, M. K., & Smith-Caroff, K. (2002). Traumatic loss and the syndrome of complicated grief. *PTSD Research Quarterly, 13,* 1–7.

Shin, L. M., Whalen, P. J., Pitman, R. K., Bush, G., Macklin, M. L., Lasko, N. B., Orr, S. P., McInerney, S. C., & Rauch, S. L. (2001). An fMRI study of anterior cingulate function in posttraumatic stress disorder. *Biological Psychiatry, 50,* 932–942.

Siegel, D. J. (1999). *The developing mind: Toward a neurobiology of interpersonal experience.* New York: Guilford.

Siegel, D. J. (2003). An interpersonal neurobiology of psychotherapy: The developing mind and the resolution of trauma. In M. F. Solomon & D. J. Siegel, D., *Healing trauma: Attachment, mind, body, and brain* (pp. 1–54). New York: Norton.

Siegel, K., & Schrimshaw, E. W. (2000). Perceiving benefits in adversity: Stress-related growth in women living with HIV/AIDS. *Social Science and Medicine, 51,* 1543–1554.

Silver, R. C., Holman, E. A., McIntosh, D. N., Poulin, M., & Gil-Rivas, V. (2002). Nationwide longitudinal study of psychological responses to September 11. *Journal of the American Medical Association, 288,* 1235–1244.

Simon, R. I. (Ed.). (1995). *Posttraumatic stress disorder in litigation: Guidelines for forensic assessment.* Washington, DC: American Psychiatric Press.

Simpson, G. M., El Sheshai, A. E., Rady, A., Kingsbury, S. J., & Fayek, M. (2003). Sertraline and monotherapy in the treatment of psychotic and nonpsychotic depression. *Journal of Clinical Psychiatry, 64,* 959–965.

Simpson, J. A., & Rholes, W. S. (Eds.). (1998). *Attachment theory and close relationships.* New York: Guilford.

Singer, M. I., Anglin, T. M., Song, L. Y., & Lunghofer, L. (1995). Adolescents' exposure to violence and associated symptoms of psychological trauma. *Journal of the American Medical Association, 273,* 477–482.

Sokolski, K. N., Denson, T. F., Lee, R. T., & Reist, C. (2003). Quetiapine for treatment of refractory symptoms of combat-related post-traumatic stress disorder. *Military Medicine, 168,* 486–489.

Solomon, M. F., & Siegel, D. J. (2003). *Healing trauma: Attachment, mind, body, and brain.* New York: Norton.

Solomon, S., Laor, N., & McFarlane, A. C. (1996). Acute posttraumatic reactions in soldiers and civilians. In B. A. van der Kolk, A. C. Mc Farlane, & L. Weisaeth (Eds.), *Traumatic stress: The effects of overwhelming experience on mind, body and society* (pp. 102–114). New York: Guilford.

Solomon, Z., & Benbenishty, R. (1986). The role of proximity, immediacy, and expectancy in frontline treatment of combat stress reaction among Israelis in the Lebanon war. *American Journal of Psychiatry, 143,* 613–617.

Southwick, S. M., Bremner, J. D., Rasmusson, A., Morgan, C. A., Arnsten, A., & Charney, D. S. (1999). Role of norepinephrine in the pathophysiology and treatment of posttraumatic stress disorder. *Biological Psychiatry, 46,* 1192–1204.

Southwick, S. M., Morgan, C. A., Charney, D. S., & High, J. R. (1999). Yohimbine use in a natural setting: effects on posttraumatic stress disorder. *Biological Psychiatry, 46,* 442–444.

Southwick, S. M., Morgan, C. A., Vythilingam, M., & Charney, D. S. (2003). Emerging neurobiological factors in stress resilience. *PTSD Research Quarterly, 14,* 1–8.

Spinazzola, J., Blaustein, M., & van der Kolk, B. A. (2005). Treatment outcome research: The study of unrepresentative samples? *Journal of Traumatic Stress, 18,* 425–436.

Sroufe, L. A., Carlson, E. A., Levy, A. K., & Egeland, B. (1999). Implications of attachment theory for developmental psychopathology. *Development and Psychopathology, 11,* 1–13.

Stamm, B. H. (Ed.). (1996). *Measurement of stress, trauma and adaptation.* Lutherville, MD: Sidran.

Stein, D. J., Davidson, J., Seedat, S., & Beebe, K. (2003). Paroxetine in the treatment of post-traumatic stress disorder: pooled analysis of placebo-controlled studies. *Expert Opinion on Pharmacotherapy, 4,* 1829–1838.

Stein, M. B., Jang, K. L., Taylor, S., Vernon, P. A., & Livesley, W. J. (2002). Genetic and environmental influences on trauma exposure and posttraumatic stress disorder symptoms: a twin study. *American Journal of Psychiatry, 159,* 1675–1681.

Stein, M. B., Kline, N. A., & Matloff, J. L. (2002). Adjunctive olanzapine for SSRI-resistant combat-related PTSD: A double-blind, placebo-controlled study. *American Journal of Psychiatry, 159,* 1777–1779.

Steinberg, M. (1994). *Structured Clinical Interview for DSM-IV Dissociative Disorders-Revised (SCID-D-R).* Washington, DC: American Psychiatric Press.

Stern, D. N. (1985). *The interpersonal world of the infant: A view from psychoanalysis and developmental psychology.* New York: Basic Books.

Straus, M. A. & Gelles, R. J. (1990). *Physical violence in American families: Risk factors and adaptation to violence in 8,145 families.* New Brunswick, NJ: Transaction.

Styron, T., & Janoff-Bulman, R. (1997). Childhood attachment and abuse: Long-term effects on adult attachment, depression and conflict resolution. *Child Abuse and Neglect, 21,* 1015–1023.

Talbot, N. L., Houghtalen, R. P., Cyrulik, S., Betz, A., Barkun, M., Duberstein, P. R., & Wynne, L. C. (1998). Women's safety in recovery: group therapy for patients with a history of childhood sexual abuse. *Psychiatric Services, 49,* 213–217.

Taylor, F., & Raskind, M. A. (2002). The alpha1-adrenergic antagonist prazosin improves sleep and nightmares in civilian trauma posttraumatic stress disorder. *Journal of Clinical Psychopharmacology, 22,* 82–85.

Taylor, S. (2003). Outcome predictors for three PTSD treatments: Exposure therapy, EMDR, and relaxation training. *Journal of Cognitive Psychotherapy, 17,* 149–162.

Terzano, M. G., Rossi, M., Palomba, V., Smerieri, A., & Parrino, L. (2003). New drugs for insomnia: Comparative tolerability of zopiclone, zolpidem and zaleplon. *Drug Safety, 26,* 261–282.

Tjaden, P., & Thoennes, N. (2000). *Full report of the prevalence, incidence, and consequences of violence against women: Findings from the National Violence*

Against Women Survey (NCJ Publication No. 183781). Washington, DC: U.S. Department of Justice, Centers for Disease Control and Prevention.

Ullman, S. E., & Filipas, H. H. (2001). Predictors of PTSD symptom severity and social reactions in sexual assault victims. *Journal of Traumatic Stress, 14,* 393–413.

Updegraff, J. A., & Taylor, S. E. (2000). From vulnerability to growth: Positive and negative effects of stressful life events. In J. H. Harvey & E. D. Miller (Eds.), *Loss and trauma: General and close relationship perspectives* (pp. 3–28). Philadelphia: Brunner-Routledge.

Ursano, R. J., Fullerton, C. S., Epstein, R. S., Crowley, B., Kao, T-C., Vance, K., Craig, K. J., Dougall, A. L., & Baum, A. S. (1999). Acute and chronic posttraumatic stress disorder in motor vehicle accident victims. *American Journal of Psychiatry, 156,* 589–595.

Ursano, R. J., Fullerton, C. S., Kao, T-C, & Bhartiya, V. R. (1995). Longitudinal assessment of posttraumatic stress disorder and depression after exposure to traumatic death. *Journal of Nervous and Mental Disease, 183,* 36–42.

Ursano, R. J., Fullerton, C. S., & McCaughey, B. G. (1994). Trauma and disaster. In R. J. Ursano, B. G. McCaughey, & C. S. Fullerton (Eds.), *Individual and community responses to trauma and disaster: The structure of human chaos* (pp. 3–27). Cambridge: Cambridge University Press.

U.S. Surgeon General. (1999). *Mental Health: Culture, Race, and Ethnicity: A Supplement to Mental Health: Report of the Surgeon General.* Retrieved October 19, 2005, from http://www.namiscc.org/newsletters/August01/Surgeon General Report.htm

van der Kolk, B. A., McFarlane, A. C., & Weisaeth, L. (1996). *Traumatic stress: The effects of overwhelming experience on mind, body, and society.* New York: Guilford.

van der Kolk, B. A., Pelcovitz, D., Roth, S., Mandel, F. S., McFarlane, A., & Herman, J. L. (1996). Dissociation, somatization, and affect dysregulation: The complexity of adaptation of trauma. *American Journal of Psychiatry, 153*(Suppl.), 83–93.

van der Kolk, B. A., Roth, S., Pelcovitz, D., Sunday, S., & Spinazzola, F. (2005). Disorders of extreme stress: The empirical foundation of a complex adaptation to trauma. *Journal of Traumatic Stress, 18,* 389–399.

van Emmerik, A. A., Kamphuis, J. H., Hulsbosch, A. M., & Emmelkamp, P. M. (2002). Single session debriefing after psychological trauma: A meta-analysis. *Lancet, 360*(9335), 766–771.

Van Etten, M. L., & Taylor, S. (1998). Comparative efficacy of treatments for posttraumatic stress disorder: A meta-analysis. *Clinical Psychology and Psychotherapy, 5,* 126–144.

Van Ommeren, M., Sharma, B., Sharma, G. K., Komproe, I. H., Cardeña, E., & De Jong, J. T. V. M. (2002). The relationship between somatic and PTSD symptoms among Bhutanese refugee torture survivors: examination of comorbidity with anxiety and depression. *Journal of Traumatic Stress, 15,* 415–421.

Vaiva, G., Ducrocq, F., Jezequel, K., Averland, B., Lestavel, P., Brunet, A., & Marmar, C. R. (2003). Immediate treatment with propranolol decreases posttraumatic stress disorder two months after trauma. *Biological Psychiatry, 52,* 947–949.

Vesti, P., & Kastrup, M. (1995). Refugee status, torture, and adjustment. In J. R. Freedy & S. E. Hobfoll (Eds.), *Traumatic stress: From theory to practice* (pp. 213–235). New York: Plenum.

Villarreal, G., & King, C. Y. (2004). Neuroimaging studies reveal brain changes in posttraumatic stress disorder. *Psychiatric Annals, 34,* 845–856.

Walker, E. A., Katon, W. J., Roy-Byrne, P. P., Jemelka, R. P., et al. (1993). Histories of sexual victimization in patients with irritable bowel syndrome or inflammatory bowel disease. *American Journal of Psychiatry, 150,* 1502–1506.

Walker, E. A., Katon, W. J. Russo, J. E., Ciechanowski, P., Newman, E., & Wagner, A. W. (2003). Health care costs associated with posttraumatic stress disorder symptoms in women. *Archives of General Psychiatry, 60,* 369–374.

Walker, L. E. (1984). *The battered woman syndrome.* New York: Springer.

Weathers, F. W., Litz, B. T., & Keane, T. M. (1995). Military trauma. In J. R. Freedy & S. E. Hobfoll (Eds.), *Traumatic stress: From theory to practice* (pp. 103–128). New York: Plenum.

Weiss, S. R. B., & Post, R. M. (1998). Sensitization and kindling phenomena in mood, anxiety, and obsessive-compulsive disorders: The role of serotonergic mechanisms in illness progression. *Biological Psychiatry, 44,* 193–206.

West, C. M. (2002). Battered, black, and blue: An overview of violence in the lives of black women. *Women and Therapy, 25,* 5–27.

Westen, D., Novotny, C. M., & Thompson-Brenner, H. (2004). The empirical status of empirically supported psychotherapies: Assumptions, findings, and reporting in controlled clinical trials. *Psychological Bulletin, 130,* 631–663.

Williams, L. M. (1994). Recall of childhood trauma: A prospective study of women's memories of child sexual abuse. *Journal of Consulting and Clinical Psychology, 62,* 1167–1176.

Wilson, J., & Keane, T. (Eds.). (2004). *Assessing psychological trauma and PTSD: A practitioner's handbook* (2nd ed.). New York: Guilford.

Wolpe, J. (1958). *Psychotherapy by reciprocal inhibition.* Stanford, CA: Stanford University Press.

Yehuda, R. (2002). Status of cortisol findings in PTSD. *Psychiatric Clinics of North America, 25,* 341–368.

Yehuda, R. (2004). Posttraumatic stress disorder. *New England Journal of Medicine, 346,* 108–114.

Yehuda, R., Halligan, S. L., Golier, J. A., Grossman, R., & Bierer, L. M. (2004). Effects of trauma exposure on the cortisol response to dexamethasone administration in PTSD and major depressive disorder. *Psychoneuroendocrinology, 29,* 389–404.

Young, B. H., Ford, J. D., Ruzek, J. I., Friedman, M. J., & Gusman, F. D. (1998). *Disaster mental health services: A guidebook for clinicians and administrators.* St. Louis, MO: National Center for PTSD, Department of Veterans Affairs Employee Education System.

Zayfert, C., Becker, C. B., Unger, D. L., & Shearer, D. K. (2002). Comorbid anxiety disorders in civilians seeking treatment for posttraumatic stress disorder. *Journal of Traumatic Stress, 15,* 31–38.

Zayfert, C., De Viva, J. C., Becker, C. B., Pike, J. L., Gillock, K. L., & Haynes, S. A. (2005). Exposure utilization and completion of cognitive behavioral therapy for PTSD in "real world" clinical practice. *Journal of Traumatic Stress, 18,* 637–645.

Zayfert, C., Dums, A. R., Ferguson, R. J., & Hegel, M. T. (2003). Health functioning impairments associated with posttraumatic stress disorder, anxiety disorders, and depression. *Journal of Nervous and Mental Disease, 190,* 233–240.

Zimmerman, M., & Mattia, J. I. (1999). Psychotic subtyping of major depressive disorder and posttraumatic stress disorder. *Journal of Clinical Psychiatry, 60,* 311–314.

Zisook, S., Chentsova-Dutton, Y. E., & Shuchter, S. R. (1998). PTSD following bereavement. *Annals of Clinical Psychiatry, 10,* 157–163.

Zlotnick, C., Donaldson, D., Spirito, A., & Pearlstein, T. (1997). Affect regulation and suicide attempts in adolescent inpatients. *Journal of the American Academy of Child and Adolescent Psychiatry, 36,* 793–798.

Appendix 1

Initial Trauma Review–3 (ITR-3)

<u>CHILDHOOD QUESTIONS</u>:

1. [**Physical abuse questions**] *"<u>Before you were age 18</u>, did a parent or another adult ever hurt or punish you in a way that left a bruise, cut, scratches, or made you bleed?"*

    Yes__   No__   [Yes = physical abuse]

    If yes:

    "When this happened, did you ever feel very afraid, horrified, or helpless?"

    Yes__   No__

    "Did you ever think you might be injured or killed?"

    Yes__   No__

2. [**Sexual abuse questions**] *"<u>Before you were age 18</u>, did anyone who was <u>5 or more years older</u> than you ever do something sexual with you or to you?"*

    Yes__   No__   [Yes = sexual abuse]

    If yes:

    "Did the person ever put their penis, a finger, or an object into your vagina, or anus, or a penis in your mouth?"

    Yes__   No__   [Yes = sexual abuse with penetration]

"Was this ever done against your will or when you couldn't defend yourself (for example, when you were asleep or intoxicated)?"

Yes__ No__ [Yes = sexual abuse]

"When this happened, did you ever feel very afraid, horrified, or helpless?"

[NOTE: For sexual abuse only; this part is not necessary for PTSD Criterion A]

Yes__ No__

"Did you ever think you might be injured or killed?"

[NOTE: For sexual abuse only; this part is not necessary for PTSD Criterion A]

Yes__ No__

3. **[Peer sexual assault questions]** *"Before you were age 18, did anyone who was less than 5 years older than you ever do something sexual to you that was against your will or that happened when you couldn't defend yourself (for example, when you were asleep or intoxicated)?"*

Yes__ No__ [Yes = peer child sexual assault]

If yes:

"Did the person ever put their penis, a finger, or an object into your vagina, anus, or mouth?"

Yes__ No__ [Yes = peer child rape if any insertion in vagina or anus, or penile insertion in mouth]

"When this happened, did you ever feel very afraid, horrified, or helpless?"

Yes__ No__

"Did you ever think you might be injured or killed?"

Yes__ No__

4. **[Disaster questions]** *"Before you were age 18, were you ever involved in a serious fire, earthquake, flood, or other disaster?"*

Yes__ No__ [Yes = childhood exposure to disaster]

If yes:

"When this happened, did you ever feel very afraid, horrified, or helpless?"

Yes___ No___

"Did you ever think you might be injured or killed?"

Yes___ No___

5. **[Motor vehicle accident questions]** *"Before you were age 18, were you ever involved in a serious automobile accident?"*

Yes___ No___   [Yes = childhood exposure to MVA]

If yes:

"When this happened, did you ever feel very afraid, horrified, or helpless?"

Yes___ No___

"Did you ever think you might be injured or killed?"

Yes___ No___

6. **[Witnessing trauma questions]** *"Before you were age 18, did you ever see someone else get killed or badly hurt?"*

Yes___ No___   [Yes = childhood witnessing trauma]

If yes:

"When this happened, did you ever feel very afraid, horrified, or helpless?"

Yes___ No___

"Did you ever think you might be injured or killed?" *[Not required for PTSD Criterion A]*

Yes___ No___

ADULTHOOD QUESTIONS:

1. **[Adult sexual assault questions]** *"Since you were 18 or older, has anyone done something sexual to you against your will or when you couldn't defend yourself (for example, when you were asleep or intoxicated)?"*

Yes___ No___   [Yes = Adult sexual assault]

If yes:

"Did the person ever put their penis, a finger, or an object into your vagina or anus, or a penis in your mouth?"

Yes__   No__   [Yes = adult rape]

"*When this happened, did you ever feel very afraid, horrified, or helpless?*"

Yes__   No__

"*Did you ever think you might be injured or killed?*"

Yes__   No__

"*Did this ever happen on a date, or with a sexual/romantic partner or spouse?*

Yes__   No__   [Yes = date/partner/marital sexual assault or rape]

2. **[Spouse/partner abuse questions]** "*Since you were 18 or older, have you ever been slapped, hit, or beaten in a sexual or marital relationship?*"

Yes__   No__   [Yes = partner battering]

"*Since you were 18 or older, have you ever been shot, shot at, stabbed, or nearly strangled in a sexual or marital relationship?*"

Yes__   No__   [Yes = partner battering and possible attempted murder]

If yes to either:

"*When this happened, did you ever feel very afraid, horrified, or helpless?*"

Yes__   No__

"*Did you ever think you might be injured or killed?*"

Yes__   No__

3. **[Non-intimate assault questions]** "*Since you were 18 or older, have you ever been physically attacked, assaulted, stabbed, or shot at by someone who wasn't a sex partner or husband/wife?*"

Yes__   No__   [Yes = non-intimate assault and possible attempted murder]

If yes:

"*When this happened, did you ever feel very afraid, horrified, or helpless?*"

Yes__   No__

"Did you ever think you might be injured or killed?"

Yes__   No__

4. **[War questions]** *"Since you were 18 or older, have you ever experienced combat, fought in a war, or lived in a place where war was happening?"*

Yes__   No__   [Yes = combat exposure]

<u>*If yes:*</u>

"When this happened, did you ever feel very afraid, horrified, or helpless?"

Yes__   No__

"Did you ever think you might be injured or killed?"

Yes__   No__

5. **[Motor vehicle accident questions]** *"Since you were 18 or older, were you ever involved in a serious automobile accident?"*

Yes__   No__   [Yes = motor vehicle accident]

<u>*If yes:*</u>

"When this happened, did you ever feel very afraid, horrified, or helpless?"

Yes__   No__

"Did you ever think you might be injured or killed?"

Yes__   No__

6. **[Disaster questions]** *"Since you were 18 or older, were you ever involved in a serious fire, earthquake, flood, or other disaster?"*

Yes__   No__   [Yes = disaster exposure]

<u>*If yes:*</u>

"When this happened, did you ever feel very afraid, horrified, or helpless?"

Yes__   No__

"Did you ever think you might be injured or killed?"

Yes__   No__

7. **[Torture questions—If client is an immigrant from another country]** *"In the country where you used to live, were you ever tortured by the government or by people against the government?"*

Yes__   No__   [Yes = torture]

If yes:

"When this happened, did you ever feel very afraid, horrified, or helpless?"

Yes__   No__

"Did you ever think you might be injured or killed?"

Yes__   No__

8. **[Police trauma questions]** *"In this country, have you ever been hit, beaten, assaulted, or shot at by the police or other law enforcement officials, during or after an arrest, or at some other time?"*

Yes__   No__   [Yes = police trauma]

If yes:

"When this happened, did you ever feel very afraid, horrified, or helpless?"

Yes__   No__

"Did you ever think you might be injured or killed?"

Yes__   No__

9. **[Witnessing trauma questions]** *"Since you were 18 or older, did you ever see someone else killed or badly hurt?"*

Yes__   No__   [Yes = adult witnessing trauma]

If yes:

"When this happened, did you ever feel very afraid, horrified, or helpless?"

Yes__   No__

"Did you ever think you might be injured or killed?" [NOTE: For witnessing trauma, this part is not necessary for DSM-IV Criterion A]

Yes__   No__

Appendix 2

BIPD

Brief Interview for Posttraumatic Disorders

A semi-structured interview for the diagnosis of Acute Stress Disorder, Posttraumatic Stress Disorder, and Brief Psychotic Disorder with Marked Stressor

Date: ___/___/___

Patient Name: _____

Sex: _____ Age: _____

Evaluator Name: _____

Instructions for completing the Brief
Interview for Posttraumatic Disorders

First: Determine whether the traumatic event occurred within the last month or longer in the past, and whether psychotic symptoms are part of the clinical presentation.

If the trauma has occurred within the last month, and there are no significant psychotic symptoms, use the <u>Acute Stress Disorder</u> screen.

If the trauma occurred in the last month, but significant psychotic symptoms are present, use the <u>Brief Psychotic Disorder</u> with Marked Stressor screen.

If the trauma occurred a month or more ago, use the <u>Posttraumatic Stress Disorder</u> screen.

Second: For each numbered diagnostic criterion, place a ✓ mark in the ( ) space for each symptom that is present for the patient you are evaluating.

For example, if a nonpsychotic patient reported recent recurrent, intrusive, and distressing dreams and thoughts about a traumatic event that happened three months ago, and intense psychological distress upon exposure to environmental reminders of the event, you would mark the following in the "B" PTSD section of the BIPD:

B. Has the traumatic event been persistently reexperienced in <u>at least one</u> of the following symptom categories <u>within the last month?</u>

  (1) recurrent and intrusive distressing recollections of the event, including images ( ), thoughts (✓), or perceptions ( )
  (2) recurrent distressing dreams of the event (✓)
  (3) acting or feeling as if the event were recurring, including a sense of reliving the experience ( ), nonpsychotic hallucinations of the event ( ), and flashbacks ( ), including those which occur upon awakening or when intoxicated
  (4) intense psychological distress (e.g., fear, anger) upon exposure to internal or external/environmental cues that symbolize or resemble the traumatic event (✓)
  (5) physiological reactivity (e.g., sweating, flushing, dizziness, increased heart rate, shortness of breath) upon exposure to internal or external cues that symbolize or resemble the traumatic event ( )

Third: Review all check marks to see if they indicate sufficient symptoms to satisfy the lettered criterion. If so, check the "Yes" box. For example, for this patient, your response to the following question would be "yes" and you would check the box:

Yes, criterion B is met (at least one numbered category checked) ☐

Fourth: Review all checked boxes to determine if sufficient criteria have been met to meet the diagnosis. For example, if criteria A, C, D, E, and F were also met in this example, you would check yes to the following:

G. Yes, PTSD diagnostic criteria are all met ('Yes' responses to criteria A through F) ☐

Based on this example, you would assign a diagnosis of posttraumatic stress disorder.

Fifth: If you determine that a disorder is present, complete the "associated features" section to document additional difficulties associated (or comorbid) with posttraumatic stress.

Acute Stress Disorder (ASD) screen

Diagnosis potentially relevant to this patient *(trauma occurred within the last month and there are no significant psychotic symptoms)* __

Diagnosis not relevant to this patient (skip to PTSD section) __

A. Has the patient been exposed to a traumatic event in which <u>both</u> of the following were present <u>within the last month:</u>
  (1) the patient experienced/witnessed/was confronted with an event that
   • involved the death of another person(s) ( ) or
   • potential death of the patient ( ) or
   • serious potential or actual injury to the patient ( ) or
   • a threat to the physical integrity of the patient or others ( ) or
   • had developmentally inappropriate sexual experiences in childhood (e.g., sexual abuse), in which case there need not be threatened or actual violence or injury ( )

<u>AND</u>

  (2) the patient's response to this event involved intense fear ( ), helplessness ( ), or horror ( ) <u>OR</u>, in children, disorganized or agitated behavior ( )

Yes, both criteria A1 and A2 are met (at least one check in each category) ☐

No, criteria A1 and A2 are not both met ☐

<u>If no,</u> stop ASD screen. (Check here __ if screen stopped)

<u>If yes,</u> briefly describe the trauma, including when it occurred:

B. <u>During the event</u> or <u>within the last month,</u> has the patient had at least three of the following dissociative symptom categories?
  (1) Numbing (not being able to feel emotions as well or at all), emotional detachment (feeling emotionally distant or uninvolved), or an absence of emotional responsiveness ( )
  (2) Reduced awareness of his or her surroundings ( )
  (3) Derealization: an altered perception/experience of the external world so that it seems strange or unreal ( )
  (4) Depersonalization: an altered perception or experience of self so that the person feels detached from—or an outside observer on—his/her mental processes or body (e.g., out-of-body experiences, distorted sense of one's body or body parts) ( )
  (5) An inability to recall an important aspect of the trauma ( )

Yes, criterion B is met (at least three numbered categories checked) ☐

No, criterion B is not met ☐

C. Has the traumatic event been persistently reexperienced in at least one of the following ways <u>within the last month</u>: recurring images ( ), thoughts ( ), dreams ( ), flashbacks ( ), or reliving the experience as if it were happening again ( ); or distress upon exposure to reminders of the event ( )?

Yes, criterion C is met (at least one symptom checked) □

No, criterion C is not met □

D. Has there been marked avoidance of stimuli that might cause recollections of the trauma [e.g., avoidance of thoughts ( ), feelings ( ), conversations ( ), activities ( ), places ( ), people ( )] within the last month?

Yes, criterion D is met (at least one symptom checked) □

No, criterion D is not met □

E. Have there been marked symptoms of anxiety ( ) or increased arousal [e.g., difficulty sleeping ( ), irritability ( ), poor concentration ( ), hypervigilance ( ), exaggerated startle response ( ), motor restlessness ( )] that were not present before the trauma and that occurred <u>within the last month</u>?

Yes, criterion E is met (at least one symptom checked) □

No, criterion E is not met □

F. Have these symptoms caused clinically significant distress or impairment in social ( ), occupational ( ), or other important areas of functioning ( ), or impaired the patient's ability to pursue some necessary task ( ) <u>within the last month</u>?

Yes, criterion F is met (at least one form of impairment checked) □

No, criterion F is not met □

G. Have these symptoms both
(1) lasted for a minimum of 2 days and a maximum of 4 weeks ( ) and
(2) occurred within 4 weeks of the trauma ( )?

Yes, both G1 and G2 are met □

No, both G1 and G2 are not met □

Assign an ASD diagnosis?

Yes, ASD criteria are all met ('yes' responses to criteria A through G) □

No, ASD criteria are not all met □

Posttraumatic Stress Disorder (PTSD) screen

Diagnosis potentially relevant to this patient (*trauma occurred a month or more ago*) __

Diagnosis not relevant to this patient (skip to BPDMS section) __

A. <u>Prior to the last month</u>, was the patient exposed to a traumatic event in which <u>both</u> of the following were present:
   (1) the patient experienced/witnessed/was confronted with an event that
- involved the death of another person(s) ( ) or
- potential death of the patient ( ) or
- serious potential or actual injury to the patient ( ) or
- a threat to the physical integrity of the patient or others ( ) or
- had developmentally inappropriate sexual experiences in childhood (e.g., sexual abuse), in which case there need not be threatened or actual violence or injury ( )

<u>AND</u>

   (2) the patient's response to this event involved intense fear ( ), helplessness ( ), or horror ( ) <u>OR</u>, in children, disorganized or agitated behavior ( )

Yes, both criteria A1 and A2 are met (at least one check in each category) ☐

No, criteria A1 and A2 are not both met ☐

If no, stop PTSD screen. (Check here __ if screen stopped)

If yes, briefly describe trauma, including when it occurred:

B. Has the traumatic event been persistently reexperienced in at <u>least one</u> of the following symptom categories <u>within the last month</u>?
   (1) recurrent and intrusive distressing recollections of the event, including images ( ), thoughts ( ), or perceptions ( )
   (2) recurrent distressing dreams of the event ( )
   (3) acting or feeling as if the event were recurring [including a sense of reliving the experience ( ), nonpsychotic hallucinations of the event ( ), and flashbacks ( )], including those which occur upon awakening or when intoxicated
   (4) intense distress upon exposure to internal or external cues that symbolize/resemble the traumatic event ( )
   (5) physiological reactivity (e.g., sweating, flushing, dizziness, increased heart rate, shortness of breath) upon exposure to internal or external cues that symbolize or resemble the traumatic event ( )

Yes, criterion B is met (at least one numbered category checked) ☐

No, criterion B is not met ☐

C. Has there been persistent avoidance of stimuli associated with the trauma and numbing of general responsiveness that was not present before the trauma, as indicated by at least three of the following symptom categories, within the last month?

   (1) efforts to avoid thoughts ( ), feelings ( ), or conversations ( ) associated with the trauma
   (2) efforts to avoid activities ( ), places ( ), or people ( ) that might stimulate or trigger recollections of the trauma
   (3) inability to recall an important aspect of the trauma ( )
   (4) markedly diminished interest or participation in significant activities ( )
   (5) feelings of detachment/estrangement from others ( ), or restricted range of affect (e.g., unable to have loving feelings) ( )
   (6) sense of foreshortened future (e.g. patient does not expect to have a career, marriage, children, or a normal life span) ( )

   Yes, criterion C is met (at least three numbered categories checked) □

   No, criterion C is not met □

D. Have there been persistent symptoms of increased arousal that were not present before the trauma, as indicated by at least two of the following symptom categories:

   (1) difficulty falling or staying asleep ( )
   (2) irritability or outbursts of anger ( )
   (3) difficulty concentrating ( )
   (4) hypervigilance ( )
   (5) exaggerated startle response ( )

   Yes, criterion D is met (at least two numbered categories checked) □

   No, criterion D is not met □

E. Have these symptoms lasted for more than one month?

   Yes, criterion E is met □

   No, criterion E is not met □

F. Have these symptoms caused clinically significant distress or impairment in social ( ), occupational ( ), or other important areas of functioning ( )?

   Yes, criterion F is met (at least one form of impairment checked) □

   No, criterion F is not met □

   Assign a PTSD diagnosis?

   Yes, PTSD criteria are all met ('yes' responses to criteria A through F) □

   No, PTSD criteria are not all met □

If yes, Specify: **Acute** (the duration of symptoms has been less than three months to date) __

Chronic (the duration of symptoms has been three months or longer) __

With Delayed Onset (the onset of symptoms was at least six months after the stressor) __

Brief Psychotic Disorder with
Marked Stressors (BPDMS) screen

Diagnosis potentially relevant to this patient (*trauma occurred in the last month and psychotic symptoms are present*) __
Diagnosis not relevant to this patient __

A. Has the patient been exposed to one or more traumatic events within the last month that, alone or in combination, would be markedly stressful to almost anyone in similar circumstances in his or her culture ( )?

Yes □   No □

If no, stop BPDMS screen. (Check here ___ if screen stopped)

If yes, briefly describe trauma:

B. Has the patient's response to this trauma(s) involved the development of at least one of the following symptoms:
   (1) **Delusions** ( )
      If yes, describe briefly:

   (2) **Psychotic hallucinations** ( )
      If yes, describe briefly:

   (3) **Psychotically disorganized speech** ( )
      If yes, describe briefly:

   (4) **Grossly disorganized or catatonic behavior** ( )
      If yes, describe briefly:

   Yes, criterion B is met (at least one numbered category is checked) □

   No, criterion B is not met □

Assign a BPDMS diagnosis?

   Yes, BPDMS criteria are both met ('yes' responses to criteria A and B) □

   No, BPDMS criteria are not met □

Associated features
(for any diagnosis documented on BIPD)

Mark "Yes" for currently present, "No" for not currently present, and/or "Premorbid" if the problem or symptom was present when the trauma occurred (regardless of whether or not it is present now). NOTE: "Premorbid" can be marked along with either "Yes" or "No" for the same problem.

(1) Suicidal ideation: Yes __   No __   Premorbid __

(2) Suicidal behavior: Yes __   No __   Premorbid __

If yes or premorbid for either, describe (including estimate of probable <u>current</u> lethality):

(3) Current or recent aggressive behavior: Yes __   No __   Premorbid __

If yes or premorbid, describe (including estimate of potential current danger to others):

(4) Significant alcohol abuse: Yes __   No __   Premorbid __

(5) Significant substance abuse: Yes __   No __   Premorbid __

If yes or premorbid for either, describe (including if addiction present):

(6) Other associated features (evaluate for each):

A.	Significant despair or hopelessness	Yes __ No __ Premorbid __	
B.	Significant depression	Yes __ No __ Premorbid __	
C.	Significant fears or phobias about people, animals, places, or things	Yes __ No __ Premorbid __	
D.	Significant guilt or shame	Yes __ No __ Premorbid __	
E.	Lack of concern about personal health or safety	Yes __ No __ Premorbid __	
F.	Impulsive behavior	Yes __ No __ Premorbid __	
G.	Unnecessary risk-taking	Yes __ No __ Premorbid __	
H.	Unstable affect or mood swings	Yes __ No __ Premorbid __	
I.	Significant dissociative symptoms	Yes __ No __ Premorbid __	
J.	Somatic symptoms or bodily preoccupation	Yes __ No __ Premorbid __	
K.	Significant social withdrawal	Yes __ No __ Premorbid __	
L.	Chronic perception of danger in environment or relationships	Yes __ No __ Premorbid __	
M.	Sexual dysfunction or distress	Yes __ No __ Premorbid __	
N.	Significant personality change	Yes __ No __ Premorbid __	
O.	Other significant feature (describe):	Yes __ No __ Premorbid __	

Appendix 3

Breath Training Protocol

Introductory Information

- Explain that learning to pay attention to breathing, and learning to breathe deeply, can both help with relaxation and reduce anxiety. Note that when we get anxious or have a panic attack, one of the first things that happens is that our breathing becomes shallow and rapid.
- Explain that, initially, some people become dizzy when they start breathing deeply—this is a normal reaction. For this reason, they should not try breathing exercises standing up until they have become experienced and comfortable with them.
- Explain that the exercises may feel strange at first because the client will be asked to breathe into his or her belly. Most of us are used to holding our stomachs in, because of tight clothes or because we are self-conscious of weight or how we look.

Practicing Breathing in the Session

- Have the client sit in a comfortable position.

- Go through the sequence below with the client—the whole process should take about 10 to 15 minutes. After each step, "check in" to see how the client is feeling, and if there are any problems or questions.

1. If the client is comfortable with closing his or her eyes, ask him or her to do so. Some trauma survivors will feel more anxious with their eyes closed, and will want to keep them open. This is entirely acceptable.

2. Ask the client to try to stay "in the moment" while doing breathing exercises. If his or her mind wanders (e.g., thinking about what to make for dinner, ruminating over an argument with someone), he or

she should gently try to bring it back to the immediate experience of breathing.

3. Ask the client to begin breathing through the nose, paying attention to the breath coming in and going out. Ask him or her to pay attention to how long each inhalation and exhalation lasts. Do this for 5 or 6 breaths.

   It is usually helpful for the clinician to breathe along with the client at the beginning of this exercise. You can guide him or her for each inhalation and exhalation, saying "in" and "out" to help him or her along.

4. Instruct the client to start breathing more deeply into his or her abdomen. This means that the belly should visibly rise and fall with each breath. This sort of breathing should feel different from normal breathing, and the client should notice that each breath is deeper than normal. Do this for another 5 or 6 breaths.

5. Ask the client to imagine that each time he or she breathes in, air is flowing in to fill up the abdomen and lungs. It goes into the belly first, and then rises up to fill in the top of the chest cavity. In the same way, when breathing out, the breath first leaves the chest, and then the abdomen. Some people find it helpful to imagine the breath coming in and out like a wave. Do this for another 5 or 6 breaths.

6. Explain that once the client is breathing deeply and fully into the belly and chest, the next step is to slow the breath down. Ask the client to slowly count to three with each inhalation and exhalation—in for three counts, out for three counts. With practice, the client may begin to slow his or her breath even further. Tell him or her that there is no specific amount of time necessary for each inhalation and exhalation, only that he or she try to slow his or her breathing. Do this for 5 or 6 breaths.

• Ask the client to practice this sequence at home for 5 to 10 minutes a day. He or she should choose a specific time of day (e.g., in the morning, before work or school), and make this exercise a regular part of his or her daily routine. The client should sit or lie down at home in a comfortable position, with no distractions, for this practice.

• Eventually, the client can extend this exercise to other times in the day as well, especially when relaxation would be a good idea (e.g., before important meetings, in stressful social situations, or whenever he or she feels especially anxious). Remind the client to count during each inhalation and exhalation, since counting, itself, will come to stimulate the relaxation response.

Index

About the Authors

John Briere, PhD, is Associate Professor in the departments of Psychiatry and Psychology at the Keck School of Medicine, University of Southern California, Director of the Psychological Trauma Program at Los Angeles County + USC (LAC+USC) Medical Center, and Co-Director of the MCAVIC-USC Child and Adolescent Trauma Program, National Child Traumatic Stress Network. He is a past president of the International Society for Traumatic Stress Studies (ISTSS). He is author or coauthor of a number of books, articles, and psychological tests in the areas of trauma and interpersonal violence. His Web site is www.JohnBriere.com.

Catherine Scott, MD, is Assistant Professor of Clinical Psychiatry at the Keck School of Medicine, University of Southern California, Medical Director of the Psychological Trauma Program at LAC+USC Medical Center, and attending psychiatrist at the Psychiatric Emergency Service of LAC+USC Medical Center. She teaches and supervises resident physicians and medical students in the assessment and treatment (including psychopharmacology) of trauma-related issues and disorders. Her clinical and research interests include human rights, women's issues, forensics, and the remediation of sexual violence and its effects.